Improving Prosecution?

Recent Titles in
Contributions in Political Science
Series Editor: Bernard K. Johnpoll

Furious Fancies: American Political Thought in the Post-Liberal Era
Philip Abbott

Politicians, Judges, and the People: A Study in Citizens' Participation
Charles H. Sheldon and Frank P. Weaver

The European Parliament: The Three-Decade Search for a United Europe
Paula Scalingi

Prelude to the Presidency: The Political Character and Legislative Leadership Style of Governor Jimmy Carter
Gary M Fink

Presidential Primaries: Road to the White House
James W. Davis

The Voice of Terror: A Biography of Johann Most
Frederic Trautmann

Presidential Secrecy and Deception: Beyond the Power to Persuade
John M. Orman

The New Red Legions
Richard A. Gabriel

Contemporary Perspectives on European Integration: Attitudes, Nongovernmental Behavior, and Collective Decision Making
Leon Hurwitz, editor

The Italian Communist Party: Yesterday, Today, and Tomorrow
Simon Serfaty and Lawrence Gray, editors

The Fiscal Congress: Legislative Control of the Budget
Lance T. Leloup

Iran, Saudi Arabia, and the Law of the Sea: Political Interaction and Legal Development in the Persian Gulf
Charles G. MacDonald

Improving Prosecution?

THE INDUCEMENT AND IMPLEMENTATION OF INNOVATIONS FOR PROSECUTION MANAGEMENT

David Leo Weimer

Contributions in Political Science, Number 49

Greenwood Press
Westport, Connecticut • London, England

Library of Congress Cataloging in Publication Data
Weimer, David Leo.
Improving prosecution?

(Contributions in political science ; no. 49
ISSN 0147-1066)
Bibliography: p.
Includes index.
1. Information storage and retrieval systems—
Criminal justice, Administration of—United States.
2. Prosecution—United States—Data processing.
I. Title. II. Series.
KF242.C72W44 345.73'05042'068 79-6190
ISBN 0-313-22247-9 lib. bdg.

Library of Congress Catalog Card Number: 79-6190
ISBN: 0-313-22247-9
ISSN: 0147-1066

First published in 1980

Greenwood Press
A division of Congressional Information Service, Inc.
88 Post Road West, Westport, Connecticut 06881

Printed in the United States of America

10 9 8 7 6 5 4 3 2 1

Copyright Acknowledgments

Portions of chapters 1 and 9 are taken from David L. Weimer, "Federal Intervention in the Process of Innovation in Local Public Agencies: A Focus on Organizational Incentives," *Public Policy*, Winter 1980. Copyright 1980 by the President and Fellows of Harvard College. Reprinted by permission of John Wiley & Sons, Inc.

Portions of chapter 4 were taken from David L. Weimer, "CMIS Implementation: A Demonstration of Predictive Analysis," *Public Administration Review*, May/June 1980. Reprinted for *Public Administration Review*, Copyright 1980 by the American Society of Public Administration, 1225 Connecticut Avenue, N.W., Washington, D.C. All rights reserved.

To the memory of my mother

Contents

Figures

Exhibits

Tables

Acknowledgments

Many people assisted me in the research for this book. Lee Friedman helped by pointing me in the proper direction. Bart McGuire provided sound advice and encouragement as he did throughout my days at the Graduate School of Public Policy of the University of California at Berkeley. Phillip Johnson, of the School of Law, provided helpful suggestions and also shared with me some of the insights he has gained as an assistant prosecutor. Aaron Wildavsky guided my initial study of management information systems and provided helpful comments on my preliminary work. Eugene Bardach, Robert Biller, Alan Kalmanoff, and Aidan Vining gave me valuable advice during the early stages of my research. Bruce Bueno de Mesquita, Eric Hanushek, Richard Niemi, William Riker, and Aaron Wildavsky offered helpful stylistic suggestions. The final organization of the work benefited greatly from the thoughtful comments of Stephen Wasby.

The research effort was aided by numerous public officials. D. Lowell Jensen, the Alameda County (California) district attorney, encouraged the research and provided complete access to his office and helped me gain access to other sources. Many other members of the Alameda County District Attorney's Office, particularly Richard Nishamoto, cheerfully answered numerous questions. Other prosecutors who allowed me to visit their offices were: District Attorney George Darden of Cobb County, Georgia; District Attorney Harry Connick of New Orleans, Louisiana; U.S. Attorney Earl Silbert of the U.S. Attorney's Office in Washington, D.C.; and Prosecuting Attorney William Cahalan of Wayne County, Michigan.

In each of these jurisdictions, others were particularly helpful: Joseph LeCroy, Larry Donaghue, William Wessel, Richard Cys, and Michael Fried. I would also like to thank Paul Gentile of the Bronx District Attorney's Office and the personnel I communicated with in the following jurisdictions: Sixth Judicial District, Arkansas; City of San Diego and County of San Diego, California; Clark County, Nevada; Kalamazoo County, Michigan; New York County, New York; Marian County, Indiana; Milwaukee County, Wisconsin; Salt Lake County, Utah; Louisville, Kentucky; and the Second Judicial District, Florida.

William Hamilton and Dean Merrill of the Institute of Law and Social Research provided me with information, documents, and work space during my visit to Washington. Joan Jacoby and Charles Work, pioneers of prosecution management, adjusted their schedules to accommodate my interviews. Alvin Ash and Mary Ann Beck of the Law Enforcement Assistance Administration quickly provided information I requested.

I would like to thank the National Institute of Mental Health, whose generous traineeship made it possible for me to conduct research free of financial burden, and Leroy Gramer, administrative dean of the Graduate School of Public Policy, who advised me on how to fund computer time, telephone interviews, and travel. Finally, I am grateful to Claire Sundeen for her expert typing of the final manuscript draft.

Abbreviations

CCJP Council on Criminal Justice Planning (Calif.)
COBOL common business oriented language
CMIS case management information system
CRT cathode ray tube
DALITE District Attorney's Automated Legal Information System
DPC data processing center
INSLAW Institute for Law and Social Research
JUSTIS Milwaukee County (Wisc.) version of PROMIS
LEAA Law Enforcement Assistance Administration
MIS management information system
MOB Major Offense Bureau
NCJISS National Criminal Justice Information and Statistics Service
OCA Office of Crime Analysis (D.C.)
OTT Office of Technology Transfer
PL/1 Programming Language Number 1
PREPARE Prosecutors' Evaluation, Preparation, and Response
PERT Program Evaluation and Review Technique
PROMIS Prosecutor's Management Information System
PX preliminary examination
RFP request for proposal
TRACE Washington, D.C. project to develop offender based transaction statistics
WALES Washington Area Law Enforcement System

PART 1

Innovation in Prosecution: Theory

. . . the people also recognize that the national Government can and the national Government should help the cities and states in their war on crime to the full extent of its resources and constitutional authority. And this we shall do.

This does not mean a national police force. It does mean help and financial support: To develop state and local master plans to combat crime. To bring the most advanced technology to the war on crime in every city and county in America.

And there is no more urgent business before Congress than to pass the Safe Streets Act this year that I proposed last year. That law will provide these required funds.

President Lyndon B. Johnson's State of the
Union Message to Congress,
January 17, 1968

chapter 1

The Law Enforcement Assistance Administration and Induced Innovation

"Law and order" emerged as a national issue in the 1964 presidential election campaign, becoming a problem of ever-increasing saliency during subsequent years as urban riots, campus disorders, and increasing crime rates attracted public attention. Between 1965 and 1968 Congress responded by appropriating modest funds for experimental, demonstration, and planning projects in state and local law enforcement agencies. Under pressure to make the federal government a more active ally in the "war on crime," Congress created the Law Enforcement Assistance Administration (LEAA) to administer funding programs begun under the Omnibus Crime Control and Safe Streets Act of 1968.[1] LEAA was expected to contribute to the control of crime by improving the criminal justice system through the certification of criminal justice master plans submitted by states receiving formula-based block grants and through the administration of discretionary grants intended to stimulate innovation in state and local criminal justice agencies. In its first seven years of existence, LEAA disbursed approximately $3.4 billion in state block grants and $600 million in discretionary grants. Despite these expenditures the national crime rate continued to rise.

Although LEAA remained popular among the state and local agencies that received its grants, criticisms of its operations were voiced increasingly by members of Congress, other federal agencies, professional groups, and criminal justice researchers. Early critics viewed LEAA funding of expensive police equipment as wasteful, describing LEAA itself as the conservatives' version of "throwing money at a problem." Some based their criticism on the failure of LEAA programs to halt the increasing crime rates. Others realized that it was probably unrealistic to expect the LEAA contribution of approximately 5 percent to criminal justice system expenditures to have a noticeable short-term impact on the national crime rates. Nevertheless, they voiced concern over the failure of LEAA to develop systematic knowledge from the thousands of projects (over 80,000 in the first seven years) it had funded that would contribute to crime reduction in the future. Specifically, LEAA was criticized for not adequately evaluating the projects it did fund and for not identifying successful projects that could be widely replicated.

One response of LEAA was the establishment of the Exemplary Projects Program to certify certain projects as worthy of replication. Another was the development of a number of programs to induce the diffusion of specific innovations. Instead of simply identifying or developing innovative technologies and disseminating information about them, the programs combine marketing activities, funding or assistance in securing funding, and direct technical assistance to encourage adoption and facilitate implementation. An indication of the increased emphasis placed on the diffusion of innovations is the dramatic rise, from $1.2 million in 1970 to an estimated $15 million in 1979, of LEAA expenditures for technical assistance services provided as a supplement to direct funding.

Two programs designed to improve prosecution through the spread of innovations have been cited repeatedly by officials of LEAA as among the agency's top successes.[2] One program is the PROMIS Transfer Project that was begun in 1973 to induce the diffusion of PROMIS (Prosecutor's Management Information System), a computerized case management information system. Currently, PROMIS is operational in twenty jurisdictions and at various stages of implementation in seventy others. The Career Criminal Program is the other LEAA proclaimed success in improving prosecution. It was begun in 1975 to induce prosecutors' offices to establish special units that focus prosecutorial resources on the cases of defendants with serious criminal histories. Within two years of the initiation of the Career Criminal Program, eighteen prosecutors' offices were operating such units and the number has increased to a current total of thirty-eight. At least in terms of the number of participants, the PROMIS Transfer Project and the Career Criminal Program appear to be successful in inducing the diffusion of innovations in prosecution.

But extensive diffusion is not necessarily a good measure of success. It is conceivable that some of the adoptions might be socially undesirable, either because they involve an excess of costs over benefits or because they have precluded the adoption of other innovations that would have yielded greater net benefits. In extreme cases in which no adopters achieve positive net benefits, rapid and widespread diffusion would indicate failure rather than success.

To what extent should the diffusion induced by the PROMIS Transfer Project be viewed as socially desirable? This book attempts to provide an answer by looking at the experiences of the first twenty PROMIS adopters. Because the answer depends in part on what other innovations in prosecution management are available, we shall consider several other innovations including special prosecution units of the type being diffused by the Career Criminal Program. Throughout, attention will be given to implementation as the crucial link between hypothetical benefits and those actually realized.

At a more general level, this book considers the advantages and disadvantages of federal efforts intended to accelerate the process of innovation in local public agencies. Despite the existence of a voluminous and diffuse literature dealing with theories of innovation in the private, as well as public sectors, little attention has been given to the institutional mechanisms that might best be employed to facilitate innovation.[3] The PROMIS Transfer Project provides a case study of a particularly powerful institutional mechanism for inducing diffusion that inherently creates incentives of a socially undesirable nature.[4] In the following section, we develop a framework for viewing federal intervention in the process of innovation in local public agencies in general, and the PROMIS Transfer Project in particular.

FEDERAL INTERVENTION IN LOCAL PUBLIC AGENCY INNOVATION

The case for federal intervention rests on the argument that local public agencies lack the incentives, resources, knowledge, and expertise needed to achieve a socially desirable rate of innovation and diffusion of new technologies. Federal assistance is needed to overcome these deficiencies. The process of technological change in private-sector industries provides a frame of reference for this discussion as well as a standard for judging whether or not the rate of public sector innovation is too slow.

Technological change can be viewed as consisting of three phases: invention, innovation, and diffusion. Invention is the creation of a design for improving the way inputs are converted to outputs. The invention phase is often called research and development: promising ideas are identified, modified, and tested on a limited scale. Innovation is the adaption of the invention by some firm to its production process. Innovation introduces the invention to a potential market—the other firms in the innovator's industry. If the innovation is judged successful in reducing costs or improving product quality by these firms, it will diffuse through the industry as other firms follow the innovator's lead.

Each phase of the process is driven by market incentives. Patent laws allow firms to capture a portion of the industry-wide benefits from successful research and development. The innovating firm may be able to secure a competitive advantage over other firms by being the first to use the invention. The benefits of being among the first to adopt innovations provide an added incentive for conducting research and development. Once one firm in the industry has successfully innovated, the other firms have an incentive to adopt the innovation so that they will not be subject to a competitive disadvantage.

In order to apply the three-phase model to public agencies, like-functioned agencies might be grouped into "industries" that employ similar production functions.[5] For example, local prosecutors' offices employ similar inputs (lawyer time, trial capacity, investigative effort, and so on) to produce similar products (conviction of the guilty and evenhanded treatment of defendants). Based on these similarities, the "prosecution industry" could be defined as the collection of all local prosecutors' offices.

Although such artificially defined public industries specify potential markets for innovation, they do not exhibit the product competition that serves as an incentive for technological change in private-sector industries.[6] Each unit in a public industry generally enjoys a monopoly position in its jurisdiction and may rarely seek comparison of practices and performance with units in other jurisdictions. Whereas a private-sector monopoly has a positive incentive to seek technological change in order to advance objectives, such as increasing profit or achieving increased sales subject to a profit constraint, it does not usually face the negative incentives of a competitive disadvantage for not adopting a favorable technological change. The managers in the public industry see a similar asymmetric reward structure: they may gain from adopting an innovation (in terms of prestige from increasing service levels or increased organizational slack to make management easier), but they will not be punished for not adopting one. In addition, managers in the public industry cannot rely on a competitive product market to signal the availability of desirable innovations.

Even when a public manager is motivated to seek innovation, he may find it more difficult to secure investment resources than his private-sector counterpart. Most innovations have start-up costs, and typically innovations must initially operate "at a loss" in order to achieve anticipated benefits or cost reductions in the future. Local budgetary sponsors may be unwilling to raise taxes (or reduce the resources available to other local agencies) to support an uncertain research and development project. Reluctance may be especially great in the case of proposed innovations that are intended to result in difficult-to-quantify improvements in service quality rather than reductions in operating costs. The competition for local resources may even make it difficult for agency managers to secure funding for the adoption of innovations that appear to have been successful in other jurisdictions. Unlike the private-sector manager, the agency manager cannot use the anticipation of future revenues to enter into capital markets where investment funds can be secured. Although organizational "slack" may provide a source of resources for adopting some innovations, it is unlikely to be adequate for those that require high start-up costs, even though these may yield the greatest net benefits in the future.

Lack of knowledge about potentially desirable innovations may also hinder the public manager. Whereas private managers can rely on the profit levels of competitors to indicate which innovations have been successful, the public manager must generally rely on fragmentary testimonial accounts from other jurisdictions. It is difficult for the public manager to judge the validity of claims that particular innovations have resulted in service improvements. Consequently, the public manager may opt for inaction in the face of uncertainty about which innovations, if any, are desirable.

The public manager may realize that anticipated benefits will not result immediately from the act of adoption; most innovations in service delivery will require a substantial implementation effort before yielding benefits. Special types of technical expertise may be required during the implementation and use of innovations. The necessary managerial and engineering skills may not be internally available to potential adopters. Even when the availability of a transferable prototype reduces the amount of specialized expertise needed, other skills may be required to adapt the prototype design to local circumstances. At the very least, skills in project management will probably be needed. But service agencies employing professionals, such as prosecutors' offices employing lawyers, or welfare agencies employing social workers, may have very small pools of personnel with management experience to draw upon for special projects. Even when funds are available to secure the services of outside consultants, the agency may not have sufficient expertise to ensure that the technical skills of the consultants are effectively applied during the implementation of the innovation in an organizational context.[7] Where lack of expertise is anticipated, potentially beneficial innovations may be declined; where the deficiency is not taken into account, adopted innovations may not be successfully implemented.[8]

It is generally believed that the rates of invention, innovation, and diffusion are slower than optimal in private-sector industries.[9] In the relatively less advantageous milieu of local public agencies the rates of invention, innovation, and diffusion are even slower.[10] Federal intervention, therefore, may be desirable to stimulate the development of new service delivery technologies and to encourage the diffusion of those that appear promising.

Because deficiencies in knowledge, investment funds, and technical expertise hinder innovation in local public agencies, it seems reasonable to classify federal programs intended to support innovation in terms of the resources directed at these three deficiencies. *Information* is intended to increase the local manager's knowledge of innovations that might or should be adopted; it may range in normative content from a simple description of what has been tried by local agencies in a public industry to the certification of specific innovations as beneficial for agencies facing certain circumstances. *Funding* is provided to defray some portion of the otherwise prohibitive start-up costs likely to be incurred during the implementation of innovations. *Technical assistance* involves the provision of types of expertise that will be needed by agencies to design or adapt innovations and manage their implementation.[11] Technical assistance can be thought of as the provision of agency-specific information. For example, publishing a document telling agencies how they should write requests for proposals (RFPs) from contractors would be considered information, whereas helping a specific agency write an RFP would be considered technical assistance for purposes of the typology.

Four types of programs represent two general strategies. The first strategy is labeled in Table 1 as "endogenous generation and lateral transfer." It includes programs that attempt to encourage locally initiated research and development, as well as accelerate the diffusion of innovations that result from one agency's imitating the apparent successes of others. The second strategy is labeled "centralized generation and transfer." It includes programs that attempt to encourage the demonstration and diffusion of innovations selected by the federal sponsors. The first strategy encourages local managers to expand their search for innovations; the second encourages them to adopt innovations judged potentially beneficial by the federal sponsor.

Before discussing some of the behavioral consequences of the federal interventions, we shall briefly describe each of the program types:

General support programs are the most common types of federal intervention. They can be thought of as supporting the philosophy of "letting a hundred flowers bloom." Local managers are encouraged to apply for funds to cover the start-up costs of introducing new technologies that are either endogenously developed or adopted from other agencies. Typically, the sponsoring agency will encourage the local agencies in a specific public industry to submit proposals for projects falling under a number of broad categories. The sponsoring agency then chooses projects from among those submitted for funding. Studies of the process of intergovernmental

Table 1. Types of Federal Support for Innovation in Local Public Agencies

---

Endogenous Generation and Lateral Transfer

1. General Support
   a. Projects
      Funding is provided for projects suggested by recipients.
   b. Capacity Building
      Funding is provided to increase the capacity of recipients to evaluate information and utilize expertise, or *technical assistance* is made available for recipient selected projects.
2. Improved Communication
   Mechanisms are introduced to accelerate the lateral transfer of information.

Centralized Generation and Transfer

3. Research and Development
   Funding is provided to research organizations, factor suppliers, and potential providers of technical assistance to prepare new technologies for introduction into local agencies.
4. Demonstrations
   Funding and *technical assistance* are provided to selected recipients to generate information about the demonstrated innovation.
5. Dissemination
   Information endorsing specific innovations is provided to potential adopters.
6. Induced Diffusion
   a. Cost Reduction
      Information is provided and *funding* is offered to encourage the adoption of endorsed innovations.
   b. Management Support
      Information and *technical assistance* help managers choose and implement endorsed innovations.
   c. Full Support
      Information, funding, and *technical assistance* encourage the adoption and assist the implementation of endorsed innovations.

---

grants suggest that organizational incentives may lead program sponsors to socially inefficient decisions.[12] For example, the desire to "move money" so as not to be left with undisbursed funds at the end of the fiscal year and the desire to increase political support through geographic distribution may lead the sponsoring agency to fund projects that either reinvent the wheel or have minimal or even negative expected net benefits. Consequently, in designing general support programs it is crucial that we consider organizational incentives in developing procedures for determining which projects are to be funded for how long and with what local requirements.

Even with federal funding, local agencies will be hindered in their innovative efforts by their limited capacity to evaluate information and utilize expertise. Recognizing these limitations, several investigators have recommended that the federal government attempt to increase the capacity of local governments to select and implement innovations efficiently.[13] Unfortunately, there is almost no research to help determine the practicality of this intuitively appealing recommendation. In fact, it is unclear what mechanisms should be used. One approach would be the funding of local analytical units, probably at the city or county level, because most local agencies would be too small to support their own units economically. Being one step removed from the substantive business of local agencies, however, such units are likely to develop an orientation toward cost reduction rather than quality improvement through innovation.[14] Another approach would be for the federal government to make technical assistance available for locally initiated projects, perhaps through regional centers or through personnel exchanges. Although they deal with individuals and private firms rather than local public agencies, the Cooperative Extension Service of the U.S. Department of Agriculture and the Technology Utilization Program of the National Aeronautics and Space Administration (NASA) provide examples of the direct provision of general technical assistance by the federal government.[15] The question of how technical assistance of a general nature could be allocated on a large scale to local public agencies remains to be answered.

Researchers have noted the importance of professional communication networks in the diffusion process.[16] One way for the federal government to increase diffusion rates, therefore, is to facilitate improved communications among agencies in the public industries.[17] A direct approach is to establish clearinghouses that receive and disseminate information about innovations that have been tried by agencies in the public industries.[18] Grants can be given to professional organizatons to enable them to do more than simply disseminate testimonial accounts of "successful" innovations provided by their members.[19] Several important questions need to be explored to determine the circumstances under which programs of improved communications are desirable: Do innovators present balanced information to potential adopters, or do they emphasize benefits and deemphasize costs? How useful is the information to potential adopters in helping them choose innovations and secure resources for their implementation? What organizational structures are most effective in securing and transmitting information?

We can consider research and development as ranging from studies of the problems facing public industries that might be solved through innovation, to the translation of innovative concepts to limited experiments and pilot projects. It includes the evaluation of innovations arising endogenously in the public industries and the investigation of innovations in the private sector that might be adapted for use by local public agencies. Funding may be provided to private firms for the development of equipment for use in areas such as public safety and sanitation, where fragmented and small markets preclude profits from unsupported research and development.[20]

Federal programs supporting domestic research and development have come under considerable criticism for not yielding practical knowledge that can be readily translated into innovative projects and programs.[21] Several researchers have offered recommendations for improving the organization and utilization of research and development programs.[22] Greater attention must be given to ways of improving the identification of promising innovations that arise endogenously, with or without general support funding, in local public agencies.

Demonstration projects, often included under the heading of research and development, involve the application of technologies in real-world environments on a scale that will yield information about their probable impacts when replicated. Usually a single site is selected for the demonstration project. Funding and technical assistance are provided by the federal sponsor who documents project activities and outcomes. Walter S. Baer, Leland L. Johnson, and Edward N. Merrow identify three levels of success in their study of twenty-four federally sponsored demonstration projects: satisfaction of participants, elimination of uncertainties about use of the technology in an organizational setting, and the diffusion of the technology as a result of the information generated.[23] Demonstration projects may be the only way to gain information about the impacts and implementation problems likely to result from technologies, such as management innovations, that cannot be adequately tested on less than agency scale. Just as with research and development projects, however, the information generated is unlikely in itself to overcome the barriers to diffusion.[24]

Programs of dissemination are intended to provide a higher quality of information than programs of improved communication. Promising innovations, perhaps arising through general support programs or demonstration projects, are evaluated in terms of effectiveness and transferability. Potential adopters are then provided with information that endorses the innovations most likely to be replicated successfully.[25] Because of the wide variability in the characteristics and capabilities of agencies in a public industry, any one of the innovations may be appropriate for only a small fraction of potential adopters. Will the information provided enable potential adopters to determine whether the endorsed innovation is likely to be successful in their agencies? The answer to this question depends as much on the way information is gathered and evaluated as on the way it is transmitted to potential adopters. Consequently, both selection and transmission mechanisms need be considered in the design of effective programs of dissemination.

Similar to programs of dissemination, programs of induced diffusion endorse specific innovations. In addition to information, they provide either funding or technical assistance to encourage adoption and facilitate implementation. Three types of programs of induced diffusion can be identified: cost reduction, management support, and full support. Cost reduction programs offer grants to agencies that adopt endorsed innovations.[26] Management support programs do not directly provide funding; rather they provide assistance in the preparation of proposals to other funding sources.

Technical assistance is also intended to mitigate deficiencies in managerial skills that may hamper agencies in their planning and implementation efforts. The full-support program provides both funding and technical assistance to encourage adoption and facilitate the implementation of endorsed innovations.[27]

Programs of induced diffusion go the furthest toward mitigating the limitations that retard endogenous innovation in local public agencies. An inherent danger in the use of programs of induced diffusion is that they may go too far. To understand this danger, we need to outline two important considerations.

First, successful diffusion involves not only the decisions of agencies to adopt a technology, but also the degree to which they can successfully implement their decisions. Studies of diffusion of innovation in the private sector have paid little attention to the implementation problem. In addition to other criticisms, classical economic models of innovation-adopting firms leave little room for modeling implementation. Managers need only adjust the levels of fully manipulable factor inputs. Failure to specify the right combination means simply that, if uncorrected, the firm will be driven from the market. Empirical studies of innovation and diffusion have tended to ignore implementation problems because they focused on the diffusion of artifacts or pieces of practical knowledge. Adoption and implementation are operationally identical for these types of innovation: doctors either write prescriptions for the new drug being studied or they do not. In the case of management and service delivery technologies, the decision to adopt may be only the starting point of a long process of managerial activity needed to make the technology useful.

Second, our simple diffusion model assumes that firms can conduct a rational evaluation of innovations. Innovations judged beneficial to the firm will be adopted; those judged unbeneficial will not be adopted. These judgments are facilitated by observing the success of the innovating firm in the marketplace.[28] Because public agencies generally do not have their outputs valued in the marketplace, it may be difficult for one public agency to judge the success of an innovation instituted by another.

The implementation and evaluation problems merit elaboration.

IMPLEMENTATION

When the managers of local agencies decide to adopt innovations for use in their organizations, they believe or hope certain consequences will result from their decisions. They expect the innovations to lead to results such as increased managerial control, improved or less expensive methods for the delivery of services, or increased prestige and larger budgets. Federal agencies supporting the innovative efforts also hypothesize sets of consequences (possibly different from those anticipated by the local public agency managers) that provide a rationale for supporting the local activities. According to Jeffrey L. Pressman and Aaron Wildavsky, implementation is the process by which the hypothesized consequences result in varying degrees after the project has been initiated.[29]

The importance of the organizational environment in the implementation process as well as its open-ended and dynamic characteristics suggests that attempts to develop general models of the implementation process from a formal rational behavioral framework are likely to produce few new insights. A loose descriptive model that is flexible enough to fit the particulars of different types of program implementation may be an adequate conceptual tool. One descriptive model that will be useful for illuminating the implementation process has been developed by Eugene Bardach. Implementation can be viewed as the assembly of the diverse elements required to build and operate a program in the context of the playing out of a number of games whereby the elements are either delivered or withheld from the program assembly.[30] For example, the implementation of a new policy in a prosecutor's office may require as an element a change in the routine of assistants. If the assistants withhold their cooperation, office managers will have to resort to threats or promises to complete the implementation process.

Several implications for programs of induced innovations can be readily drawn out from the model of implementation as an assembly process. First, the greater the complexity of the project, in terms of the number of elements that must be assembled, the greater the chances of project failure. Consider the example of a district attorney attempting to implement a management innovation within his office.

Funds may have to be secured from the local legislative body to match federal grants. Cooperation may have to be secured from other local criminal justice agencies (such as police departments) making up what has been called the "nonsystem of criminal justice." Although the district attorney may rely on the reciprocal nature of relationships with the other criminal justice agencies, he may have little leverage for securing cooperation from local agencies, such as the county data processing center, whose services may be required for the development or operation of the innovation. Cooperation must be secured from office personnel, who may view the innovation as an inconvenience or a threat. Even though the district attorney may be able to gain the nominal cooperation of his staff, special pains may be required to elicit the full or extra effort required to make the innovation a success. Civil service regulations and fixed pay scales for professional employees may make it more difficult for public managers to secure full cooperation from their staffs through punishments, rewards, or replacements than for managers of private firms attempting innovation.

A second implication, relevant to those designing programs of support for innovation, is that the organizational variability of the target agencies means that different sets of assembly problems may predominate in different agencies. For example, the prosecution industry was previously defined as the collection of local prosecution offices employing similar inputs to produce similar outputs. Yet no two prosecutors' offices are organized exactly the same way. Nor do any two prosecutors face exactly the same political and bureaucratic environments. Some prosecutors' offices, given a large enough dollar grant, would be able to purchase critical component elements through consulting contracts and transfers to other agencies. Other prosecutors' offices may not have sufficient managerial or political resources to use contractors effectively or formulate viable agreements with other agencies whose cooperation is required. The designers of programs of induced diffusion must determine whether assistance can be provided to local agencies in sufficient magnitude and duration to carry the assembly of project elements to completion. The variability in the organization of local public agencies, even among those in the same "industry," and the difficulty of anticipating problems that will be encountered in assembling the program elements suggest that attempts to design a fixed package of assistance adequate for a large number of agencies are likely to be frustrated. In order for a program of induced diffusion to be effective for a large number of agencies, it must allow for flexibility in the mix and packaging of the various forms of assistance to be provided.

RATIONAL EVALUATION

It was previously noted that models of the diffusion of innovations among private firms assume that it is possible to anticipate the costs and benefits of imitating the innovations. The experience of the innovating firm and each of the successive imitators serves as an empirical base for the rational anticipation of the innovation's impact for potential innovators. For several reasons the assumption that impacts can be rationally evaluated is unlikely to be satisfied for programs inducing the diffusion of management or service delivery technologies among local public agencies.

First, the valuation of an innovation's impact on the quantity and quality of services produced by public agencies (which are not readily revealed in the marketplace as changes in sales or profits) is technically difficult. There is often a measurement problem, particularly in cases in which the innovation is intended to enhance the quality of services provided. When reasonable measurements can be developed, the absence of benchmark data is likely to reduce the possibility of comparing the preinnovation measures with postinnovation measures. Conclusions drawn concerning before/after comparisons may be suspect because changing conditions that could explain the results have not been accounted for.

As an illustration of these points, consider the problem of evaluating an innovation intended to increase uniformity of case handling in a prosecutor's office. (Chapter 2 shows that the uniformity in case handling has many dimensions.) In plea-bargaining practices, for example, uniformity might be measured by grouping plea-bargained cases according to the seriousness of the offense and the prior record of the defendants and then comparing the variance in the plea-bargaining sentences within groups homogeneous in these characteristics. It is unlikely that data for such measures would be readily at hand. Thus a sampling of old, and possibly incomplete, files would be necessary. It might also be believed that the strength of the case against the defendant is a legitimate source of variation in plea-bargained sentences. Although it might be possible to collect data on the strength of the cases handled after the introduction of the innovation, it would probably be impossible to gather this data for the sample of preinnovation cases unless the evaluation process had been started long enough before the innovation had been introduced to allow data collection on active cases. The resulting before/after comparison would be of questionable validity if the size of the prosecutor's staff increased, independently of the innovation, during the comparison period. Moreover, answering such questions would be difficult for experienced and skilled researchers, let alone for the personnel typically available in local prosecutors' offices.

Second, even when it is possible to conduct methodologically sound evaluations of the impact of an innovation on the quantity and quality of services produced by a public agency, bureaucratic incentives may discourage the conduct of evaluations or the communication and utilization of negative findings. In addition to the putative goals of the innovation project, the local public agency manager may be interested in some of the subsidized project elements for their intrinsic value to the office. For example, an innovation with the prospect of only marginally improving management or service delivery might be accepted and protected because participation in the project leads to an increase in the organization's budget and staff.[31]

Once an innovation has been incorporated into the agency, the manager has little to gain from a rigorous evaluation of its impact on the quantity or quality of services produced. Although positive findings might yield the local manager some additional prestige, negative findings might cost him the resources associated with the introduction of the innovation as well as a loss of prestige.

The federal administrators of the program of induced diffusion are also likely to face bureaucratic incentives that will discourage their pursuit of rigorous evaluations. The unit administering the program of induced diffusion will be dependent upon some legislative or administrative body for its budget. Once a mandate is secured to begin a program of induced diffusion, the program administrators will be under pressure to identify innovations to support so that the current budget and future budget requests can be justified. The program administrators may be pushed toward innovations that are promising in theory, but have been tested only on a limited basis. In promoting the innovation to local public agencies, the program administrators must set an enthusiastic tone in order to encourage the diffusion of the innovations so that money can be "moved." Such enthusiastic support, however, commits the program administrators to specific innovations. Evaluations that reveal an innovation to be ineffective could jeopardize the survival of the program and the bureaucratic position of the administrators. Because the innovation was originally marketed to local public agencies as effective, positive evaluation results are likely to be of only marginal value in increasing diffusion. The potential for high costs and only small benefits should discourage program administrators from seeking rigorous program evaluations.

A third reason why the rational evaluation of the impacts of innovations is likely not to be an important factor in the induced diffusion process is that the time needed to conduct a rigorous evaluation may be lengthy compared with the rate of diffusion. For example, a federal agency is concerned with improving the administration of justice. There is a search for "inventions" that have the potential for improving management within prosecutors' offices (possibly by funding a number of ideas in local prosecutors' offices). When a promising invention has been identified, efforts are made to market it to the prosecution industry. The federal agency intends to evaluate the new idea thoroughly based on the experiences of the first few prosecutors' offices in adopting it.

Figure 1 illustrates a situation in which the innovation has diffused to a large number of agencies prior to their knowing the results of a rigorous evaluation of the impact of the innovation on the quantity or quality of services produced.

The diffusion curve in Figure 1 is assumed to describe the cumulative percentage of the industry of local agencies adopting the

Figure 1. Evaluation and Fast Diffusion

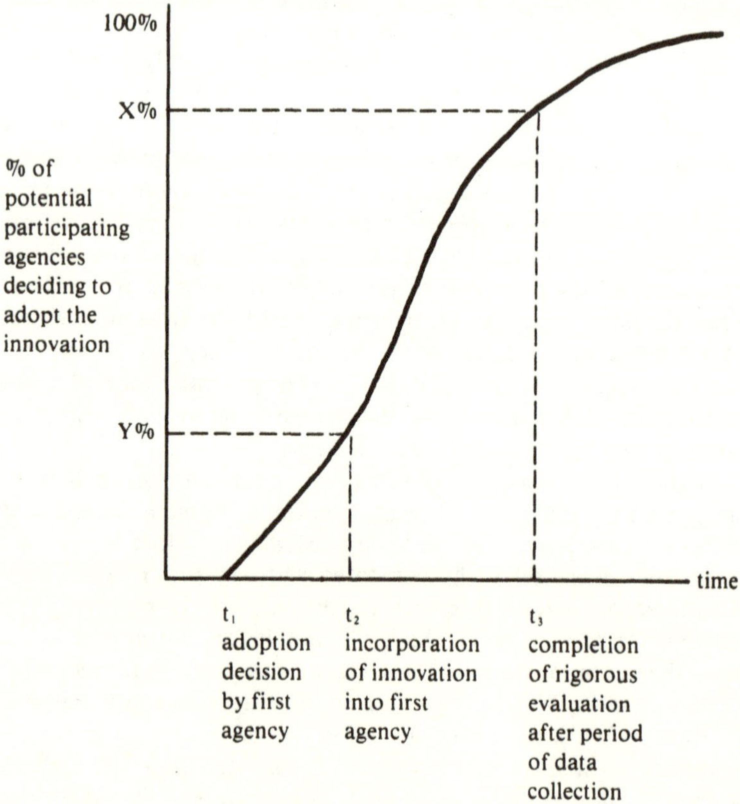

innovation as a result of program marketing efforts and in the absence of available evaluation results. The period between t_1 and t_2 is the time required to implement fully the innovation in the first adopting agency. The period between t_2 and t_3 is the time required to collect data on the services produced after the implementation of the innovation. At t_3, evaluation results become available. If the results are negative, the program may be terminated or no new agencies may adopt the innovation. But by t_3, however, X percent of the agencies that are potential adopters of the innovation have begun to implement it.

Thus even when rigorous evaluations of the impact of the innovation on the production of services are technically feasible, and program administrators and the innovating local public agency are willing to carry them out, the time delay in the availability of evaluation results means that negative findings may be too late to prevent the adoption of the innovation in a number of other agencies. The alternative is to delay marketing activities until the innovation can be fully implemented and evaluated in the first agency adopting it. Such a delay, however, may be inconsistent with bureaucratic incentives facing the program administrators to "move money."

The PROMIS experience readily illustrates the evaluation problem. As noted previously, the research for this book was completed in 1977, almost three years after the beginning of LEAA efforts to induce the diffusion of PROMIS. The diffusion of PROMIS has accelerated during the past two years. Yet during this five-year period, LEAA has neither funded independent evaluations of the desirability of continued PROMIS diffusion nor sponsored systematic studies of PROMIS implementation. Although a major purpose of this book is the demonstration of how implementation analyses should be used in the evaluations of programs of induced innovations, it also serves as the only systematic and independent evaluation of the PROMIS Transfer Project.

ORGANIZATION OF THIS VOLUME

Having set out an overview of the process of induced diffusion generally applicable to federal intervention in the wide range of locally provided public services, we next turn to important aspects of prosecution and its management. Chapter 2 examines the importance of improving prosecution and the major innovations that have led to improvement in the past decade. The chapter concludes with an outline of the potential benefits that might be obtained from computerized case management information systems.

Chapters 3 and 4 present the experiences of two prosecutors' offices with case management information system prototypes (one was with PROMIS), in an attempt to predict potential benefits for subsequent adopters. The implementation analysis suggests that several major problems, centered on the difficulty of achieving and maintaining an accurate data base, make the LEAA decision to diffuse PROMIS highly premature. Chapter 5 evaluates the criteria LEAA employed in its decision and describes the marketing, funding, and technical assistance LEAA provides to induce the diffusion of PROMIS.

The experiences of the first twenty PROMIS adopters are investigated in chapter 6 to determine the accuracy of the implementation analysis based on the prototypes and to provide a basis for evaluating the PROMIS Transfer Project. (An apparent catch-22 is identified.) The same factors that make case management information systems desirable also make them difficult to implement successfully.

The analysis of the implementation of case management information systems and several other innovations in prosecution management, particularly case ranking systems (which are discussed in chapter 7), provide a framework (in chapter 8) for viewing the implementation of innovations. An attempt is made to determine the characteristics of appropriate innovations for improving the management of prosecution.

Chapter 9 reviews the PROMIS Transfer Project to illustrate the mixed blessings of induced diffusion: rapid diffusion and an increased chance of successful implementation are obtained at the cost of creating organizational incentives that can result in adoptions that do not yield positive net benefits. The chapter concludes with a consideration of some institutional mechanisms that might be employed to reduce the dangers involved in launching programs of induced diffusion.

NOTES

1. For a review of LEAA history see Susan O. White and Samuel Krislov, eds., *Understanding Crime: An Evaluation of the National Institute of Law Enforcement and Criminal Justice* (Washington, D.C.: National Academy of Sciences, 1977); Richard E. Cohen, "Renewal of LEAA Likely Despite Doubts on Crime Impact," *National Journal* 7, no. 38 (September 20, 1975): 1319-48; Lawrence O'Connell and Susan O. White, "Politics and Evaluation in LEAA: The New England States," in *Management and Policy Science in American Government: Problems and Prospects,* ed. Michael White, Michael Radnor, and David Jansik (Lexington, Mass.: D. C. Heath, 1975); and The Twentieth Century Fund Task Force on the Law Enforcement Assistance Administration, *Law Enforcement: The Federal Role* (New York: McGraw-Hill, 1976).

2. For example, see the interview with James M. H. Gregg, former acting administrator of LEAA, in *LEAA Newsletter* 7, no. 8-9 (October/November 1978): 8-10.

3. Richard Nelson and Sidney Winter, "In Search of a Useful Theory of Innovation," *Research Policy* 6 (1977): 36-76; and J. David Roessner, "Federal Technology Policy: Innovation and Problem Solving in State and Local Governments," *Policy Analysis* 5, no. 2 (Spring 1979): 181-200.

4. Warner has raised the possibility of such adverse effects of federal intervention and the importance of studying them. Kenneth Warner, "The Need for Some Innovative Concepts of Innovation: An Examination of Research on the Diffusion of Innovations," *Policy Sciences* 5, no. 4 (December 1974): 433-51.

5. For example, see Lee S. Friedman, "The Evolution of a Bail Reform," *Policy Sciences* 7, no. 3 (September 1976): 281-313.

6. In the private sector, firms supplying capital equipment often serve as a source of innovations. Roessner argues that limited resources from fragmented purchasing practices limit the incentive for suppliers of capital goods to serve a similar function for local agencies. J. David Roessner, "The Local Government Market as a Stimulus to Industrial Innovation," *Research Policy* 8 (1979): 340-62.

7. Brewer provides an extreme illustration of the problems involved in the use of consultants in his study of the failure of large-scale simulation models. Garry Brewer, *Politicians, Bureaucrats, and the Consultant* (New York: Basic Books, 1973). Use of consultants may also undermine the development of inhouse skills needed to maintain adopted innovations. See Elliot H. Kline and C. Gregory Buntz, "On the Effective Use of Public Sector Expertise or Why the Use of Outside Consultants Often Leads to the Waste of In-house skills," *Public Administration Review* 39, no. 3 (May/June 1979): 226-29.

8. For a discussion of the importance of considering the implementation process in studying innovations see, Paul Berman and Milbrey McLaughlin, *Federal Programs Supporting Educational Change,* vol. 1, R-1589/1-HEW (Santa Monica, Calif.: Rand Corporation, September 1974); Neal Gross, Joseph Giacquinta, and Marilyn Bernstein, *Implementing Organizational Innovations* (New York: Basic

Books, 1971); Richard Nelson and Douglas Yates, eds., *Innovation and Implementation in Public Organizations* (Lexington, Mass.: D. C. Heath, 1978); Robert Yin, Karen Heald, and Mary Vogel, *Tinkering with the System* (Lexington, Mass.: Lexington Books, 1977).

9. Richard Nelson, "The Allocation of Research and Development Resources: Some Problems of Public Policy," in *Ohio State University Conference on the Economics of Research and Development* (Columbus: Ohio University Press, 1962).

10. For somewhat different arguments leading to a similar conclusion, see J. David Roessner, "Incentives to Innovate in Public and Private Organizations," *Administration and Society* 9 (November 1977): 341-65.

11. Federal technical assistance to local governments has received almost no attention from students of innovation. The major exception is Robert K. Yin et al., who include technical assistance among the independent variables they use to explain the degree of implementation success; see Yin et al., *Tinkering with the System*.

Technical assistance is provided by a variety of federal agencies: the Health Services Administration of HEW, the Technology Utilization Office of NASA, and a variety of programs in the Department of Transportation. The Law Enforcement Assistance Administration (LEAA) has greatly expanded its provision of technical assistance from $1.2 million in 1970 to an estimated $15 million in 1979. The LEAA expenditures include support of general technical assistance provided by the National Clearinghouse for Criminal Justice Information Systems and the National Center for State Courts, as well as for innovation-specific technical assistance for participants in the PROMIS Transfer Project and the Career Criminal Program. Law Enforcement Assistance Administration, *Ninth Annual Report: Fiscal Year 1977* (Washington, D.C., 1978).

12. Jeffrey Pressman, *Federal Programs and City Politics* (Berkeley: University of California Press, 1975).

13. Robert K. Yin, Karen A. Heald, Mary E. Vogel, Patricia D. Fleishauer, and Bruce C. Vladeck, *A Review of Case Studies of Technological Innovations in State and Local Services,* R-1870-NSF (Santa Monica, Calif.: Rand Corporation, February 1976); and Roessner, "Federal Technology Policy."

14. One of the most highly developed and active units of this kind is the San Diego County Office of Program Evaluation. For a description of its activities, see Gale G. Whiteneck, *Assessment of State and Local Government Evaluation Practices: An Evaluation Unit Profile,* HEW-100-76-0158 (Denver, Colo.: Denver Research Institute/University of Denver, March 1977).

15. Samuel I. Doctors, *The Role of Federal Agencies in Technology Transfer* (Cambridge, Mass.: The MIT Press, 1969).

16. See, for example, Irwin Feller and Donald Menzel, "Diffusion Milieus as a Focus of Research on Innovation in the Public Sector," *Policy Sciences* 8, no. 1 (March 1977): 49-68; and Everett Rogers and Floyd Shoemaker, *The Communication of Innovations* (New York: Free Press, 1971).

17. Yin suggests using such "natural" points of entry as professional organizations. Robert K. Yin, *R&D Utilization by Local Services: Problems and Prospects for*

Further Research, R-2020-DOJ (Santa Monica, Calif.: Rand Corporation, December 1976).

18. For example, LEAA funds Project SEARCH as a clearinghouse for information provided by criminal justice agencies that have developed computerized information systems. See Gordon Karl Zenk, *Project SEARCH: The Struggle for Control of Criminal Information Systems in America* (Westport, Conn.: Greenwood Press, 1979).

19. For example, the National Science Foundation provides grants to the International City Management Association for preparation of case studies of municipal innovations. Fred S. Knight and Michael D. Rancer, eds., *Tried and Tested: Case Studies in Municipal Innovation* (Washington, D.C.: International City Management Association, 1978).

20. Michael Radnor, *Studies and Action Programs on the Law Enforcement Equipment R&D System: Evaluative Study of the Equipment Systems Improvement Program,* 74-NI-99-0004-G (Evanston, Ill.: Northwestern University, 1975).

21. See, for example, the account of policy research supported by the Office of Economic Opportunity. Walter Williams, *Social Policy Research and Analysis* (New York: American Elsevier, 1971).

22. Howard R. Davis and Susan E. Solasin, "Strengthening the Contribution of Social R&D to Policy Making," in *Knowledge and Policy: The Uncertain Connection,* ed. Laurence E. Lynn, Jr. (Washington, D.C.: National Academy of Sciences, 1978); and Yin, *R&D Utilization by Local Services.*

23. They also report that, although more than 10 percent of the $5.9 billion obligated for civilian research and development in fiscal year 1974 was for demonstration projects, there have been relatively few studies of their role in the innovation process. Walter S. Baer, Leland L. Johnson, and Edward N. Merrow, *Analysis of Federally Funded Demonstration Projects: Final Report,* R-1926-DC (Santa Monica, Calif.: Rand Corporation, April 1976).

24. "Demonstration projects appear to be weak tools for tackling institutional and organizational barriers to diffusion." Baer, Johnson, and Merrow, *Analysis of Federally Funded Demonstration Projects,* p. vi.

25. For example, the Office of Policy Development and Research of the U.S. Department of Housing and Urban Development endorses the use of policy analysis and program evaluation teams by local and state governments. Public Technology, Inc., *Program Evaluation and Analysis* (Washington, D.C.: Government Printing Office, 1978).

26. An example is LEAA's Career Criminal Program, which provides grants to local prosecutors for the establishment of special units for prosecuting habitual offenders.

27. Programs of induced diffusion have received almost no attention from researchers. In fact, a survey of federal technology transfer programs completed in 1975 did not explicitly distinguish induced diffusion from grant and dissemination programs. National Science Foundation, "Directory of Federal Technology Transfer" (Washington, D.C.: National Science Foundation, 1975).

28. Even private firms may be misled by the direct observation of early innovations. Sapolsky describes how firms falsely attributed the success of the U.S. Navy's Fleet Ballistic Missile Program to the use of the widely ballyhooed Program Evaluation and Review Technique (PERT). PERT was more successful as a shield from interference from governmental actors than as an actual aid to managing the Polaris project. Nevertheless, PERT diffused widely among large corporations in the mid-sixties. See Harvey M. Sapolsky, *The Polaris Systems Development* (Cambridge, Mass.: Harvard University Press, 1972), chap. 4, "PERT and the Myth of Managerial Effectiveness," pp. 94-130.

29. Jeffrey L. Pressman and Aaron Wildavsky, *Implementation* (Berkeley: University of California Press, 1975), p. xv.

30. Eugene Bardach, *The Implementation Game: What Happens After a Bill Becomes a Law* (Cambridge, Mass.: MIT Press, 1977), p. 37.

31. For empirical evidence see Yin et al., *A Review of Case Studies,* p. 151. The public manager may also receive prestige simply by being considered an innovator. Lawrence B. Mohr, "Determinants of Innovation in Organizations, *American Political Science Review* 63 (March 1969): 111-26.

chapter 2

The Management of Prosecution

> *Viewed in broad perspective, the American legal system seems to be shot through with many excessive and uncontrolled discretionary powers but the one that stands out above all others is the power to prosecute or not to prosecute.*[1] —Kenneth Culp Davis

As the chief law enforcement officer of his county or district, the chief prosecutor (or district attorney) enjoys immense discretionary power in setting policies for the charging, processing, and disposition of criminal cases. Although state criminal procedure laws and the requirements of due process place some bounds on the way cases are handled, the chief prosecutor is free to decide who will be prosecuted, on what charges, and with what degree of vigor.[2] In general, the courts will not interfere with decisions not to prosecute or to terminate prosecutions already begun.[3] The discretion of the chief prosecutor is checked by the electorate, which periodically has the opportunity to vote him out of office. In theory, the ballot box provides a mechanism for voters to change the character of prosecution in their jurisdiction. In practice, the low visibility of most prosecutorial decisions limits the effectiveness of electoral control. The divergence between established policy and the actions of assistant prosecutors limits the amount of change that can be achieved by replacement or threat of replacement of the chief prosecutor.

The chief prosecutors of populous jurisdictions may employ scores or even hundreds of assistant prosecutors. Where policies are absent, incompletely formulated, inadequately communicated, or unenforced, the preferences and prejudices of assistants will assert themselves. The less strict the adherence to office-wide policies, the more prosecution will take on an idiosyncratic character.

Some deviations from office policies are unlikely to come under administrative review. If the assistant declines to file charges, the case is unlikely to be reconsidered by the office unless a particularly irate witness or arresting officer complains to office management. The defense is likely to accept immediately an overly lenient plea-bargaining offer rather than take the chance that it will be withdrawn when the case is reviewed prior to trial. In the typical prosecutor's office, detection of these deviations would require a time-consuming review of original case documents by office managers who often have difficulty keeping up with the active case load.

Other types of deviations are more likely to come under administrative review but can nevertheless involve costs to defendants or the office even if corrected. A case that is charged more severely than is consistent with office policy may eventually be refiled with more appropriate charges. But in the meantime the defendant may have failed to secure pretrial release because of the higher bail corresponding to the more serious charges. An overly harsh stance in plea bargaining is likely to move the case toward trial status. As the case is prepared for trial, a more appropriate plea bargain may be offered. If the offer had been made originally, the ultimate disposition might have been reached without the additional costs of preparing the case for trial. Failure to oppose unwarranted requests by the defense for continuance delays disposition, perhaps weakening the state's case as apparent injuries to the victim heal and witnesses forget, lose interest, or move away.

These illustrations suggest three major reasons why idiosyncratic prosecution—charging, handling, and disposition decisions reflecting the preferences of assistant prosecutors rather than the policies of the chief prosecutor—should be a matter of public concern.

First, it violates our conception of equitable treatment under the law. According to Arthur Rosett, "Our legal tradition demands that decisions be made dispassionately and rationally, pursuant to generally applicable rules. Idiosyncratic choice, whereby the individual's fate depends upon which official happens to be on duty that day, is repellent."[4] In the context of the criminal justice system, the "individual's fate" ranges from mere inconvenience to incarceration for varying periods of time. The denial of freedom through incarceration is a most serious matter in a democratic society. Witness the rulings of the Warren Court that extended the procedural protections given to criminal suspects and defendants with a recognition of the rulings' increased costs for the procedural mechanisms of the criminal justice system and possible costs to society in terms of crime control. Increased administrative efforts aimed at reducing idiosyncratic prosecution would be consistent with the judicial attention given to the protection of the defendant's rights in criminal procedures.

Second, idiosyncratic prosecution leads to an inefficient use of society's crime control resources. As previously noted, an overly harsh stance in plea bargaining (or the filing of charges that must eventually be dismissed) can inflict unnecessary trial preparation costs. On the other hand, excessive leniency can reduce the deterrent effects of prosecution. Although there is controversy over its importance in crime reduction, there is general agreement that the deterrent effect of punishment is a function of the certainty and swiftness of its application.[5] Idiosyncratic prosecution reduces the certainty of punishment by increasing the chances that defendants can avoid the level of punishment consistent with the prosecutor's policies. It reduces the swiftness of punishment by increasing the opportunity for skillful defense attorneys to delay disposition by maneuvering cases to assistants who will not strenuously oppose continuances.

Finally, idiosyncratic prosecution may undermine public respect for the criminal justice system as defendants, victims, and witnesses come in contact with its arbitrary workings. Order in society depends largely on the willingness of individuals to obey the law voluntarily. To the extent public respect influences the willingness of individuals to obey the law, idiosyncratic prosecution may lead to a reduction in societal order. Citizens who view the criminal justice system as arbitrary may not be willing to report crimes, press charges, or volunteer as witnesses.

So idiosyncratic prosecution is a problem of public concern. But how serious a problem? Perhaps the common experience of law school leads assistant prosecutors to share similar outlooks on the substantive law. Perhaps typically employed management procedures limit deviations from policy to a negligible level. Unfortunately, a large body of empirical research suggests otherwise by demonstrating the prevalence of idiosyncratic prosecution and the incapacity of endogenously evolved management procedures to control it effectively.[6] Before reviewing the major innovations in prosecution management that have appeared in this decade, we shall draw from the empirical research a sketch of the "typical" management procedures employed by large prosecutors' offices in the early 1970s. Even today, despite the introduction and diffusion of a number of innovations, many urban prosecutors' offices have management styles similar to the one outlined.

Perhaps the most fundamental managerial responsibility is the assignment of tasks to employees. Heavy case loads, the segmented nature of the adjudication process, and the commonly found bifurcation of courts into lower (municipal) and superior (county or district) branches necessitates horizontal organization for the prosecution of all or almost all cases. Under horizontal organization, assistants are assigned to specific courtrooms where they handle a single phase of case processing. For example, an assistant assigned to a municipal court that is set aside for the conduct of preliminary hearings for felony cases would handle only this phase of case processing. Horizontal organization eliminates the need to have assistants follow cases from one courtroom to another and therefore permits them to spend a maximum of time in court session. Just as an industrial assembly line enables mass production, horizontal organization allows a prosecutor's office to handle a heavier case load than would be possible if each case was handled throughout by a single assistant.

The assignment of assistants to the various stages of the disposition process only partly specifies the tasks they must perform. At each stage assistants must exercise discretion in making decisions concerning the dismissal of charges and the offering of concessions to secure guilty pleas. Because facilities are available to provide trials for only a fraction of the total case load, it is presumed that assistants will exercise their discretion to dispose of a majority of cases in the stages preliminary to trial. Unless the prosecutor is successful in communicating general policies to the assistants, the pattern of dispositions that result will lack uniformity. In practice, the communication of policies is neither formal nor comprehensive. Typically, junior assistants discover implicit policies through informal consultation with their seniors. Such informal communications may be effective in small, geographically centralized offices where personal contact with the prosecutor and his chief assistants can occur on a regular basis. In large, geographically decentralized offices having a rapid turnover in personnel, consistency in the promulgation and interpretation of policies would be surprising.

A manual of office policy and procedure may constitute the only formal statement of charging and disposition policies. The manual will usually include a general statement of office policy that is too vague to be of practical use to any but the newest assistants, whose training consists of a rotation through the various courtroom assignments, perhaps beginning with traffic court and eventually advancing to a felony trial court. The manual may also include a collection of the various memoranda that the prosecutor issues in response to serious errors in case dispositions that come to his attention. As such, the manual is useful only in indicating a limited number of specific actions that should be avoided. Not surprisingly, office manuals are rarely referred to by assistants.[7]

Deficiencies in communicating general policies would be of less concern if the performance of assistants could be constantly monitored and evaluated so that uniform practices might develop inductively. Some observers of the courts have pointed out how the interaction of the assistant prosecutors with other court actors tends to lead to inductive learning of standard views and behaviors.[8] Such informal learning can be viewed within the general framework of "organized work groups" developed recently by James Eisenstein and Herbert Jacob.[9] The assistant prosecutor develops a mutually acceptable view of substantive issues with the judge and defense attorney forming the work group so that over time we might expect similar cases to receive similar treatment by each work group. Unfortunately, the views adopted by different work groups are likely to be different, depending upon the interaction of their particular members. The influence of judges and defense attorneys on the outcomes of cases complicates the task the chief prosecutor faces in evaluating his assistants. In addition, several other factors hinder systematic monitoring and evaluation.

The sampling of performance is difficult and expensive. Because manual case files are not indexed by the various assistants who participated in case processing, it is time consuming to retrieve a sample of cases that has been handled by a particular assistant. Once the sample has been drawn, the chief prosecutor or one of the office managers would have to cull sufficient data from the case folders to allow an estimation of what the correct case decisions (in terms of office policies) should have been. Gathering the necessary data would be onerous, requiring the reading of the criminal complaint and other documents the cases had generated prior to disposition. The segmented case handling of horizontal organization may make it difficult to attribute responsibility for errors to a particular assistant. These factors make routine sampling of performance infeasible, or at least unlikely.

Instead, sampling is initiated as a reaction to specific criticism or questioning, usually from outside the office. Gross deviations from office policy are likely to trigger such complaints. From the perspective of the assistants, it may appear that performance is subject to management by "random terror": no feedback on performance is provided until a serious error happens to be caught. In response, assistants may attempt to avoid complaints from the defense by being overly lenient. The absence of managerial feedback on performance is compounded by the difficulty of learning by doing. By handling only one segment of case processing, assistants often do not have an opportunity to see the final dispositions of cases. Consequently, assistants cannot link their actions to final outcomes. In sum, assistants receive little feedback concerning their exercise of discretion.

The inherent difficulty of managing prosecutorial discretion is often compounded by a lack of managerial expertise and interest. The prosecutor and his chief assistants are lawyers who may have had no managerial experience outside the criminal justice system. As lawyers, they tend to view trial work as the most professionally interesting prosecutorial activity. The prosecutor, concerned about reelection, realizes that the media rarely pay attention to what happens to cases between arraignment and trial. Consequently, the monitoring of trial work and the handling of notorious cases receives relatively more attention than the more mundane activities of training new assistants and monitoring pretrial dispositions.

The innovations we shall discuss, however, suggest a growing realization among prosecutors of the importance of improving their control of delegated discretion. The first two classes of innovations discussed—enhanced case screening and clearance procedures—have arisen largely endogenously within prosecutors' offices without federal intervention. Although the other major innovations—vertical prosecution units and case management information systems—have been developed with federal funding and initiative, they are being adopted by an increasing number of prosecutors' offices. Our brief discussions of enhanced case screening and clearance procedures will include some practical as well as conceptual considerations. Our discussions of vertical prosecution units and case management information systems, however, will deal only with conceptual considerations because the remaining chapters focus on the extent of realization of their potential benefits in practice. Subsequent chapters will describe how LEAA has invested heavily in the diffusion of vertical prosecution units and case management information systems. Our discussion of the other innovations—enhanced screening and clearance procedures—is intended to illustrate alternatives LEAA might have chosen.

ENHANCED CASE SCREENING

In many offices case screening is performed by the least experienced assistants who often file the charges requested by law enforcement officers as long as they believe a conviction could be gained on some offense. The product of this kind of screening is a stream of cases with widely varying levels of strength of evidence and case seriousness for any given nominal charge.[10] The charges filed convey little information to other assistants concerning the disposition that should be sought. The low correlation between the charged offense and the level of disposition consistent with office policy also makes post-disposition monitoring difficult because it is a very weak presumption that like-charged cases should receive similar disposition.

Enhanced case screening can be conceived of as the centralization of the responsibility for selecting charges in the hands of a limited number of experienced assistants. Their experience enables them to make more reliable estimates of the strength of evidence and to select charges that reflect office policies. Assistants who handle the cases at latter stages receive guidance on appropriate dispositions implicitly through the more accurate charges and explicitly through comments made on the case folders by the more experienced assistants. The reduction in the number of assistants involved in case screening increases the chances that informal communication will lead to a common perception and application of the prosecutor's policies.

In her multi-jurisdictional study of pretrial screening projects, Joan Jacoby reports that the idea of screening cases before they enter the court system has widely diffused.[11] She also reports, however, that prosecutors tend to view case screening as a way of increasing efficiency by eliminating cases with insufficient evidence before they receive prosecutorial attention rather than as a way of ensuing that the charges filed are consistent with office policy. Screening units are often staffed with inexperienced assistants who have insufficient knowledge of office policies to charge cases in a way that reflects the disposition that is to be sought.

The greatest difficulty in implementing an enhanced screening unit is convincing experienced assistants to give up desirable assignments as trial prosecutors for work generally viewed as professionally unchallenging. In fact, in one office visited in conjunction with this study, assignment to screening duty has been in recent years considered a punishment for poor performance at trial. Nevertheless, two other offices visited demonstrated that it is possible to design the screening assignment so that experienced assistants will find it both attractive and at the same time continue to develop their understanding of office policies.

Prior to 1970, the Alameda County (California) District Attorney's Office employed all its personnel assigned to the seven municipal court branch offices to case charging in the hours prior to the arraignments held each morning. Not only did this method of case charging lead to excessive inter- and intra-branch variation, but it also enabled police officers to shop for assistants who would be most likely to file the charges they desired. In an attempt to introduce greater uniformity, the district attorney established a Felony Task Force of assistants who had had at least one year of trial experience. The Felony Task Force members handle all case charging.

The apparent success of the Felony Task Force is in large part due to the authority and status given its members. Municipal court assistants must obtain their approval before disposing of certain felony cases. Felony Task Force members meet regularly with the district attorney to discuss office policy as it has been applied to specific cases. The meetings encourage uniformity in the interpretation of policies and give members status as a select group in direct contact with the district attorney.

In April 1974 a new district attorney was elected for Orleans Parish (Louisiana). Under his direction, there have been major changes in office policies, accompanied by the transformation of office organization and the expansion of office resources to facilitate their implementation. One of the major changes has been the introduction of an enhanced screening unit.

Assistants assigned to the screening unit receive an increase in salary. Assignment to the screening unit has been made more attractive by occasionally allowing screening assistants to handle cases they have screened and expect to be professionally challenging at trial. The office rule that all dismissals must be cleared by the assistant who filed charges not only serves as a check on the dismissal decisions of less experienced assistants, but also provides screening assistants with feedback on the quality of their charging decisions and increases the status of the screening assignment by vesting in it management authority. Increased salary, status, and opportunity to handle the trials of professionally challenging cases has been successful in making screening service desirable to experienced assistants. Notification of dismissals and continuing trial experience provide information to the charging assistants about the consequences of their charging decisions.

Although the opportunity to grant pay increases may not be readily available to many prosecutors, the types of organizational rewards used in New Orleans and Alameda County could enable many prosecutors to implement and maintain enhanced screening units. Not only is enhanced screening in itself a valuable innovation for increasing control over idiosyncratic prosecution, it also facilitates the implementation of the other innovations that will be discussed shortly.

CLEARANCE PROCEDURES

With its enhanced screening unit, the Orleans Parish District Attorney's Office operates on the principle that dispositions should reflect the charges filed. Assistants wishing to dismiss charges or offer charge reductions to secure guilty pleas are required to seek prior approvals—clearances—from office managers. It represents the most direct control of discretion.

The primary responsibility for approving charge reductions rests with the two trial division chiefs, each of whom manages teams of ten assistants. When a trial section assistant wishes to reduce a defendant's charges, or chooses not to invoke the state's habitual-offender status, he must submit a written memorandum to the chief of his trial division outlining the reasons for these types of actions. If a case involves hard narcotics, approval for charge reduction must also be secured from either the district attorney or his first assistant.

The office management has adopted the philosophy that the dismissal of a case represents a failure: either the case has not been properly charged at screening, or sufficient contact has not been maintained with witnesses. Consistent with this philosophy, a two-stage clearance system has been established for dismissals. First, the trial section assistant wishing to dismiss a case must contact the screening division assistant who charged the case. If the screening division assistant gives his approval for dismissal, the second stage of the clearance system requires that the approval of the first assistant district attorney be secured.

The combined effect of the introduction of the screening division and clearance system has been to reduce greatly the number of cases in which charge reductions are made to secure guilty pleas.

Before the office reorganization, it is estimated that 75 to 85 percent of the convictions secured were the result of plea bargains. In 1975, the percentage of convictions resulting from plea bargains dropped to 12 percent and appeared to be approaching 8 percent in 1976.[12]

Defendants may enter guilty pleas without the offer of inducements from the prosecution. Some expect to be convicted and therefore wish to avoid the expense and ordeal of trial by entering a guilty plea. Other defendants enter guilty pleas in the hope that the judge will reward their admission of guilt with a lenient sentence. As might be expected, however, the limitations placed on plea bargaining by the clearance system has greatly increased the number of defendants demanding trials. In 1973, the year before the reorganization, 187 defendants demanded jury trials. In the first year after the reorganization, the number of defendants demanding jury trials rose to 531. A decreased crime rate and reduction of case docket intake in 1976, however, helped lead to a 20 percent reduction in the number of jury trials from the previous year.

What are the advantages and disadvantages of the clearance system? First, it has limited the exercise of discretion by trial section assistants. One of the trial division chiefs reported that he approved only about half of the requests made for charge reductions. The majority of the approvals were based on problems with evidence that would have made trial convictions on the original charges unlikely. The rejection of a portion of the requests made for charge reductions indicates that the clearance system has had some impact on the degree to which plea bargaining conforms to office policy. The commitment of office management to its operation is illustrated by willingness to use firings and pay reductions as punishment for assistants failing to follow the clearance procedures. On the other hand, it may be that the inconvenience of preparing memoranda discourages trial section assistants from making requests for charge reductions that would be consistent with office policy. To the extent that the screening unit is effective in selecting appropriate initial charges, there should be few instances where charge reductions would be consistent with office policy. In addition, it is unlikely that the inconvenience of preparing a written memorandum will deter a trial section assistant from seeking permission to reduce the charges for a seriously flawed case. If the assistant does not secure permission for a reduction in charges, he or she faces the prospect of losing the case when it goes to trial—a consequence more onerous than the writing of memoranda.

Second, the clearance system has altered the nature of the trial section assistant's job. One negative aspect of the change may be the reduction in job satisfaction resulting from the limitation placed on the discretion exercised over case disposition. The loss in job satisfaction is likely not to be at a level that will seriously erode job preference because the trial section assistants retain the exercise of their professional judgment in the presentation of cases at trial that constitutes their primary work effort.

In one way, the introduction of the clearance system has made the job of the trial section assistant easier. The clearance system shields the trial section assistant from dissatisfaction expressed by the defense attorney when charge reductions are not offered. One trial section assistant who was interviewed commented:

> You're not under constant pressure from defense attorneys—you don't have to worry about maintaining friendly working relationships. You're off the hook . . . same in dealing with the judges. The clearance system helps keep administrative considerations out of case decisions.[13]

The clearance system does not appear to exhibit the dysfunctions that Lief Carter reported finding in connection with the clearance system operated in "Vario" County.[14] One of the dysfunctional consequences of the "Vario" County clearance system was that the office regularly became "locked in" to trying cases that ought to have been dismissed or reduced. Two factors explain the lock-in effect that Carter observed. First, the assistant whose job it was to approve all charge reductions or dismissals of cases that reached superior court tended to be overly rigid in considering requests. This behavior was not realistic in view of the second factor explaining the undesirable lock-in effect: there was little effort made to ensure that cases were charged in a uniform manner. As a result, many cases reached superior court that were similar to cases prosecuted as misdemeanors. Weak cases also tended to reach superior court because assistants who put on preliminary hearings tended to overestimate the probability that case weaknesses could be corrected during preparation for trial.

In contrast with the lax screening procedures employed in "Vario" County, the Orleans Parish District Attorney's Office devotes considerable manpower and managerial resources to its screening division. Experienced assistants charge cases according to the policy that the office should be willing to go to trial on the particular charges filed. Assistants in the screening division have an opportunity to contact witnesses to assess potential case weaknesses prior to making a filing decision. Decisions by screening division assistants not to file the charges requested by the arresting officer are routinely subject to review by the division chief. The resulting case flow to the Trial Divisions is likely to exhibit charge levels much more consistent with office policy than would be expected from "Vario" County-style case screening. Consequently, there is much less potential for being locked in on unreasonable charges.

Carter argues that segmentation of case handling will have the undesirable consequence of preventing assistants who handle the case during its early stages from learning about errors in judgment they made that only become apparent in later stages. The clearance system for dismissals employed by the Orleans Parish District Attorney's Office appears to close the feedback loop to the assistants in the screening division by bringing to their attention all the cases they charged that eventually are discovered to be unsuitable for trial.

Is it likely that other prosecutors' offices would be able to replicate the apparently successful use of comprehensive clearance procedures by the Orleans Parish District Attorney's Office? Orleans Parish enjoyed three favorable circumstances that may not hold in other offices. First, Louisiana criminal procedure allows the prosecutor ten days from time of arrest to decide the charges that are to be filed. During this period, witnesses can be directly contacted by assistant prosecutors, increasing the chances that the case will be correctly charged from the outset. In most other states arraignments must be held within a much shorter period, limiting the extent to which information can be gathered to file the correct charges initially. The less frequently the correct charges are initially filed, the greater the number of clearances that need be sought from the presumptive dispositions and therefore the greater the cost of operating the clearance system.

Second, the spatial centralization of the Orleans Parish District Attorney's Office readily permitted face-to-face contact between assistant prosecutors and office managers. The direct contact added flexibility to written request procedures, allowing managers to advise and question assistants about their requests. It would be logistically more difficult for spatially decentralized offices to employ clearance procedures.

Finally, the Orleans Parish District Attorney's Office enjoyed a more than doubling of budget and more than 50 percent increase in staff during the period in which the screening division and clearance procedures were introduced. The added resources permitted an increase in control without a significant decrease in the number of cases handled. Without such an increase in resources, it may not be possible for many prosecutors' offices to introduce a comprehensive system of clearance procedures.

Although it is likely to be impractical for many prosecutors' offices to employ a comprehensive system of clearance procedures, it may be possible and desirable to employ a selective system of clearance procedures that requires clearances only for those cases with the greatest expected loss from decentralized decision making.[15] Ideally, all cases could be ranked according to their expected loss. Starting with the case with the greatest expected loss, cases would be successively added to the set upon which clearance procedures were imposed until the additional cost of inclusion exceeded the expected loss that could be avoided. The selective system of clearance procedures can only be employed if there is a method for identifying, a priori, the cases with the greatest expected loss.

Since 1974, the Alameda County District Attorney's Office has employed a case weighting system in support of its selective use of clearance procedures. Felony Task Force members employ a predetermined procedure to derive case weights for all prosecution requests that are filed as felonies. They begin by assigning points to each case in three categories: the characteristics of the defendant, the harm suffered by the victims, and other case characteristics believed relevant to the community. One, two, or three points are given in each of these three case categories. Next, the total points accumulated over the three dimensions is used to find a tentative letter weight. Finally, the tentative letter weight can be adjusted upward (where "A" is the highest and "C" is lowest) if certain specified circumstances hold.

The "A," "B," and "C" case weights specify the level of clearance that must be obtained prior to a case disposition. Whereas municipal court assistants may dispose of "C" cases without prior approval, the disposition of "A" and "B" cases requires prior approval from either the Felony Task Force member who charged the case or the branch manager, who in turn are expected to consult with a superior court manager before permitting the disposition of "A" cases. At the superior court level, disposition of "A" cases requires prior approval of the assistant's team leader. The three levels of clearance suggest the description "hierarchic" case weight ing system. Does the case weighting system involve a reasonable allocation of clearance resources? Three observations suggest an affirmative answer.

First, as discussed previously, assistants are more likely to err in the direction of leniency than in being overly harsh. If an assistant offers the defense an overly lenient disposition as part of a plea bargain, the defense will be likely to accept the bargain out of fear that the next assistant handling the case will offer a bargain more consistent with the office policy. On the other hand, if the assistant offers a bargain harsher than is consistent with office policy, the defense will be unlikely to accept it. Consequently, there is an asymmetry in the defense's response to the assistant's offer of bargains inconsistent with the office policy. In addition, the assistant's desire to maintain good working relations with defense attorneys may lead to a greater frequency of error in the direction of leniency.

The second observation is that the potential magnitude of excessive leniency increases as the seriousness of the case increases. If the district attorney believes that a certain set of cases should result in sentences of straight probation (the lowest level of punishment) or short jail terms, there is little room for excessive leniency. If the district attorney believes that another set of cases should result in state prison sentences, there is considerable room for excessive leniency. Namely, the defendant might receive the mildest punishment of straight probation when, according to the district attorney's policy, the defendant should have received the much more severe sentence of a term in state prison.

The third observation is really an assumption about the effectiveness of the classification procedure. If "A" cases are truly those whose dispositions should result in severe punishments to be consistent with the district attorney's policies, then it is appropriate that the "A" cases be subjected to the most stringent clearances because they have the greatest expected loss in light of the first two observations. If "C" cases are truly those whose dispositions should result in mild punishment to be consistent with office policy, then it also follows that they should have the weakest clearance requirements or no clearance requirement. It is at least plausible that the intermediate expected loss associated with "B" cases is not high enough to exceed the costs of requiring clearance by upper-level (superior court) managers, but is high enough to justify requiring clearances by middle-level (municipal court) managers. The latter involve lower cost, even after taking into consideration the fact that the middle-level management clearances will be less effective than upper-level management clearances in preventing dispositions inconsistent with office-wide policies. Middle-level management clearances are assumed to be less costly because they can be based on face-to-face communication and because the opportunity costs to the office of devoting time to handling clearances is lower for middle-level managers than upper-level managers. Middle-level managers may be less effective in increasing consistency with office-wide policies than upper-level managers because the middle-level managers may have varying policy interpretations and preferences.

There is statistical evidence that the selective clearance procedures employed in Alameda County have resulted in greater uniformity in plea bargaining.[16] The effectiveness of the clearance procedures and the supporting case weighting system have been enhanced by the ease with which implementation and modification have been achieved. It is likely that many offices could successfully implement similar systems, especially if they are coupled with enhanced screening units.

VERTICAL PROSECUTION UNITS

Although it involves higher per case costs than horizontal organization, the vertical assignment of cases offers several advantages. Continuous contact with cases may enable assistants to gather more or better evidence, increasing the chances of gaining a conviction if the cases go to trial. Victims and witnesses are likely to be more cooperative when they deal with a single assistant rather than with different ones at each of several court appearances. Defense attorneys lose the opportunity to try to delay disposition until their cases are handled by assistants who make overly lenient plea bargain offers. Additionally, assistants may be able to speed up the disposition process when doing so is advantageous to the prosecution.

When resource constraints make the vertical prosecution of the entire case load impractical, it may be possible to operate mixed systems. A common pattern involves the horizontal prosecution of all cases except a small number of homicides or otherwise notorious cases. A major innovation in recent years has been the introduction of the special prosecution unit that vertically prosecutes a larger fraction of the case load. The operation of a vertical prosecution unit permits the selective allocation of prosecutorial resources: for similar cases, the increased probability of trial conviction and the greater control over plea bargaining resulting from vertical prosecution will tend to yield higher levels of convictions and more severe sentences than the routine handling of horizontal prosecution. A prosecutor could increase the correspondence between the actual disposition pattern and that consistent with his policies by assigning those cases he believes most deserving of severe dispositions to the vertical prosecution unit.

In 1974, LEAA began inducing the diffusion of the vertical prosecution unit concept through its Career Criminal Program, which provides funding and on-site technical assistance to participating offices. By the end of 1976, eighteen prosecutors' offices had established vertical prosecution units (career criminal bureaus) with assistance from the Career Criminal Program.[17] Although a variety of criteria are employed for determining which cases will be handled by the units, all tend to prosecute defendants with the most serious criminal histories. Prosecutors who have established career criminal bureaus are implicitly adopting the policy that the defendants with the worst criminal records should receive the most severe punishments. If prior record is a good predictor of future criminal activity, this policy is consistent with maximizing the reduction in the number of future offenses that can be obtained through the isolating effect of incarceration. This policy may also reduce the number of offenses through the deterrent effect of the increased swiftness, certainty, and severity of punishment anticipated by persons with a high propensity for committing offenses.

It is not surprising that evaluations of career criminal bureaus report that they do in fact increase the swiftness, certainty, and severity of punishment for the cases they handle—higher levels of prosecutorial effort should yield such gains. To determine whether the career criminal bureaus are cost effective, however, requires reliable estimates of the magnitude of these gains. Several limitations in the evaluation methodologies so far employed cast doubt on reported estimates of the size of increases in the swiftness, certainty, and severity of punishment obtained through career criminal bureau prosecution.

First, the increases are measured relative to samples of routinely handled cases that are usually not comparable. If the career criminal bureau is handling the most serious cases, the comparison sample will consist of less serious cases that would be expected to result in less severe dispositions even if both groups were handled routinely. When the career criminal bureau handles only a portion of the most serious cases, the comparison may be confounded by the selection procedures employed. In particular, bureau directors are likely to choose cases that have an initially high probability of conviction so that it will be easy to maintain a high conviction rate. Anticipating that impressive statistics will make it easier to obtain continued funding from LEAA or replacement funding from local sources, the chief prosecutor may even encourage the selection of the strongest cases.[18]

Second, the comparisons ignore the higher utilization rates of trial capacity associated with the career criminal bureaus. With a fixed number of court days available, a higher rate of disposition through trial for career criminal bureau cases means a lower rate for routinely handled cases. The lower rate must be achieved either by more lenient plea-bargaining offers or by increasing the delay between arraignments and trials. The former will affect the comparison of severity, the latter the comparison of swiftness, and because cases tend to become weaker with the passage of time, conviction rates. Ignoring the opportunity costs of increased use of trial capacity not only biases the comparison of career criminal prosecution with routine case handling, but it may also lead to an expansion of the career criminal bureau when expanding trial capacity instead would be a more cost-effective way of improving dispositions.

The apparent success of the career criminal bureaus is likely to encourage greater use of vertical prosecution units. The extent to which their use increases the efficiency and equity of dispositions will be largely determined by whether or not they handle the cases viewed by the chief prosecutor as most deserving of severe punishment. If it were possible for the chief prosecutor personally to review all requests for prosecution, it is conceivable that he could rank them according to their priority for vertical prosecution. Those cases with the highest priority could then be assigned to the vertical prosecution unit.

In all but the smallest offices it is impractical for the chief prosecutor personally to assign priorities to all cases. The prosecutor may attempt to communicate his preferences to assistants in the form of specific policies. We have already discussed the limitations inherent in this communication process and the use of enhanced screening units to overcome them. Another approach is to communicate policies implicitly through the establishment of a case ranking system.

A case ranking system can be defined as a formal procedure for the evaluation of cases yielding a summary measure for each case that reflects the chief prosecutor's policies concerning its handling or disposition. The formal procedures involve the assessment of each case in terms of a number of predetermined dimensions that may be "objective" in the sense of requiring assistants to make direct observations of some case characteristics. For example, is the defendant accused of carrying a firearm while committing the offense? Subjective assessments by the assistants, such as an estimate of the chances of gaining a conviction of the defendant on the charges at trial, might also be included. The formal procedures also involve some rule or rules for combining the assessment dimensions into some metric (such as rank, weight, or priority) that facilitates the comparison of different statutory offenses in terms of an underlying scale. In addition to facilitating the selection of cases for special prosecution, the case ranking system provides a standard that could be useful in the monitoring of dispositions.

The case weighting system used by the Alameda County District Attorney's Office is a simplified form of a case ranking system. In subsequent chapters we shall investigate the implementation and use of more complicated case ranking systems by the U.S. Attorney's Office for the District of Columbia, the Wayne County Office of the Prosecuting Attorney, and the Bronx County District Attorney's Office. In the latter office, a case ranking system has been used to select cases for handling by the Major Offense Bureau, a vertical prosecution that serves as a prototype for the Career Criminal Program.

CASE MANAGEMENT INFORMATION SYSTEMS (CMIS)

The systematic monitoring of charging, handling, and disposition decisions is impractical for prosecutors offices relying solely on manual case files. The clerical costs of producing more than simple summary statistics is usually prohibitive. An approach to controlling delegated discretion is to increase the ability of the prosecutor to detect and investigate apparent deviations from established policies or common practices through the introduction of management information systems.

A case management information system (CMIS) can be defined as a computerized data processing system that collects, on a case-by-case basis, data describing defendants, their cases, and the way their cases have been handled at various points in the prosecution process; and stores the data so that it can be readily retrieved for individual cases as well as for sets of cases sharing given case characteristics. The increased sampling capabilities provided by the CMIS can improve management control in three major ways.

First, where explicit policies have been established, apparent deviations can be detected. For example, the prosecutor might have a policy that nighttime burglaries not be reduced to misdemeanors in plea bargaining unless the defendant has no prior convictions. A listing of all nighttime burglaries reduced to misdemeanors where defendants had prior convictions could be used for identifying assistants who were either ignorant of the policy or unwilling or unable to enforce it.

Second, the increased capacity to compare charging, disposition, and delay patterns across branch offices and assistants facilitates "management by exception": attention is focused on performance that deviates most from the observed norm. The detection of deviation in this manner allows performance appraisal in the absence of well-defined evaluation criteria. The CMIS can enable comparisons to be made in terms of simple descriptive statistics such as the percentage of cases filed by each branch office in which the court dismisses all charges (an indication of how well weak cases are screened out at the charging stage) or the percentage of cases handled by a trial team in which a trial conviction results in a straight probation sentence (a possible indication of an unrealistic plea-bargaining stance). The CMIS might even be designed to sample automatically certain types of cases for management attention. For example, a listing might be produced showing cases that were taking longer than normal to complete a certain stage of case handling, such as the preliminary hearing. Managers could investigate the listed cases to determine whether there were legitimate reasons for delay.

Third, in addition to permitting office managers to provide corrective feedback to assistants where deviations are detected, the CMIS may help assistants assigned to the early stages of prosecution learn about the consequences of their decisions by providing them with disposition reports for the cases they handle. For example, if an assistant assigned to a municipal court receives a report indicating that all the shoplifting cases she charged as grand thefts (subsequently sent to superior court) were reduced to misdemeanors in plea bargaining, she may be more willing to accept misdemeanor pleas for similar cases instead of sending them to superior court as felonies.

The CMIS thus appears to be a very effective tool for improving the management of prosecution. Our discussion has assumed, however, that the potential benefits we outlined can actually be realized in practice. We have ignored the problems that are likely to be encountered during the implementation of a CMIS. Unlike the other innovations—enhanced screening units, clearance procedures, and vertical prosecution units—we discussed, whose implementation could be accomplished by altering the responsibilities of office personnel, the implementation of a CMIS requires the introduction of technologies and the employment of managerial expertise not commonly found in prosecutors' offices. Consequently, what appears to be a desirable innovation in theory may not be so in practice.

Since 1974, LEAA has been successfully inducing the diffusion of a particular CMIS design. The experiences of the first twenty adopters will provide a basis for determining to what extent the hypothesized benefits of a CMIS are likely to be realized in practice. Obviously, it would be much better to make such a determination before the program of induced diffusion is launched. Although LEAA did not attempt to do so, we shall investigate in the next two chapters the experiences of two CMIS prototypes in an attempt to predict the implementation problems that are likely to delay or deny the realization of potential benefits. Our implementation analysis will bring into question the wisdom of the decision made by LEAA to induce CMIS diffusion.

NOTES

1. Kenneth Culp Davis, *Discretionary Justice: A Preliminary Inquiry* (Chicago: University of Illinois Press, 1971), p. 188.

2. In some jurisdictions the police, rather than the prosecution, decide whether or not to file charges. Once these cases reach the preliminary hearing stage, however, the discretion of the prosecution becomes dominant.

3. For a review see Sarah J. Cox, "Prosecutorial Discretion: An Overview," *The American Criminal Law Review* 13, no. 3 (1976): 387-89.

4. Arthur Rosett, "Discretion, Severity and Legality in Criminal Justice," *Southern California Law Review* 46, no. 1 (December 1972): 16.

5. Franklin E. Zimring and Gordon J. Hawkins, *Deterrence: The Legal Threat in Criminal Control* (Chicago: University of Chicago Press, 1973), pp. 158-72.

6. For example, see Albert Alschuler, "The Prosecutor's Role in Plea Bargaining," *University of Chicago Law Review* 36, no. 1 (Fall 1968); George J. Cole, *Politics and the Administration of Justice* (Beverly Hills, Calif.: Sage Publications, 1973); George J. Felkenes, *A Sociological Study of the Prosecutor's Office*, dissertation, Doctor of Criminology, Berkeley, June 1976; Joan E. Jacoby, "Pre-Trial Screening in Perspective," U.S. Department of Justice, National Institute of Law Enforcement and Criminal Justice, January 1976; Milton Heumann, *Plea Bargaining* (Chicago: University of Chicago Press, 1978); Frank Miller, *Prosecution: The Decision to Charge a Suspect with a Crime* (Boston: Little, Brown, 1969); Donald J. Newman, *Conviction: The Determination of Guilt or Innocence Without Trial* (Boston: Little, Brown, 1968); "Prosecutorial Discretion in the Initiation of Criminal Complaints," *Southern California Law Review* 42, no. 3 (Spring 1969); and Milton Heumann and Colin Loftin, "Mandatory Sentencing and the Abolition of Plea Bargaining: The Michigan Felony Firearm Statute," *Law and Society Review* 13, no. 2 (Winter 1979). Two intensive studies of prosecutors' offices are particularly relevant. Lief H. Carter's study of "Vario" County, California, led him to conclude that not only are commonly employed management procedures ineffective in reducing idiosyncratic prosecution, but also that attempts to increase their use may produce undesirable behavior on the part of those being managed. Lief H. Carter, *The Limits of Order* (Lexington, Mass.: D. C. Heath, 1974). The Rand Corporation study of Los Angeles County, California, also found a variety of idiosyncratic behavior and recommended the adoption of several new management technologies. Peter Greenwood, Sorrell Wildhorn, Eugene Pogoio, Michael Strumwasser, and Peter De Leon, *Prosecution of Adult Felony Defendants: A Policy Perspective* (Lexington, Mass.: D. C. Heath, 1976).

7. For a discussion of the use of office manuals see Carter, *Limits of Order*, pp. 120-22; Jacoby, "Pre-Trial Screening," pp. 62-63; and "Uniform Crime Charging Standard," California District Attorneys Association, December 1974, p. i.

8. John Kaplan, "The Prosecutorial Discretion—A Comment," *Northwestern University Law Review* 60, May-June 1965; David Sudnow, "Normal Crimes: Sociological Features of the Penal Code in a Public Defender Office," *Social Problems* 12, no. 3 (Winter 1965); and Jerome Skolnick, "Social Control in the Adversary System," *Journal of Conflict Resolution* 11, no. 1 (March 1967).

9. James Eisenstein and Herbert Jacob, *Felony Justice* (Boston: Little, Brown, 1977).

10. See, for example, Carter, *Limits of Order*, pp. 127-30.

11. Jacoby, "Pre-Trial Screening," pp. 54-58.

12. The plea-bargaining rate is measured as the ratio of pleas involving charge reductions or dismissals to the total number of dispositions.

13. Interview with New Orleans Trial Section deputy, November 30, 1976.

14. Carter, *Limits of Order*, pp. 127-30.

15. Expected loss would be computed by assigning a dollar value (or other metric) to the loss associated with each of the possible outcomes that could result if no clearance requirement is imposed, and then summing these values weighted by their respective probabilities of occurrence. For a theoretical discussion of the

selective use of clearance procedures, see David L. Weimer, "A Note on the Optimal Use of Clearance Procedures, *Public Choice* 34, no. 3-4 (1979).

16. David L. Weimer, "Plea Bargaining and the Decision to Go to Trial: The Application of a Rational Choice Model," *Policy Sciences* 10, no. 1 (August 1978); and David L. Weimer, "Prosecution Management: Evaluating an Innovation," in *Courts and Decision*, ed. Patricia L. Brantingham and Thomas Bloomberg (Beverly Hills, Calif.: Sage Publications, 1979), pp. 47-62.

17. David McGillis, *Major Offense Bureau: An Exemplary Project* (Washington, D.C.: Office of Technology Transfer, Law Enforcement Assistance Administration, November 1976).

18. The gains from vertical prosecution are likely to be lowest for cases with initially high probabilities of trial conviction. Adding an additional witness or locating another piece of evidence will have a greater impact in a weak case than in one that already is strong. For a formal analysis of this issue, see David L. Weimer, "Vertical Prosecution and the Career Criminal Program: How Many and Who?" Public Policy Analysis Discussion Paper No. 7903, University of Rochester, March 1979. (Forthcoming in *Journal of Criminal Justice*.)

PART 2

Innovation in Prosecution: Practice

Nearly ten years ago I wrote that the billions of dollars the federal government was then preparing to spend on crime control would be wasted, and indeed might even make matters worse if they were merely pumped into the existing criminal justice system. They were, and they have.

—James Q. Wilson
Thinking About Crime (1975)

chapter 3

The PROMIS Prototype

The origins of innovations in the administration of justice are often lost with the passage of time. Occasionally, however, we can point to circumstances that are the source of substantial changes in criminal justice institutions. For example, the Manhattan Bail Project conducted by the Vera Institute of Justice was instrumental in demonstrating the feasibility of the increased use of own recognizance as an alternative to money bail. Another example, central to our study of innovation in prosecution management, is the development of the PROMIS (Prosecutor's Management Information System) prototype, which represents not only the source of the case management information system selected by LEAA for widespread diffusion, but also early experimentation with vertical prosecution units and statistically derived case ranking systems. In this chapter we briefly describe the PROMIS prototype and its implementation, providing background for the analysis that subsequently follows.

OVERVIEW

PROMIS is operated by the Superior Court Division of the U.S. Attorney's Office for the District of Columbia. Assistant U.S. attorneys, District of Columbia Metropolitan Police Department officers, and U.S. Attorney's Office clerical personnel record data on all misdemeanor and felony cases handled by the Superior Court Division. For each case, approximately 170 data elements are collected in six general categories: characteristics of the accused or defendant, description of the alleged crime, circumstances of the arrest, description of charges including reasons for alteration of those initially filed, history of court events including outcomes and reasons for actions taken, and description of witnesses.[1]

At the end of each day, a contractor uses the PROMIS data collection forms to prepare a tape for updating a file of active cases that is maintained on a District of Columbia Metropolitan Police Department computer. The update tape contains data for newly charged cases and data on court event results for cases that were charged at an earlier date. The nightly update procedure means that there is generally a twenty-four-hour delay before court events are reflected in the active case file. An editing program prevents inconsistent or incorrectly formulated data from being entered into the active case file. Detected errors must be corrected and added to the update tape used the next day.

In the autumn of 1975, the Office of Management and Finance of the U.S. Department of Justice conducted an evaluation of PROMIS.[2] Developmental costs were reported to have been approximately $700,000, and recurring yearly nominal operating costs were estimated to be $156,863. In addition to the nominal operating costs that involved a measurable cash flow, the Justice Department study estimated that PROMIS operations involved indirect costs of $14,429 in attorney time expended in the recording data specifically needed by PROMIS.[3] The sum of the direct and indirect costs, $171,292, can serve as an estimate of the costs of PROMIS that are in excess of the costs needed to operate the manual case information system previously in use.[4] Or, an additional cost of approximately $10.70 per case was being incurred through the use of PROMIS in 1975.

The Justice Department study, involving interviews with fifty of the seventy-five assistant U.S. attorneys employed in the Superior Court Division and other employees having responsibilities related to PROMIS operations, concluded:

> Although this evaluation revealed a number of deficiencies in PROMIS operations, the benefits gained from the use of PROMIS are too great to discontinue the operation of the system. . . . To attempt to replace the

PROMIS system with a manual procedure does not appear to be feasible, considering the volume of cases prosecuted annually by the Superior Court Division and the prosecutors' need for timely and diverse case information.[5]

INFORMATION OUTPUTS

There are three modes by which data can be extracted from the PROMIS system: on-line access through remote terminals, regularly generated batch reports, and specially generated batch reports. Since 1975, on-line access has been providing operational information outputs, regularly generated batch reports have been used primarily to help maintain the PROMIS data base, and specially generated reports have been used almost exclusively by an outside agency for purposes of general research. By the end of 1976, PROMIS was not being used by the U.S. Attorney's Office for provision of the management control information described in the previous chapter.

The Justice Department study of PROMIS found that 85 percent of the assistant prosecutors in the Superior Court Division at least occasionally use the PROMIS on-line data access capability. In the first eight months of 1975, approximately 92,800 terminal queries of the data base were made. The queries provide operational information that aids assistant prosecutors in more efficiently carrying out the mechanics of case handling. Some examples of specific operational uses include: checking a defendant's status in the prosecution process, checking to see whether a defendant has other charges pending in Superior Court, and finding out which assistant prosecutor is assigned to the case. The on-line access eliminates the need for fetching case folders manually from the active files to obtain case data. Some of the operational information, such as checking to see whether a defendant has other charges pending, would be less timely and involve much higher expenditures of personnel time if performed manually. The conclusion of the Justice Department's study that it would not be feasible to replace PROMIS with a manual information system is based on an assessment of the value of the operational information it provides. The conclusion implies that the average benefit from an on-line query is in excess of \$1.80 (the estimated operating costs divided by the number of queries). The Justice Department study, however, does not actually attempt to measure the magnitude of the average benefit (in terms of employee time saved) of a PROMIS query.

The PROMIS system produces a number of regularly generated batch reports that nominally provide operational, logistical support, and management control information. The Justice Department study, however, found that these reports were rarely used as information sources by assistant prosecutors and their supervisors. For example, at the operational level, the Subpoena Summary Listing is not being used currently. It was introduced as a device to monitor the automatic generation of witness subpoenas by PROMIS. The level of data quality, however, has not been sufficiently high to allow the automatic generation of subpoenas.

At the logistical support level, the reports serve primarily as turn-around documents for updating and correcting the data base rather than as sources of information outputs for scheduling and workload monitoring. Assistant prosecutors indicated that the major use to which they put the regularly generated calendars was to check the data they accumulated on a manual basis. Discrepancies are recorded on the calendars and returned to PROMIS personnel so that errors in the data base can be corrected.

At the management control level, reports that list, in order of "seriousness," misdemeanor cases scheduled for trial on a given day were used at one time to ensure that the most serious cases received individualized pretrial preparation. With the organization of the misdemeanor trial section so that all cases are individually assigned, the misdemeanor trial listings are no longer needed or used for control purposes.

At the time of the Justice Department study, PROMIS was not being used by the U.S. Attorney's Office to generate special reports that could provide information for management analysis or planning. Extensive use of PROMIS was and is being made by the Institute for Law and Social Research (INSLAW), which has received over $1.2 million in LEAA funds in support of analysis of the PROMIS data base. The objectives of this research are "to develop measures of prosecutory effectiveness and even-handedness and to determine the impact on those measures of various discretionary decisions, policies, and other actions exercised by prosecutors."[6]

Although the general research information they generate is only of general interest to the U.S. Attorney's Office, it has supported criminal justice system innovation in a number of jurisdictions.

For example, INSLAW research on data collected by the PROMIS system since 1973 found that 7 percent of all the persons arrested accounted for nearly 25 percent of the 72,160 cases analyzed.[7] This finding encouraged LEAA to develop the Career Criminal Program, which provides support to prosecutors' offices for the establishment of units that give special attention to defendants with extensive prior records.

The following description of the implementation history of PROMIS will help provide an explanation for the current dominance of operational and general research information as the major PROMIS outputs.

ORIGINS

In 1968, the District of Columbia Office of Crime Analysis (OCA) received a mandate from the U.S. Congress to develop an offender-based criminal justice tracking and data system for the District of Columbia. The plan formulated by OCA for the development of the statistical system was named Project TRACE. The plan called for an "integrated file approach"—separate information systems would be built for the police, courts, and corrections with a view to their respective operational needs. The statistical system would be built by linking together the otherwise independent police, courts, and corrections information systems by means of common offender (suspect) and offense codes.

Joan E. Jacoby, the director of OCA, chose to work first with the District of Columbia Metropolitan Police Department, which already operated the Washington Area Law Enforcement System (WALES), an automated crime and arrest data system. OCA designed and implemented an offender status register to provide the names of all defendants on conditional release so that bail violations might be more easily monitored.

Consideration was given next to corrections within the District of Columbia. An automated inmate accounting system was developed to track all defendants sentenced to jail or a reformatory within the District of Columbia. An index of the police and corrections offender identification numbers was constructed to allow the eventual construction of an integrated file.

MOVES TOWARD A PROSECUTORIAL INFORMATION SYSTEM

Then OCA turned its attention to the courts, a crucial link for an offender-based statistical system. The presiding judge of the District of Columbia Superior Court Division, however, would not allow the development of an automated court system that would be a part of a larger criminal justice information system on the grounds that it would violate the separation of judicial and executive power—the courts being a part of the judicial branch and the police, prosecution, and corrections a part of the executive branch of government.

Through a common friend at the local LEAA office, Jacoby became acquainted with Charles R. Work, a member of the U.S. Attorney's Office. Work was the deputy chief for the District of Columbia Court of General Session, which handled the prosecution of all misdemeanor cases. He had been with the U.S. Attorney's Office since 1966. His belief that the function of the district attorney was not just to prosecute cases but to "fight crime" made him sympathetic to management innovation that would enable more efficient utilization of prosecutorial resources in dealing with repeat offenders and more serious offenses. Thomas A. Flannery, then the U.S. attorney for the District of Columbia, agreed to allow Work to develop a model prosecutor's information system for the Court of General Session in conjunction with OCA. At the time, the Court of General Session handled only misdemeanors.

Cooperation with the district attorney's office appeared promising to OCA for several reasons. First, the U.S. Attorney's Office had problems managing the prosecution of misdemeanor cases. The increasing case load of the late 1960s overburdened misdemeanor prosecution to the point that case files were often lost or misplaced. Court appearances were postponed to the extent that cases were often dismissed without an opportunity to decide the charges on their merits.[8] The existence of these management problems meant that there was potential for operational benefits to accrue to the U.S. Attorney's Office, leading OCA to believe that a favorable partnership could be built upon the mutual anticipation of benefits.

Second, the prosecutor's office could collect all the information desired for the offender-based statistical system except pretrial custody status. In fact, given the discretionary power of the prosecutor to dismiss charges without court approval, the prosecutor's office would facilitate more comprehensive data collection than the court administration. Finally, although the Court of General Session handled only misdemeanors at that time, it was known that plans were being developed to group misdemeanor and felony prosecution into a single court sometime in the future. A successful system might be expanded to include felonies when the courts were joined, completing the offender-based statistical system.

INITIAL EFFORTS: STARTING FROM SCRATCH AND SETTING GOALS

In 1969, advanced management techniques were not being employed in the prosecution of cases in the Court of General Session. In describing the record-keeping practices then in use, Work claims that the introduction of the manila folder case-jacket was literally a "management revolution." OCA received a grant of $73,419 from LEAA to develop automated management procedures for the office. From September 1969 to April 1970, OCA, in conjunction with Work, developed management procedures for the office and placed active case files in standardized case-jackets.

While developing management procedures, the OCA questioned personnel about the kinds of management information they wanted. Three general goals for an automated CMIS emerged. First, on the logistical support and management control levels, a system was desired for the identification of cases requiring or deserving special attention. Assistant prosecutors usually did not have time to prepare cases prior to trial. One assistant is reported to have commented:

> Our system did not allow us the time or resources to prepare the cases individually. So we looked at a case the day the police officer brought it in and made a judgment of whether to prosecute—nobody looked at the case

again until the day of trial. Consequently, we were losing, through the cracks in the system, over 40 percent of the cases.

I don't mean losing them through jury verdicts of not guilty—I mean losing because files were misplaced or because cases got continued so many times that witnesses failed to appear or a judge ultimately dismissed the case.[9]

The need to identify special cases for more extensive pretrial preparation motivated the development of PROMIS.

The second goal that emerged was the development of capability to track individual cases and collect aggregate statistics for office management. During the initial study period, a simple manual statistical system was introduced—the first statistical system for misdemeanor cases.

The third goal of developing a data base for general research into crime and prosecution was of primary interest to the OCA. This goal led to the inclusion of data items (such as the breakdown of the defendant's arrest records) that would not be of direct operational or management value to the prosecutor. Some data items were included because they were of *potential* research interest. A reappraisal was planned after an empirical analysis of the data collected during the first year of operation.

IMPLEMENTATION

In April 1970 a contract of $30,000 was awarded by the U.S. Attorney's Office to the consulting firm of Peat, Marwick, Mitchell and Company for the development of the computer software necessary for the automated case management information system. A supplement of $30,000 was later awarded to the contractor for the implementation of the computer software. A project team was formed headed by Joan Jacoby with William A. Hamilton, the senior consultant for Peat, Marwick, Mitchell and Company, as project manager. In addition to Charles Work, the project team included management analysts, criminologists, statisticians, and computer science specialists from OCA and the contractor.

The project team produced an operational version of PROMIS that began collecting data on January 1, 1971. Several of the members of the project team left the consulting firm to stay with the project and became consultants to the U.S. Attorney's Office, including William Hamilton and Dean C. Merrill. In 1973, Hamilton and Merrill left the U.S. Attorney's Office to form the nonprofit Institute for Law and Social Research (INSLAW) when LEAA requested that PROMIS software be reprogrammed so that it could be transferred to other jurisdictions. INSLAW received an LEAA grant of $89,925 to enhance and reprogram PROMIS. The second version of PROMIS included the tracking of felony cases that were added to the jurisdiction of the Superior Court Division of the U.S. Attorney's Office on August 1, 1972. It also added an on-line capacity that allowed assistant prosecutors to request case information via remote computer terminals.

We shall now focus on specific aspects of the implementation process.

DESIGN BY AN INTERDISCIPLINARY TEAM

By April 1970, Work and Jacoby had spent "literally thousands of hours" developing a system concept and preparing for automation. Nevertheless, a much more detailed specification of system characteristics was found to be necessary before computer software could be written. The project manager directed the writing of the narratives that described the operation and structure of the proposed system. The narratives served as detailed specifications for the programmer who developed the computer software.

A classic problem of multidisciplinary teams was encountered: imperfect communication among members of the team. The OCA staff had developed a detailed understanding of office operations and a general idea of how the proposed system would operate but had not worked out all the details of the design. The project manager and systems consultants had to become familiar with office operations as they were translating the general concept to the computer programmer. As an experienced scientific applications programmer rather than a business applications programmer, the programmer not only was unfamiliar with office procedures but also inexperienced in information systems work and the business applications language (COBOL, or common business-oriented language) that the contract required he use. The communications problem was magnified by the low consulting grant that was accepted by the contractor under the misconception that a detailed system design had already been prepared. There were insufficient funds in the consulting fee to allow the programmer to spend time sitting in on the time-consuming and tedious writing of the narratives.

The programmer spent four to six weeks writing COBOL code before the rest of the project team discovered that there was a misunderstanding concerning the way multiple counts against a defendant would be handled: the programmer was treating the multiple counts as separate cases whereas the prosecution usually treats them as a package in terms of court events. (The prosecutor may often drop some of the counts to secure a guilty plea.) This misunderstanding and others that became apparent meant that the programmer would almost have to begin the programming anew. The programmer had expended a large portion of his project budget in the aborted effort. There was also concern about delaying project completion. In order to ensure the timely completion of the software, the programmer was allowed to write the new version in PL/1 (Programming Language Number 1), a scientific applications-oriented language with which he was more familiar than COBOL.

During the first two years of operation of the first version of PROMIS, several design weaknesses became evident: ineffective methods for updating case status information, lack of summary case status information, duplication in the storage of data, inefficient design of the master file with respect to the extraction of data for on-line retrieval, excessively high computer case storage requirements, and excessively long processing time.[10] So when LEAA requested that PROMIS be reprogrammed in COBOL so that it would be compatible with a wide range of computer manufacturers' equipment, the U.S. Attorney's Office recognized an opportunity to deal with the PROMIS design weaknesses that had emerged. In addition, it would allow the incorporation of the felony cases that had been transferred to the jurisdiction of the Superior Court Division.

At the time PROMIS reprogramming was being considered, Work was the chief of the Superior Court Division. Although OCA was no longer directly involved in the PROMIS Project (Jacoby had left OCA on January 1, 1972, to become head of the National

Center for Prosecution Management), Hamilton and Merrill from the original project team had become consultants to the U.S. Attorney's Office. Over the two years of system operation, they had become intimately acquainted with the day-to-day operations of the office. In 1973, at INSLAW, in contrast to their experience at the time of the design of the first version of PROMIS, they not only enjoyed an understanding of system science, but also an understanding of the detailed substantive business of the office and the practical problems facing information systems operations. The revised PROMIS system that resulted eliminated the *design* weaknesses that had become apparent. In addition, the PROMIS software routines were modularized and generalized so that future adaptations could be handled more easily.

DATA QUALITY

After limited preliminary testing, data collection for PROMIS commenced on January 1, 1971, to take advantage of the yearly court docket number cycle. Data collection efforts were plagued immediately by a high error rate. As much as 33 percent of the system's case data was incomplete or inaccurate during the first year of operations.

The reason for the high error rate was technical in nature. The data coding system did not allow the clerk to verify the data that were being placed on the tape used to update case records. This problem was reduced by introducing cathode ray tube (CRT) input devices that allowed the clerks to monitor the data they typed.

The data collection problems were not only technical in nature. The project manager attributes the first year's problems to "lack of early attention to data collection procedures, lack of training for office personnel and poor forms design." As a result, members of the project team had to spend long hours adding data that had been missed or incorrectly recorded by regular data collection procedures. By the end of the first year of operations, the data error had been greatly reduced.

In February 1973, the second version of PROMIS became operational. As an on-line real-time system, assistant prosecutors could request specific pieces of case information from the PROMIS data files by means of a CRT terminal. The introduction of on-line access contributed to increased data quality. Assistants who utilized the terminals were more willing to fill out data-input forms conscientiously because they could perceive a direct benefit from the system.

In the fall of 1975 the U.S. Department of Justice conducted its evaluation of PROMIS. Almost five years after PROMIS data collection had begun, the study indicated that there were still data quality problems. The findings were based on a comparison of a sample of PROMIS case data with the source documents from which the data had been collected. Attention was given to the accuracy, completeness, and timeliness of the data. Although significant errors were identified in almost one out of every twenty cases sampled, the most troublesome problem observed as a result of the data sampling was the lengthy turn-around time for updating PROMIS. These findings may have been abnormal because of the extensive turnover in the data collection personnel that was occurring at the time. Nevertheless, the fact that INSLAW has conducted several massive PROMIS data base clean-ups as a service to the U.S. Attorney's Office suggests that the data quality problems reported by the Justice Department study were not totally transitory in nature.

ACCEPTANCE AND USE BY PROSECUTORS

The PROMIS project added an unfamiliar technology to the U.S. Attorney's Office. Having been trained as lawyers, assistant prosecutors had little or no prior experience with automation or management science. It may be that the emphasis on case law in legal training tends to focus lawyers' interest on the unusual or exceptional in cases—rather than the similarities in cases that can be captured in information system statistics. In general, the reaction of the assistant prosecutors to the new system was skepticism.

The major exception was Charles Work, the chief of the Superior Court Division. His enthusiasm for the system and the potential use of its data prompted some of the assistant prosecutors to refer to PROMIS as "Chuck Work's toy." Project team members who were interviewed credited Work's dedication to the system as a major reason for its success. The project manager describes the project team as being strongly dedicated and highly motivated in trying to make the system useful to the office despite the general apathy. Efforts at encouraging use were often frustrated by the poor quality of the data base. The Justice Department study reports that the most frequent reason cited by assistant prosecutors for not making full use of PROMIS concerned the quality of the data base: ". . . some PROMIS users described PROMIS reports as inaccurate, unreliable or not timely."[11]

A cycle developed that was adverse to increased use of the system. Poor data quality led to fewer requests for reports, which meant that there was less chance of correcting data errors and hence the possibility of further decay in data quality.

The introduction of on-line terminal inquiry capability greatly increased the use by assistant prosecutors of PROMIS as a primary source of case reference information. This in turn led to an improvement in data quality:

> Not only is this type of immediate access (to pending cases) valuable per se, but it also produces a desirable by-product in that "hands-on" utilization of terminals by prosecutors reinforces their perception of PROMIS's overall effectiveness and helps convince them that the forms they complete for PROMIS data-input purposes are worth the time it takes to complete them.[12]

Because PROMIS collects data on the reasons for assistant prosecutors' discretionary actions (such as reasons for dismissing cases), it has potential as a tool for monitoring the execution of policy and providing information to aid the analysis of policy problems. One study that realized the latter potential was an investigation into the reason why assistants dropped charges against defendants. It was found that, in 39 percent of the cases where charges were dropped, the assistants listed lack of lay (nonpolice) witness cooperation.[13] A subsequent survey of those witnesses reported as uncooperative found that, in about 20 percent of the cases, the assistants had incorrectly assumed a lack of cooperation because of communication problems between the witnesses on one hand, and the prosecution and police on the other. This led to the creation of a Witness Notification Unit that automatically notifies witnesses when scheduled court dates are changed or canceled.

PROMIS has been used to provide information for management planning. When the court proposed a speedy trial rule, PROMIS was able to provide the number of cases that would have been impacted under the proposed rule. The U.S. Attorney's Office was able to use the PROMIS data to help convince the courts that the proposed rule involved unrealistically short time periods.[14]

Why has the use of PROMIS for the generation of problem analysis and planning information not continued to the present? There are two factors that limit the value of PROMIS as a resource for these uses. First, the U.S. Attorney's Office does not have the personnel to carry out special studies of the PROMIS data base. All special requests are handled by INSLAW research personnel. Second, requests from the U.S. Attorney's Office are presently limited because of a concern about the accuracy of the historical data.[15] At the time of the Justice Department evaluation of PROMIS, the deputy chief of the Superior Court Division expressed the belief that the number of requests for quarterly and yearly statistical reports would increase after completion of the data base clean-up then in progress.

THE CASE EVALUATION SYSTEM

PROMIS computes a measure of seriousness for each case it tracks. At one time, rankings of cases according to the computed seriousness provided the U.S. Attorney's Office with management control information. The PROMIS case evaluation system will be discussed here because of the important role it played in LEAA's decision to support the transfer to PROMIS.

In the late 1960s, the misdemeanor section of the U.S. Attorney's Office faced a massive case load that precluded the pretrial preparation of all cases. Once charges had been filed, cases were generally not reviewed or prepared prior to their trial dates. Many cases were being lost as a result of the lack of preparation. The PROMIS project team decided that as long as resources were available for pretrial preparation of only a small number of the 9,000 cases being handled annually, it would be best to concentrate attention on those cases that were in some way "most serious." Although it was felt by the project team that seriousness should be judged by the chief assistant in charge of the misdemeanor section, it was not practical for the chief assistant to review personally each case prior to its trial date. This led to the concept of an automated case evaluation system that would measure the seriousness of the case by using data collected at the time charges had been filed.

The project team identified four factors that they believed should enter into the case evaluation. First, the evaluation should be related to the harm done to society by the offense. As a measure of the gravity of the offense in terms of the harm done to society, the project team chose a scale developed by the criminologists Thorsten Sellin and Marvin E. Wolfgang.[16] The second factor to be included is a measure of the seriousness of the defendant's criminal history. A version of a scale developed by D. Gottfredson was chosen to measure the gravity of the defendant's criminal history.[17] The third factor included was a measure of the strength of the case in terms of the quality of evidence available. The assistant screening the case would make a subjective estimate of the case strength. The final factor to be included was the length of time since the case had been screened by the U.S. Attorney's Office.

Jacoby developed a methodology for relating the four measurable factors to the relative seriousness the chief assistant in charge of the misdemeanor section would assign if he reviewed all the cases. As a first step in the methodology, the chief assistant of the misdemeanor section was asked to rank the seriousness of a set of 300 cases as they arose over a period of time. The next step was to relate the chief assistant's revealed preferences to the four measurable factors. A stepwise regression was used to determine a functional form for a fit of the revealed preferences to the four factors and their interactions. The resulting equation could then be used to predict a rank for new cases handled by the office.

A Special Litigation Unit of six assistants was formed to prepare (contact witnesses, and so on) the most serious cases prior to their trial date. Each day PROMIS would generate a list of all cases scheduled for trial five days hence. Cases were listed in order of decreasing predicted ranks. The idea was that the Special Litigation Unit would start at the top of the list and work down preparing as many cases as time would allow.

The case evaluation system was implemented and used by the Special Litigation Unit. Gradually over time, however, the ranks generated by the case evaluation system became less satisfactory. By 1973, the Special Litigation Unit was manually choosing cases and using the evaluation system ranks only to help identify cases they might have missed or to add cases quickly when the manually identified cases had been completed ahead of schedule.

Why did the case evaluation system fall into disuse? One major reason was that it became obsolete. It was based on the preferences of a particular assistant at a particular point in time. Changes in the environment and personnel mean that ranks generated by the evaluation system will not reflect the preferences of later managers. Because OCA no longer had a direct interest in the PROMIS project, there was no one available to reestimate the parameters of the evaluation system.

There were also several technical difficulties with the case evaluation system. First, the stepwise regression procedure used to find a functional form for relating the four measurable factors to the chief assistant's preferences led to the choice of a complicated (third-order interactions) model that may have made the choice of weights very sensitive to a specific set of cases used for their estimation. Second, several of the interaction terms in the ranking equation had case strength as a factor. The estimates of case strength were made at the time the cases were screened. Because case screening was handled by a large number of assistants, many of whom have had little experience in the office, wide variation in the case strength estimates occurred and the case evaluation ranks lost their predictive power. Because the ranking was a positive function of the case strength, it often led to the targeting of "easy" cases that required little special preparation.

When Hamilton and Merrill began the reprogramming of PROMIS in 1973, they decided that the case evaluation system had lost its usefulness. The case evaluation system was replaced by simple listings of the measures of offense and defendant seriousness. The case strength estimates were no longer collected. A report ranking cases according to the gravity of the criminal history of the defendant was designed for use by the Special Litigation Unit, which also became known as the Major Violators Unit.

The Special Litigation Unit initially made use of the new ranking report to choose cases for pretrial preparation. The Special Litigation Unit soon achieved a conviction rate for the cases it handled that was 25 percent higher than that for other cases handled by the office. Two of the PROMIS project team members emphasized the then *perceived* importance of the ranking system when they wrote: "The centerpiece of the PROMIS system, however, is the automated designation of priorities of pending criminal cases."[18]

However, the revised ranking system soon became obsolete. Its eventual disuse because of dissatisfaction with its predictions became irrelevant because of organizational changes. With an increase in the resources available to the U.S. Attorney's Office permitting misdemeanors as well as felonies to be assigned to specified deputies at the time they are accepted for prosecution, the Special Litigation Unit lost its function, and now exists in name only. Two experienced deputies do all the misdemeanor case screening and assign highly complex cases or cases involving defendants with serious records to more experienced assistants. The increase in office resources and the introduction of a more sophisticated organizational structure mitigated the problems the case evaluation system was designed to address. At the present time, the offense and defendant seriousness measures are used only by INSLAW for policy research purposes.

OVERVIEW OF PROMIS IMPLEMENTATION

Almost six years after work on PROMIS had begun, a Justice Department study concluded that it would not be feasible to replace PROMIS with a manual information system. The nominal $700,000 spent over the six years underestimates the efforts, if not the quantifiable resource costs, expended during PROMIS development. Several members of the highly dedicated project team were involved with PROMIS during the entire period, including participation in a complete redesign of the computer software and periodic efforts to "clean up" the data base. Attention had to be given not only to improving the ability of PROMIS to supply information outputs, but also to the generation of demand among an often skeptical prosecution staff.

Over the six years, there were instances when project team members demonstrated the use of PROMIS to support policy analysis activities through the provision of information for problem analysis and planning. The capacity for this type of use, however, was never institutionalized within the U.S. Attorney's Office. Current use of the PROMIS historical data base can be classified as policy research that is of only general interest to the U.S. Attorney's Office.

The introduction of on-line access to active case files greatly increased the amount of operational information produced by PROMIS. Inaccuracy and incompleteness prevented PROMIS from becoming the primary source of logistical support information. It is yet to be demonstrated that sufficient data quality can be achieved to support these uses. The major management control benefits of PROMIS resulted from the initial use of the case evaluation system to ensure serious misdemeanors received additional pretrial preparation. The case evaluation system, however, fell into disuse as the quality of its predictions appeared to deteriorate over time.

NOTES

1. Institute for Law and Social Research (cited hereafter as INSLAW), "Management Overview of PROMIS," PROMIS Briefing Series No. 1, July 1975, p. 7.
2. U.S. Department of Justice, *An Evaluation of the PROMIS System,* Fall 1975.
3. This estimate may be low. It is based on the estimate that five minutes of attorney time are required for the collection of PROMIS data for each of the 16,000 cases filed each year, or approximately 1,340 hours of attorney time. The Institute for Law and Social Research has estimated, however, that over 4,750 hours of attorney time are required annually for PROMIS data collections (INSLAW, "PROMIS Data Collection Problems," presented to PROMIS Users Group, Detroit, Michigan, July 15-16, 1976). If the INSLAW estimate is correct, the indirect costs of PROMIS would be more than triple the Justice Department estimate.
4. Because computer facilities are provided by the District of Columbia Metropolitan Police Department at below the market rental price, the estimate of operating costs will be smaller than the actual economic costs of the system. On the other hand, no direct estimate will be made of the value to police of having access to the PROMIS data base. It may be that the difference between the market rental price and the price charged by the District of Columbia Metropolitan Police Department may reflect the value they place on access to PROMIS data.
5. U.S. Department of Justice, *PROMIS Evaluation,* pp. 2, 17.
6. INSLAW, "Research Uses of PROMIS Data," PROMIS Briefing Series No. 10, July 1975, p. 7.

7. Office of Technology Transfer, National Institute of Law Enforcement and Criminal Justice, Law Enforcement Assistance Administration, "Major Offense Bureau," November 1976, p. 1.

8. INSLAW, "Final Report: PROMIS Reprogramming Grant," January 17, 1975, p. 1.

9. INSLAW, "Special Litigation (Major Violators) Unit," PROMIS Briefing Series No. 4, July 1975, p. 2.

10. INSLAW, "PROMIS Reprogramming," p. 4.

11. U.S. Department of Justice, *PROMIS Evaluation,* p. 29.

12. INSLAW, "Systems Options," PROMIS Software Documentation Series, vol. 6, 1975, pp. ii-5.

13. INSLAW, "Witness Notification Unit," PROMIS Briefing Series No. 5, July 1975, p. 2.

14. INSLAW, "Research Uses of PROMIS," PROMIS Briefing Series No. 10, July 1975, p. 5.

15. U.S. Department of Justice, *PROMIS Evaluation,* pp. 30-31.

16. Thorsten Sellin and Marvin E. Wolfgang, *The Measurement of Delinquency* (New York: John Wiley and Sons, 1964).

17. D. Gottfredson and R. Beverly, "Development and Operational Use of Prediction Methods in Correctional Work," *Proceedings of the American Statistical Association,* American Statistical Association, Washington, D.C., 1962.

18. William A. Hamilton and Charles R. Work, "The Prosecutor's Role in the Urban Court System: The Case for Management Consciousness," *The Journal of Criminal Law and Criminology* 64, no. 2 (1973): 185.

chapter 4

CMIS Implementation Analysis

In recent years students of the policy sciences have drawn attention repeatedly to the importance of trying to anticipate implementation problems before programs are launched on a large scale.[1] Drawing on the experiences of two prosecutors' offices with case management information system (CMIS) prototypes, we shall predict the implementation problems that are likely to be encountered by subsequent CMIS adopters. The prospect of serious implementation problems is evident from the abundance of accounts of management information systems failing to yield anticipated information benefits in a variety of organizational settings.[2] The existence of such problems might cause some people to question the wisdom of inducing the diffusion of the CMIS prototypes. To the extent that we gain an understanding of the problems, it may be possible to mitigate their impact by altering the design of the prototype or modifying the technical assistance provided by the program of induced diffusion.

EVALUATION CONSIDERATIONS

One approach for evaluating the impact of a CMIS is to compare the costs of its operation with the benefits resulting from the provision of information. It should be recognized that a prosecutor's office must have some kind of information system: basic case records must be kept and aggregate reports generated. The choice is not between a CMIS and no information system: it is between a

CMIS and the best manual information system that can be developed for the prosecutor's office. Because it may not be possible to identify the best manual system that the office could employ, the evaluation of impact might be operationalized by measuring the costs and benefits of the CMIS relative to those of the manual information system previously in use. If another manual information system providing the same benefits at reduced costs or increased benefits at the same cost could be envisioned, it would serve as the basis for computing the costs and benefits of the CMIS.

As is the case with many government activities, costs are much easier to quantify and measure than benefits. Costs can be measured in terms of resources that are valued in the marketplace, such as the time devoted by personnel to data collection and the rental cost of computer time. It may be difficult or impossible, however, to place a value on the information produced, not only because it is intermediate to the final product, prosecution, but also because no common metric exists for the comparison of the various prosecution outcomes that can be generated. Without dollar values for the information outputs, it is not possible to employ cost-benefit analysis. Instead, the costs of introducing the CMIS must be balanced against the array of additional information outputs it produces.

Assume that a prosecutor's office is operating a manual information system producing information outputs Q_1 and Q_2 at a cost of C_m. Assume that a CMIS could produce information outputs Q_1, Q_2, Q_3, Q_4, and Q_5 at a cost of C_c. An evaluation of the impact of the CMIS would ask whether the net costs $C_c - C_m$ were offset by the value of the additional information outputs Q_3, Q_4, and Q_5.

Information outputs can be categorized into a hierarchy paralleling the organizational levels that derive benefits from them.[3] Table 2 presents six different types of information outputs. A CMIS that is operating in a prosecutor's office might produce any subset of the information outputs depending upon its design and the extent to which the design is successfully implemented.

Operational information results from the use of the CMIS to obtain data on particular cases or defendants. The CMIS may provide daily listings of cases in a particular stage of processing or allow on-line access to computer-stored files of active cases. An assistant prosecutor who wished to find out something about a

Table 2. Hierarchy of Information Uses

Information Output	Examples	Main Users	Type of Benefit	Frequency	General Description	
Operational	case-specific references	line prosecutors	efficiency	routine	simple automation	
Logistical support	calendars and schedules	line prosecutors and middle managers	efficiency	routine		
Management control	detection of deviation from office policies	middle and top managers	efficiency and equity	routine		management information
Problem analysis	consideration of changes in case handling policies	top managers	efficiency and equity	sporadic	tool for policy analysis	
Strategic planning	reaction to proposed legislation	top managers	efficiency and organizational maintenance	externally stimulated		
General	general criminal justice research	external researchers and evaluators	general knowledge	according to external demand	policy research	

particular defendant could refer to the case lists or initiate an on-line request. For example, suppose an assistant prosecutor wanted to know whether a defendant whose case he is handling had any other charges pending in the jurisdiction. He could check a list of active cases or initiate an automatic search of the computer files for other cases against the defendant. Operational information outputs of the CMIS, although perhaps faster and more accurate, result from the simple automation of tasks that could be and previously were manually performed.

Logistical support information accrues to assistant prosecutors and their direct supervisors when reports generated by the CMIS are an aid for keeping track of case handling responsibilities. Lists of cases assigned to each assistant prosecutor, lists of cases scheduled for a certain type of court appearance on a given day, and counts of the number of cases assigned to each of the assistant prosecutors supervised by a given manager are examples of the types of reports that could yield logistical support information. The logistical support information generated by the CMIS will primarily replace information that can be manually generated on a decentralized basis by assistant prosecutors who each maintain calendars of their own court appearances. The CMIS centralizes calendar generation, allowing for greater monitoring of case loads by supervisors.

While operational and logistical support information facilitates efficiency in case handling and manpower assignment, *management control information* contributes to equity in case handling by aiding managers in their efforts to ensure that assistant prosecutors are making case processing decisions that are consonant with established office policies. The capability of the CMIS to retrieve cases sharing a particular characteristic facilitates management by exception. Case charging, disposition, and delay patterns can be compared across assistant prosecutors, office units, or time periods to highlight variation. Deviations from expected patterns may reflect case handling that is inconsistent with office policies. For example, if the cases charged by a particular assistant appear to have a much higher rate of dismissal than other cases, it might be that the assistant is employing undesirably low standards of evidence in his charging decisions. Sometimes it may be possible to detect directly deviations from established policies. For instance, a rule that offenses invoking the use of firearms not be reduced to misdemeanors during plea bargaining could be enforced by looking at the final dispositions for all cases initially recorded as involving firearm use. Assistants could then be asked to justify the apparent violations of the rule. Manual information systems can produce only a very limited amount of control information of this kind because of the heavy clerical effort needed to generate reports with disaggregated data. The control information generated by a CMIS therefore comprises one of the information outputs that is usually not available to a prosecutor's office relying on a manual information system. Thus it has potential as a major innovation in the control of idiosyncratic prosecution.

Problem analysis information refers to uses of the CMIS data that help the prosecutor and his chief assistants identify and explore aspects of office policies or procedures that need review. For example, the CMIS might reveal that there is an increase in the number of trials because fewer narcotics defendants are entering guilty pleas. Further investigation might reveal that judges no longer gave prison sentences to narcotics offenders having no prior conviction. An office policy that narcotics defendants not be offered plea bargains that do not involve prison sentences might be altered to allow greater concessions so that first-time offenders would demand fewer trials. Such a change in policy would allow the prosecutor to obtain approximately the same levels of sentencing against these defendants but at much reduced cost.

Unlike operational, logistical support and management control information that can be preprogrammed in the form of regular reports, information for problem analysis must be specifically requested. Areas of concern may be suggested by control information or the direct observation of office management. Information for problem analysis requires office managers with enough sophistication in data analysis to know how to frame questions that CMIS-generated data can help to answer. To the extent that information for problem analysis can be realized, improved office policies could lead to either increased efficiency or greater equity.

Strategic planning information aids office managers by helping them to make preparations to deal with expected changes in the organization's environment. For example, let us assume that the state legislature is considering the passage of a bill that would require grand jury presentations rather than preliminary hearings for a certain type of offense. Grand jury presentations require a greater input of prosecutorial resources than preliminary hearings. The prosecutor might use CMIS data to estimate the expected additional costs to the office by noting the number of cases that would have been covered by the bill in the preceding year. If the costs appear to be substantial, the prosecutor may decide either to testify against the bill or use the estimates to support requests to the office's budgetary sponsors for supplemental funds to cover the additional costs.

Students of management information systems (MIS) operated by private firms argue that useful information for strategic planning is less likely to be produced than for other types of management decisions.[4] Their argument rests largely on the observation that strategic planning decisions are influenced more by the organization's external environment than by the internal organizational phenomena sampled by the MIS. Unlike many other organizations, prosecutors' offices face a fairly certain environment: there are always more requests for prosecution than can be handled, and changes in criminal procedures are dictated by state legislatures, usually with long lead times. Consequently, most strategic planning decisions are made in reaction to and anticipation of externally dictated procedural changes. The information need is not to be able to predict these changes (for example, in California, the California District Attorneys Association serves as an information source for predicting procedural changes that will be dictated by the legislature and the courts), but rather to be able to determine the impact of the changes on the office so that the new procedures can be incorporated into office practice, and additional resources sought if necessary.

General research information may be generated by the CMIS for use by external researchers whose findings make a general contribution to knowledge rather than a specific contribution to improved management in the organization providing the data.

TWO CMIS PROTOTYPES

PROMIS, described in the previous chapter, and DALITE (District Attorney's Automated Legal Information System), described in Appendix A, are CMIS prototypes developed with funding provided by LEAA. PROMIS has been in operation in the U.S. Attorney's Office for the District of Columbia since 1971. DALITE has been operational in the Alameda County (California) District Attorney's Office since late 1974. By the end of 1975, PROMIS and DALITE had attained stable operating characteristics, with approximately $700,000 and $140,000 invested respectively in the development of each. Excluding these investments, average opportunity costs above those involved in the operation of manual information systems amount to approximately $11 per case for each system.

By the end of 1975, PROMIS was producing primarily operational information to the U.S. Attorney's Office. Researchers were also using PROMIS data for general criminal justice research. PROMIS initially supported a case ranking system that was used to help select cases for a special prosecution unit, but use of the ranking system was discontinued after a short period of use. At various times consultants had been able to use PROMIS to generate the other information outputs, but these uses were never institutionalized. Poor data quality, a constant problem, prevented the use of PROMIS for logistical support. The poor data quality and lack of in-house expertise discouraged further attempts by the U.S. Attorney's Office to use PROMIS as a source of management information. Nevertheless, a U.S. Justice Department evaluation of PROMIS concluded that the operational benefits alone justified continued operation.[5]

By the end of 1976, DALITE was producing all six information outputs. Operational information was produced regularly for the entire office, while logistical support information was being used primarily by Superior Court personnel. Office managers regularly used reports to detect cases moving toward disposition too slowly. Other management control information, as well as problem analysis and strategic planning information, was produced sporadically and somewhat limited by the difficulty of generating reports other than counts or listings. Like PROMIS, DALITE appears to be cost effective relative to provision of the same information by a manual system.[6]

Although the prototypes eventually reached these levels of information use, their implementation histories suggest that other prosecutors' offices can expect to encounter delay and high development costs before CMIS projects will actually begin to produce information outputs to offset a major portion of their costs of operation. The histories of the prototypes and *simple* behavioral theory will be used to outline an implementation analysis for prospective CMIS adopters. Table 3 displays four problem themes.

DESIGN AND COGNITION

If the CMIS implementation process is conceptualized as the assembly of diverse project elements, then the initial implementation effort can be described as the development of a plan that identifies the project elements to be assembled and indicates how they are to be combined. The plan must address questions such as: What data items will be collected? By whom? In what form? How will the data be stored? On what type of computer hardware? Using which computer language? What particular information outputs are desired? What regular reports should be produced? How often? For whom? In what format? How should answers to these questions be found?

The successful development of a CMIS design and implementation plan requires the application of several types of knowledge and skills: an understanding of the substantive operations of the office, knowledge of the principles of information system design, computer expertise, and skill in project management. With the exception of personnel having an understanding of the substantive operations of the office, it is unlikely that a typical prosecutor's office will include individuals with the various design and planning skills among its employees. The necessity of securing the design and planning skills from outside consultants lies at the heart of the design problem. The outside consultant may not be in contact with the office for a sufficient length of time to develop a sound understanding of the substantive operations of the office. Although office personnel assigned to the CMIS project may be able to provide adequate input concerning the substantive operations of the office, they may not have sufficient understanding of the technical aspects of the design to ensure that the skills of outside consultants are appropriately applied.

The PROMIS and DALITE experiences illustrate the difficulties involved in the integration of the technical skills of outside consultants with the substantive knowledge of office personnel. During the design of the first version of PROMIS, none of the project

Table 3. A Brief Summary of the Prototype Experiences

	PROMIS	DALITE
Information outputs	Currently produces operational and general research information; was previously used to produce management control, problem analysis, and strategic planning information	Currently produces all six information outputs—logistical support and operational information predominate
Problem themes Design and cognition	Redesign required after two years of operation to achieve current levels of information outputs	Redesign desired to facilitate greater use for management control, problem analysis, and strategic planning
Organizational cooperation	Originally failed to secure cooperation of the courts	Lack of cooperation with county data processing center; opposition from municipal court line deputies
Maintenance of data quality	Continuing problems in maintaining data completeness; delay in case updates	Eventually achieved high quality of superior court data, but municipal court data quality problems persist
Acceptance and use	Initial line-prosecutor skepticism gradually replaced by acceptance after introduction of on-line access; poor data quality and lack of in-house resources discourage management use	Full acceptance only after management personnel changes; limited programming resources restrict use

team members had both extensive substantive knowledge and technical skills. One obvious illustration of the resulting difficulties was the false start made by the software consultant. The cumulative effect of the design difficulties led to the redesign of PROMIS after two years of operation. The improvement of the PROMIS software resulting from reprogramming can at least be partially attributed to the understanding of the substantive operations gained by the consultants who maintained contact with the office over the period.

DALITE design weaknesses can also be related to the reliance on outside consultants for technical support. Before becoming a deputy attorney, the DALITE project director had had considerable experience as a systems analyst and forms designer. The case tracking system and data collection forms appear to be successful DALITE components—probably a result of the project director's combination of technical and substantive skills. On the other hand, no member of the project team was familiar with computer hardware and software. Outside consultants provided design aid with respect to these areas. Lack of in-house expertise may explain why the computer system has not been fully satisfactory. On-line remote terminals and many software features have not yet been implemented. The District Attorney's Office would like to alleviate these difficulties by switching to a new computer system.

Another design problem is related to the temporary nature of technical assistance provided by consultants. When they complete their design tasks, the consultants may leave behind a system that cannot be altered readily by office personnel. As the environment of the office changes, the original CMIS applications may become obsolete and new applications desired. For example, when the U.S. Attorney's Office began assigning misdemeanor cases to prosecutors immediately after charges are filed instead of assigning the cases to different prosecutors for each court appearance, many of the PROMIS calendar reports became obsolete.

Faced with uncertainty as to future information demands, program designers may attempt to guard against excluding some data item which in the future will be necessary by including as many data elements as possible in the initial design. Given a limited information system budget, however, the more resources expended for data collection, storage, and retrieval (all of which are increasing functions of the amount of data collected per case), the less the resources available for producing useful information.[7] Some of the data collection problems encountered with PROMIS may be related to the decision to collect a large number of data items to increase the chances of having data that would be useful in future, but unspecified, research efforts.

So far, the discussion of design problems has been in terms of prosecutors' offices developing their own prototypes. Will the problems be encountered in the implementation of an existing prototype by a prosecutor's office? The answer depends upon how much the office differs in structure and operating procedures from the office for which the CMIS was initially designed. If there are major differences, then either the organization must change to fit the CMIS, or the CMIS must be modified to fit the office. The former, perhaps a case of the tail wagging the dog, requires forceful administrative leadership to say the least. The latter has the potential of involving the design problems discussed previously.

ORGANIZATIONAL COOPERATION

The design phase identifies the project elements needed for the CMIS; the assembly phase involves efforts to collect and combine the project elements into a functioning CMIS. The greater the number and importance of the project elements controlled by agencies other than the prosecutor's office, the more difficult the assembly efforts will be. The assembly efforts will also be more difficult the greater the excess of costs over benefits expected from the introduction of the CMIS by office personnel who are required to collect data.

Recent studies of attempts to increase coordination among public agencies delivering social services through the introduction of computerized information systems illustrate the difficulties of securing cooperation among agencies that are budgetarily independent.[8] The underlying problem is that the agency requesting the program element may have no way of rewarding or coercing the potential supplier. For example, one reason why the Alameda County District Attorney's Office chose an in-house computer for DALITE rather than using the county data processing center (DPC) computer was that user priority could not be secured from the county facility. The District Attorney's Office had no leverage over the county data processing center. Although nominal cooperation could have been secured (use of the DPC computer without user priority), the full cooperation needed to ensure that management reports would be produced on a timely basis could not be secured. In the short run, the operation of an in-house computer eliminated the need for DPC cooperation. In the longer run, however, DALITE operations were hampered when arrangements could not be made with the DPC for access to data from the county-wide police booking system. The office's current difficulty in securing permission for DALITE hardware improvements may be related to the threat that in-house computerization poses to the DPC's bureaucratic "turf."

Cooperation may be easier to secure when there is mutual dependence unrelated to the CMIS. For example, the prosecution and police must cooperate on a daily basis in the selection of cases to be filed in the courts. The need to maintain a good working relationship with the U.S. Attorney's Office may help explain the Metropolitan Police Department's willingness to direct its officers to fill out the defendant history forms needed for PROMIS. On the other hand, the need to maintain good working relations may constrain the CMIS design. For example, while the District Attorney's Office would have found reports on the sentencing decisions of judges useful, the data needed to produce these reports were not collected in order to avoid a controversy with the judges with whom the office must deal on a day-to-day basis.

Intraorganizational implementation difficulties can be related to the differences between the organizational members who bear the costs of data collection and those who gain the benefits of the data's use. An individual's power within an organization results from his or her control over persons, information, and instrumentalities.[9] Anthony Downs suggests that information systems will produce "power payoffs" to certain organizational members by changing their access to or control over information.[10] Opposition to the increased workload of data collection and fear of increased administrative control from the conversion of data to information outputs may mean that prosecutors' office personnel will not give their full support to CMIS implementation efforts.

The chief prosecutor or district attorney will be able to order cooperation. Data collectors may respond with only minimal compliance, however. Data collectors can even covertly sabotage CMIS effectiveness by simply neglecting to control the quality of the data provided. The greater the organizational distance between the data collection and data processing units, the less likely the CMIS implementor will be successful in stopping data quality deterioration through spot checks or direct contacts with data collection personnel.

The PROMIS and DALITE implementation experiences each illustrate the intraorganizational cooperation problem. Getting assistant prosecutors to complete data input and error correction forms for PROMIS has always been a problem. Since the introduction of on-line access, however, assistant prosecutors have been much more faithful in completing PROMIS data collection forms because they can now realize benefits from their efforts.

The Alameda County District Attorney's Office municipal court branch offices collect a large portion of the case data while most of the management benefits go to superior court users. It was originally intended that municipal court felony department deputies (who receive no managerial benefits from DALITE) would collect court appearance data. The felony department deputies objected to having to collect this data. Consequently, clerical personnel in each of the municipal court branch offices were trained to collect the required data from the court docket. The same problem did not occur with superior court deputies, probably because they were more familiar with DALITE's benefits and had closer personal contact with the system's implementators.

The examples illustrate consequences of the divergence between the costs and information benefits accruing to data collection personnel. One can imagine, however, that if PROMIS and DALITE had been more successful in providing management control information, assistant prosecutors might have engaged in manipulation of the data to avoid the control. Increased spot checking and other data verification steps might then have to be taken to counter the counter control.

A program attempting to diffuse a CMIS prototype must anticipate a wide range of variation in the organizational environments of the adopters. While it may not be possible to predict which approach will in general be successful, the program designers should heed the following warning:

> Programs predicated on continuing high levels of competence, on expeditious interorganizational coordination, or on sophisticated methods for accommodating diversity and heterogeneity are very vulnerable. They are not necessarily doomed to failure, but they are asking for trouble.[11]

MAINTENANCE OF DATA QUALITY

Some project elements, once secured, require little or no further attention from the implementor. Other project elements require constant monitoring to ensure that they remain engaged in the project assembly. Artifacts such as data collection forms or activities such as the generation of regular reports are examples of the former. The collection of complete and accurate data is an example of the latter. The need for periodic clean-ups of the PROMIS data base and the data quality problems encountered during the implementation of DALITE suggest that the difficulty of maintaining data quality is the Achilles heel of the CMIS.

Explanations for the data quality problem have been suggested in the discussion of the preceding problem themes. The difficulty of anticipating what data items will be needed in the future prompts the CMIS designers to include too many data elements, stretching data collection resources too thinly. The net costs generally faced by the data collectors may make them unenthusiastic (and unconscientious) in the conduct of their data collection tasks. Resources may not be available for adequate monitoring of the data collection process.

Initial data collection efforts are complicated by the need to maintain the previously existing information system until the CMIS can replace it. Even if the CMIS will eventually replace the manual system, during the transition period, personnel must be available to support both systems. During the DALITE and PROMIS transition periods, there was not sufficient personnel available to keep the new systems and the manual systems they were replacing up to date. Backlogs in data entry developed, considerably delaying the time when management reports approached an accuracy level that would allow their full use.

There may be a tendency to underestimate the resources that will be required to train personnel in data collection procedures. It is not sufficient only to provide training sessions when data collection activities begin because prosecutors' offices are typically characterized by the rotation of new personnel for training purposes. Some provision must be made for a continuing training program, or each rotation may be accompanied by a decline in data quality. Almost five years after data collection had begun, the Justice Department's evaluation of PROMIS reported data errors resulting from the reassignment of personnel without proper training.

A vicious circle can result from the interaction between data quality and use. Poor data quality discourages use; lower levels of use reduce the chances of error correction, which in turn hampers efforts to improve data quality. In the DALITE experience, for example, prior to the reorganization of the superior court trial teams, assistants did not rely on DALITE reports because they often contained errors or omissions. Because of this, the DALITE manager could not generate sufficient support or interest to correct the errors. Improvement came when an organizational change required an accurate accounting of the cases assigned to the old and new trial teams, thereby generating enough support to upgrade data quality. Eventually some deputies came to rely completely on the superior court reports, guaranteeing a continuous flow of error corrections.

ACCEPTANCE AND USE

Factors other than poor data quality may discourage the acceptance and use of a CMIS. Both the PROMIS and DALITE project teams encountered skepticism from line prosecutors and middle-level managers. The PROMIS project team had to devote considerable effort to promoting the system's potential uses. The DALITE project team used preimplementation interviews with branch managers as much for public relations purposes as for the determination of information needs. Although the CMIS implementation teams attributed much of the skepticism to the professional (legal) orientation of the prosecutors, the degree of skepticism was not fixed. It increased when initial promises of system outputs were not fulfilled or fulfilled only after long delays. It was reduced when information outputs started to become visible.

Another factor hindering CMIS use is a lack of resources for special in-house studies. In-house resources for special studies are an element of the assembly process that is likely to be missing. Use of the data base as a source for the generation of problem analysis and strategic planning information requires a substantive knowledge of office operations and some familiarity with statistical methodology. In general, prosecutors' offices do not have methodologically trained personnel on their staff. The conduct of special studies also requires programming resources above the level needed simply for system maintenance and the generation of regular reports. Such slack resources are likely to be available only after the CMIS has been operating for a considerable length of time, perhaps after any initial management enthusiasm for use of the system has worn thin.

The lack of in-house resources has hindered the use of both PROMIS and DALITE. The U.S. Attorney's Office does not have the resources to conduct in-house studies of the PROMIS data base. All studies using PROMIS data have been conducted with the assistance of outside consultants. Although a number of special in-house studies have been conducted using DALITE data, limitations in programming resources have restricted the analyses to simple listings and counts of cases sharing particular characteristics.

SUMMARY

Prosecutors' offices attempting to design and implement new CMIS prototypes are likely to encounter difficulties related to the four general problem themes suggested by the PROMIS and DALITE implementation experiences. The interrelationship of the problem themes is illustrated in Figure 2. (Arrows indicate the direction of influence.) If the use of the CMIS data to produce information outputs is considered the final product, Figure 2 points to the importance of data quality as an intermediate product. A major weakness of the CMIS is the number of factors that can combine to hinder the achievement of data quality.

Figure 2. The Interrelationship of CMIS Implementation Problems

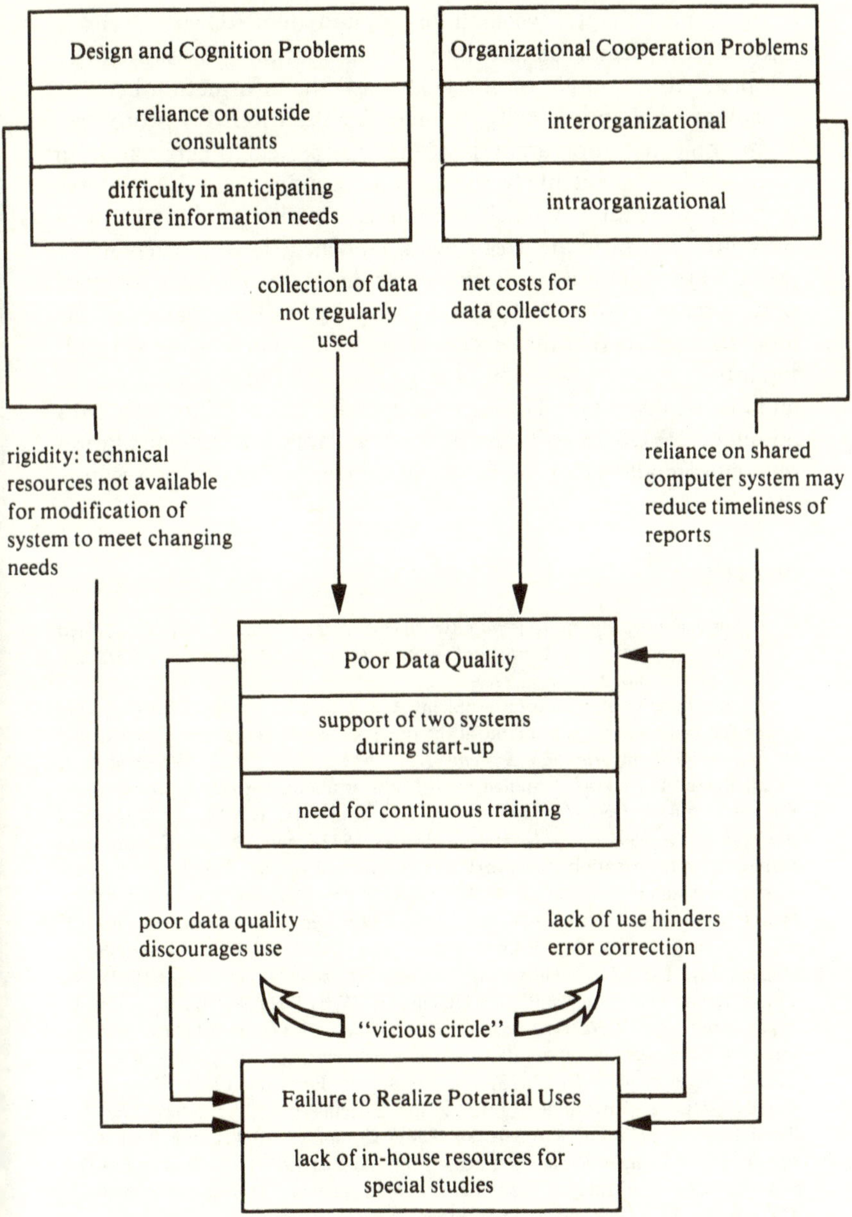

In the next chapter we shall discuss how the PROMIS Transfer Project was begun on the implicit assumption that subsequent adopters would obtain on a regular basis the information benefits that were only sporadically provided by the PROMIS prototype. If an implementation analysis of the type presented here had been conducted, it is not likely that this assumption would have been accepted so readily. Even if the implementation analysis had not prevented the program from being launched, it would have suggested ways of improving the prototype that were eventually followed only after widespread diffusion had begun. For example, our analysis suggests that the success of DALITE in producing scheduling information is the result in large part of its implementation on an in-house computer. Through the initiative of one of the PROMIS adopters, PROMIS software is now available for implementation on mini-computers that can be operated independently by prosecutors offices.

NOTES

1. For example, see the following two special issues of policy journals devoted to the implementation problem: *Policy Analysis* 1, no. 3 (Summer 1975), and *Public Policy* 27, no. 2 (Spring 1978).

2. That some implementation problems should have been expected is suggested by the following warnings available at the time: Robert V. Head, *Manager's Guide to Management Information Systems* (Englewood Cliffs, N.J.: Prentice-Hall, 1972); Russell L. Ackoff, "Management Misinformation Systems," *Management Science* 14, no. 4 (December 1967); John Dearden, "MIS Is a Mirage," *Harvard Business Review* 50, no. 1 (January-February 1972), and "Myth of Real-Time Management Information," *Harvard Business Review* 44, no. 3 (May-June 1966); Arlene Hershman, "A Mess in MIS," *Dun's Review* 91, no. 1 (January 1968); Henry Mintzberg, "The Myths of MIS," *California Management Review* 15, no. 1 (Fall 1972); Ridley Rhind, "Management Information Systems—Some Dreams Have Turned to Nightmares," *Business Horizons* 11, no. 3 (June 1968). For a more recent discussion see Regina Herzlinger, "Why Data Systems in Nonprofit Organizations Fail," *Harvard Business Review* 55, no. 1 (January-February 1977); James M. Danziger, "Computers, Local Governments, and the Litany to EDP," *Public Administration Review* 3, no. 1 (January/February 1977); Kenneth L. Kraemer, "Local Government Information Systems and Technology Transfer: Evaluating Some Common Assertions About Computer Applications Transfer," *Public Administration Review* 37, no. 4 (July/August 1977); and Phillip Ein-Dor and Eli Segev, "Strategic Planning for Management Information Systems," *Management Science* 24, no. 15 (November 1978).

3. For a general classification see Robert N. Anthony, *Planning and Control Systems: A Framework for Analysis* (Boston: Harvard University Press, 1965). Gory and Morton provide a starting point for the decision hierarchy discussed here. G. Anthony Gory and Michael S. Scott Morton, "A Framework for Management Information Systems," *Sloan Management Review* 13, no. 1 (Fall 1971), pp. 55-70.

4. See, for example, Gory and Morton, "A Framework for Management Information Systems."

5. Office of Management and Finance, U.S. Department of Justice, *An Evaluation of the PROMIS System*, Fall 1975.

6. Cost effectiveness in this context means that a manual information system could not produce the same information outputs at a lower cost. We have avoided the question of whether or not the value of the information outputs to the offices exceeds the operating costs.

7. See Herbert Simon, "Designing Organizations for an Information-Rich World," in *Computers, Communications and the Public Interest*, ed. Martin Greenberger (Baltimore: Johns Hopkins Press, 1968), pp. 38-72.

8. See, for example, Laudon's account of the Social Services Information System of Western County. Kenneth C. Laudon, *Computers and Bureaucratic Reform* (New York: John Wiley & Sons, 1974), pp. 101-73. See also, Kling's account of the Riverville Social Services Information and Referral System, Rob Kling, "The Riverville Social Services Information and Referral Service," Public Policy Research Organization, University of California, Irvine, June 1975; and Robert E. Quinn, "The Impacts of a Computerized Information System on the Integration and Coordination of Human Services," *Public Administration Review* 36, no. 2 (March/April 1976).

9. David Mechanic, "Sources of Power of Lower Participants in Complex Organizations," *Administration Science Quarterly* 7, no. 3 (December 1962): 348-64.

10. Anthony Downs, "A Realistic Look at the Final Payoffs from Urban Data Systems," *Public Administration Review* 27, no. 3 (September 1967): 204-10.

11. Eugene Bardach, *The Implementation Game: What Happens After a Bill Becomes a Law* (Cambridge, Mass.: The MIT Press, 1977), p. 253.

chapter 5

The PROMIS Transfer Project: A Program of Induced Diffusion

In 1973, the remnant of the PROMIS project team was searching for funds to support the redesign of PROMIS. Two years of operation had uncovered many deficiencies in the original design that jeopardized the continued use of PROMIS by the U.S. Attorney's Office. But by the end of 1976, less than three years later, PROMIS was being implemented in twenty-one jurisdictions. Sixteen other jurisdictions were actively planning PROMIS implementation, and it was estimated that by the end of 1976 implementation of PROMIS would be under way in over one hundred jurisdictions.[1] What explains the dramatic transformation of PROMIS from a system struggling for survival in a single jurisdiction to one that is diffusing at an increasing rate throughout the country?

One explanation concerns money. By the end of 1976, the first twenty-one jurisdictions adopting PROMIS had received over $4.7 million from the Law Enforcement Assistance Administration (LEAA) to fund their implementation efforts.[2] LEAA had also expended over $800,000 to improve PROMIS's transferability and to support its transfer.[3] By simple extrapolation additional LEAA expenditures of $20 million should be expected if one hundred jurisdictions begin implementing PROMIS over the next two years as anticipated.

The availability of federal dollars alone does not account for the diffusion of PROMIS to so many local jurisdictions. Marketing activity (including information dissemination) and technical assistance in support of PROMIS implementations have been and continue to be provided through LEAA's PROMIS Transfer Project.

Without the services provided by the PROMIS Transfer Project, many of the jurisdictions now implementing PROMIS would not have found LEAA funding alone to be a sufficient inducement to begin PROMIS implementation.

The PROMIS Transfer Project is an example of induced diffusion. Its activities have a much broader scope than the simple promulgation of information that characterizes programs of dissemination. It generates demand among prosecutors' offices by advertising the benefits that may result from PROMIS operations. It helps prosecutors' offices secure financing for PROMIS by helping them prepare proposals for LEAA grants. Once a prosecutor's office has decided to implement PROMIS, it provides direct technical assistance to the office. Finally, by providing system enhancements and by demonstrating possible uses, it encourages adopters to make maximum use of its potential.

This chapter examines the origins and operations of the PROMIS Transfer Project and includes an overview of the diffusion and mutation of PROMIS.

THE PROMIS EXEMPLARY PROJECT

The dissemination of information concerning the development and use of PROMIS by the U.S. Attorney's Office began shortly after operations had commenced. Members of the PROMIS project team reported their experiences and expectations in publications directed at local prosecutors and potential criminal justice information system users.[4] Early efforts to disseminate information about PROMIS were not limited to the project team members. In August 1971, less than eight months after data collection had begun, the administrator of LEAA sent letters to 1,300 local prosecutors, urging them to consider installing PROMIS-like systems in their offices. The administrator's letter constituted the first public step of LEAA in support of the diffusion of PROMIS.

Two general factors may have helped motivate the interest in LEAA in the diffusion of PROMIS. First, at the time, LEAA was receiving criticism for placing too much emphasis on support for police agencies relative to the courts.[5] During fiscal years 1969 to 1971, LEAA provided over five times more in grants to police agencies than the courts; during fiscal years 1972 to 1975, the ratio dropped by more than half. The change in the relative proportion of grant money going to the courts reflects the impact of external criticism. It also reflects a readjustment of goals within LEAA from programs that directly fight crime to programs aimed at improving the quality of justice. PROMIS appeared to be a way of improving the quality of the administration of justice within the courts by improving prosecution management.

The second general factor motivating interest in the diffusion of PROMIS may have been the criticism that LEAA was funding a large number of projects without finding approaches that would be appropriate for diffusion. The failure of LEAA to identify projects that should be replicated prompted Congress in 1973 to direct LEAA to increase its evaluations of funded projects. One of the responses of LEAA was to develop the Exemplary Projects Program, which includes PROMIS among the projects whose diffusion it encourages.

BEYOND DISSEMINATION

The dissemination of information about PROMIS was successful in generating interest among prosecutors and court administrators. During the first two years of operations, the U.S. Attorney's Office hosted a number of representatives from local jurisdictions who were interested in developing PROMIS-like systems. These early visits, however, did not actually lead to the development of CMISs by the interested jurisdictions.

Within LEAA, the National Criminal Justice Information and Statistics Service (NCJISS) became interested in the diffusion of PROMIS because of its potential for aiding local jurisdictions in the collection of comprehensive offender-based criminal statistics. The Systems Development Division of NCJISS believed that the diffusion of PROMIS would be more likely if the PROMIS software was more transferable. Because computer centers operated by local governments were unlikely to have personnel familiar with the scientific language in which PROMIS had been initially programmed, local jurisdictions would have difficulty adapting PROMIS software—probably to the extent that it would be easier to start the programming from scratch. The Systems Development Division therefore decided to fund the reprogramming of PROMIS in COBOL, a widely accepted business application language that can be operated on the hardware of most computer manufacturers.

The PROMIS project team viewed the reprogramming request as a golden opportunity to correct the design deficiencies that had become apparent during the first two years of PROMIS operations.[6] William Hamilton and Dean Merrill, members of the project team, who had stayed with the U.S. Attorney's Office as consultants, formed the Institute for Law and Social Research (INSLAW), a nonprofit corporation, to act as a recipient of the reprogramming grant. On January 1, 1973, INSLAW received $89,821 from the Systems Development Division of LEAA for PROMIS reprogramming and $63,285 from the U.S. Attorney's Office for the expansion of PROMIS to include the tracking of felonies. In August 1974 the reprogramming was completed.

DESIGNATION AS AN EXEMPLARY PROJECT

In 1973 the National Institute of Law Enforcement and Criminal Justice, the research arm of LEAA, began the Exemplary Projects Program. Administered by the National Institute's Office of Technology Transfer (OTT), the Exemplary Projects Program attempts to encourage the widespread use of advanced criminal justice practices. The procedure currently employed to designate a project as exemplary is outlined by the following:

> Rigorous screening procedures have been established to glean only the very best programs—those which warrant adoption on a broad scale. To be eligible for consideration, projects must:
>
> - Be operational for at least a year.
> - Have significantly reduced crime or measurably improved the operations and quality of the criminal justice system.
> - Be cost effective.
> - Be adaptable to other jurisdictions.
>
> Projects that pass initial screening by staff of the Institute's Office of Technology Transfer are validated by a contractor, working under OTT direction. The validation process includes an objective analysis of the project's achievements and an on-site assessment of its operations. The resulting report is submitted to a nine-member advisory board, which includes representatives from the State Criminal Justice Planning Agencies and LEAA Central and Regional Offices.[7]

PROMIS was only the second project to be designated as an exemplary project. Although the criteria for designation cited in the preceding passage had already been established by the time PROMIS was being considered, the procedure for determining whether the criteria were actually satisfied had not been finalized. As a result, PROMIS was *not* evaluated by an independent contractor. The evaluation was based on written material submitted by the U.S. Attorney's Office and INSLAW, and an oral presentation made to the Advisory Board by the president of INSLAW. Charles Work, the "father" of PROMIS, had, by the time, become an assistant administrator of LEAA. Although he was not directly involved with the exemplary project designation process, it may be that his association with PROMIS development favorably predisposed the review committee toward its designation.

PROMIS was designated an exemplary project primarily on the merits of its ability to select automatically high-priority cases for special pretrial preparation by a Special Litigation Unit. The cases that received special pretrial preparation during the first nineteen months of operation had a conviction rate 25 percent higher than the cases that were routinely handled.[8]

Two factors bring into question the use of this statistic as grounds for declaring PROMIS an exemplary project. First, special pretrial preparation would probably have produced a similar increase in the conviction rate for *any* set of cases to which it was applied. Second, as described in chapter 3, the automated selection of high-priority cases by PROMIS was used as a backup for manual selection during much of the first two years of operation. Eventually the automated selection of high-priority cases for special pretrial preparation was discontinued. These factors suggest that, although the PROMIS development may have been instrumental in the establishment of the Special Litigation Unit, the operation of the unit soon became relatively independent of PROMIS. A more rigorous evaluation, if it named anything, might have named the Special Litigation Unit as an exemplary project rather than the PROMIS system as a whole. A rigorous evaluation of PROMIS conducted at a later date when the benefits of on-line access began to be realized, might have found PROMIS qualified as an exemplary project on the merits of the operational and general research benefits it can provide.

When a project receives exemplary status, the Office of Technology Transfer generally supervises the preparation of a detailed handbook designed to guide policy makers and criminal justice administrators interested in implementing the project. The Office of Technology Transfer delegated its responsibility for the preparation of PROMIS documentation to the Systems Development Division of NCJISS. It was felt that the Systems Development Division was better prepared to supervise the development of computer software documentation because its staff included computer specialists. The Systems Development Division gladly accepted this responsibility because it viewed the diffusion of PROMIS as a way of furthering its objective of the development of comprehensive offender-based transaction statistics. (As noted in chapter 3, Joan Jacoby initiated the development of the PROMIS prototype for the same reason.) Grants intended to improve the transferability of PROMIS have been administered by the Systems Development Division.

INSLAW AND THE INDUCEMENT OF PROMIS TRANSFERS

INSLAW was chosen by the Systems Development Division to perform tasks designed to facilitate the diffusion of PROMIS. It was chosen as the PROMIS Transfer Project contractor because of the continuous involvement several of its personnel had had with the PROMIS system since the beginning of its implementation in the U.S. Attorney's Office. INSLAW was also in the best position to prepare PROMIS software documentation because it was still in the process of completing the PROMIS reprogramming. Other contractors were given the opportunity to submit bids for continuation of the PROMIS Transfer Project into 1975. Even though the request for proposals generated about 250 initial responses, only INSLAW actually submitted a bid. Other consultants may have been deterred by the restriction that the PROMIS Transfer Project contractor would not be allowed to accept contracts from the jurisdictions implementing PROMIS—profit-seeking firms were probably not interested in generating a market that they would have to cede to competitors.

By 1976, INSLAW was receiving approximately $325,000 per year for the continued development and operation of the PROMIS Transfer Project. The services provided by INSLAW go well beyond the dissemination of information:

> In its role as middleman-broker, INSLAW strives to bridge the communication/expertise gap that often exists between the technology and the potential user, the prosecuting attorney. Put another way, INSLAW attempts to provide the crutch, or backup, for potential PROMIS users so they will feel more confident in taking the first step and will have the security of knowing that support is available throughout their journey toward implementing PROMIS as a computer-based system, or, in the case of smaller jurisdictions, as a manual or semi-automated system. Among the many roadblocks facing potential users are the following:
>
> - Obtaining funds to support the transfer effort.
> - Planning an unfamiliar, technical project involving time schedules and procurement of services and hardware.
> - Employing new categories of personnel, such as systems analysts, to implement and monitor PROMIS.
> - Using contractors and consultants for the first time.
> - Justifying costs and benefits of PROMIS to local legislatures.
>
> In helping local jurisdictions surmount such difficulties, INSLAW does not "take charge," but serves as a catalyst, pointing out the available options which the local prosecutor may see fit to accept or reject.[9]

The activities that comprise the PROMIS Transfer Project can be divided into three general categories. The first category is marketing. It includes the activities primarily directed at selling the advantages of PROMIS to prosecutors and their jurisdictions. The second category is implementation assistance. It consists of those activities that are designed to help prosecutors' offices achieve and use operational PROMIS systems. The third category, system enhancement, includes efforts to improve the capabilities of the PROMIS prototype design. The marketing, implementation assistance, and system enhancement categories form the basis of the PROMIS Transfer Project activities executed by INSLAW.

Marketing

One component of marketing is advertising, which is the dissemination of information about the product to the potential market.

In order to advertise PROMIS, INSLAW has promoted the distribution of nontechnical descriptions of its operation and potential uses. Videotape and film presentations, demonstrations at conventions of local criminal justice system officials (such as conferences of the National District Attorneys' Association, conventions of the State District Attorneys' Associations, and meetings of criminal justice information system users), tours of and briefings on PROMIS operations in the U.S. Attorney's Office, and a series of briefing papers on various aspects of PROMIS have been used as advertising devices. Of these, demonstrations of PROMIS presented at conventions, conferences, and meetings of local officials have probably been most successful in generating initial interest in PROMIS. The other advertising devices, including the briefing papers, are useful in encouraging an already developed initial interest.

The managerial goals advanced as ones PROMIS can help to achieve are outlined in the first of twenty-one papers in the PROMIS Briefing Series:

> Some consider as the *centerpiece of PROMIS* its ability to help prosecuting attorneys identify the more serious cases among the thousands that flow through the Washington prosecutor's office each year. Typically, the relative importance of pending cases is hidden by their sheer number and by the masking effect of legal charges. . . . PROMIS cuts through these difficulties by assigning ratings to cases on the basis of data obtained by attorneys and arresting officers at the screening stage.
>
> . . .
>
> *A second major managerial objective* PROMIS addresses is the control and/or elimination of scheduling and logistical impediments that tend to block adjudication of cases on their merits.
>
> . . .
>
> *A third principle management objective* PROMIS focuses on is the monitoring and enforcing of even-handedness and consistency in the exercise of prosecutive discretion.
>
> . . .
>
> Finally, *the fourth major management objective* addressed by PROMIS pertains to the analysis and research of problems associated with the screening and prosecution of criminal cases.[10]

As indicated by our discussion of the PROMIS prototype, these expected benefits must have been advanced on historical rather than the then current uses of PROMIS by the U.S. Attorney's Office. Other papers in the briefing series suggest the use of PROMIS for policy research and PROMIS's potential for serving as a link with other criminal justice information systems.

A second component of marketing will be called salesmanship. It consists of efforts made to convince specific jurisdictions to consider the adoption of PROMIS. Salesmanship activities are applied to prosecutors' offices showing a favorable response to PROMIS advertising. The major salesmanship activities are on-site feasibility studies and cost-benefit analyses for justifying PROMIS to the budgetary sponsors of the prosecutors' offices.

During the first two years of the PROMIS Transfer Project, INSLAW conducted on-site feasibility studies for thirty-five prosecutors' offices. Each of the on-site visits, conducted free of charge, culminated in a report to the chief prosecutor on

> the adaptability (or unsuitability) of PROMIS to his jurisdiction, the modifications to manual procedures that may have to be made, the level of effort to transfer PROMIS, the use of the cost-and-benefit Briefing Paper, the level of help INSLAW can provide during transfer, and the next steps to be taken if a decision is made to transfer PROMIS.[11]

INSLAW is continuing to conduct on-site feasibility studies for interested jurisdictions. INSLAW is also attempting to facilitate greater use of the PROMIS cost/benefit methodology by automating the calculation procedures.

Customer relations, a third set of marketing activities, describes efforts to encourage prosecutors to support, use, and enhance the PROMIS systems they have implemented or are in the process of implementing. The major customer relations activity conducted by INSLAW is the administration of quarterly meetings of PROMIS users. A complimentary customer relations activity is the publication of the PROMIS newsletter.

PROMIS Users Group meetings have been held quarterly since June 1974. LEAA funds the travel expenses of a representative from each jurisdiction that has implemented or is in the process of implementing PROMIS. Jurisdictions considering the implementation of PROMIS are also invited to send representatives. The meetings started out as single-day conferences held at INSLAW facilities and attended by twenty participants. By the spring of 1977, the meetings had expanded to two-day conferences held in various PROMIS jurisdictions and attended by over one hundred participants.

The Users Group meeting typically includes a presentation on some aspects of PROMIS implementation, often in the form of a panel discussion. It provides an opportunity for INSLAW and the PROMIS jurisdictions to consider ideas for and experiences with enhancements of the PROMIS system. INSLAW uses the Users Group meetings to present research findings based on the analysis of PROMIS data. In addition to these information transfer activities, the growing number of User Group participants provides encourage- for those beginning, or planning to begin, PROMIS implementation.

The PROMIS newsletter is published quarterly and generally provides a summary of the previous Users Group meeting, including an interview with the prosecutor who hosted it. The PROMIS newsletter provides a status report on the implementation progress of the PROMIS jurisdictions. It also provides an updated listing of INSLAW's PROMIS-related publications.

Implementation Assistance

INSLAW provides a number of services, free of charge to local jurisdictions, in support of PROMIS implementation. Often the first service provided by INSLAW is help in preparing grant proposals for implementation funds. Although LEAA has no funds specifically set aside for support of PROMIS implementations, funds are generally available through either the state planning agencies (which control LEAA state block grants) or in conjunction with special LEAA programs (such as the Career Criminal, Improved Lower Court Handling programs, and, most recently, the Incentive Funding Program). INSLAW's assistance is particularly helpful to prosecutors' offices that have not previously had experience preparing grant proposals for large-scale projects.

Once funding has been secured, INSLAW may assist in the preparation of requests for proposals for consulting services needed for the implementation project. INSLAW's participation allows the jurisdictions to prepare much more detailed requests for proposals than would otherwise be possible. INSLAW may also provide assistance to local jurisdictions in evaluating bids submitted by contractors. INSLAW's accumulated experience with PROMIS implementations allows it to serve as a resource to the local jurisdiction for monitoring the execution of consulting contracts.

INSLAW provides a six-volume set of PROMIS documentation to help guide the jurisdiction through the implementation process.[12] After computer facilities have been secured, INSLAW provides a tape containing the PROMIS software. The software documentation is designed to allow the jurisdiction to test the unmodified PROMIS software quickly on sample data also provided by INSLAW. The jurisdiction can then begin to test software modifications in the context of the full software system.

During the modification of PROMIS software, INSLAW is available to provide technical assistance. Because INSLAW personnel were involved in the design of the PROMIS software, it is often possible for INSLAW to provide information by phone within hours after the request has been made. The solution to more difficult problems in software modification may require a visit by INSLAW personnel. Such visits may also be used to provide assistance in other aspects of PROMIS implementation, such as the development of training procedures for data collection personnel. Unlike the services of the consultants hired by the jurisdiction, INSLAW continues to provide technical assistance after the expiration date of the implementation grant.

System Enhancements

INSLAW continues to develop enhancements of the PROMIS system that can be incorporated into the basic software design. Several of the enhancements have been added in an attempt to make it easier for prosecutors to extract information from PROMIS. For example, an on-line inquiry package was developed to allow access to case-specific data through remote terminals. For systems operating only in the batch mode, the Generalized Inquiry Package was developed to allow access to case-specific data through a set of standard programs. Most recently, INSLAW has added the Management Report Package in an attempt to reduce the programming effort needed to produce management reports. The Management

Report Package allows the programmer to produce a wide range of statistical reports by simply setting a number of parameters.

Other enhancements are designed to increase the potential market of PROMIS by providing alternatives to the basic design. Despite initial reluctance, but at LEAA's insistence, INSLAW developed a version of PROMIS for the nonautomated or semiautomated office that has become very popular in small jurisdictions.[13] (We shall continue to refer only to the automated version as PROMIS.) INSLAW now makes available a version of PROMIS for minicomputers that can be operated by prosecutors' offices independently of shared computer systems.

DIFFUSION AND MUTATION

The PROMIS Transfer Project has been successful in fostering the diffusion of PROMIS. A jurisdiction will be considered to have adopted PROMIS at the time it has secured LEAA funding to begin the implementation process. Under this definition, PROMIS had diffused to over twenty jurisdictions by the end of 1977. Table 4 illustrates the time profile of PROMIS diffusion.

The first adoption occurred prior to the completion of the PROMIS reprogramming. In April 1973, Cobb County, Georgia, received an LEAA grant to develop a criminal justice information system that used PROMIS as the central component. Joseph LeCroy, the Cobb County System project manager, recommended the use of PROMIS in his jurisdiction after his search for a court system model had failed: ". . . everyone I called was either in the planning stage, or had tried something and given up, or were working on systems so complex it didn't appear that they would work."[14] When it was learned that INSLAW was beginning the reprogramming of PROMIS, a decision was made to wait for the new software rather than attempt to reprogram independently. Waiting was advantageous for both INSLAW and Cobb County. Cobb County had only to make software modifications rather than to mount a complete reprogramming effort. INSLAW had a direct "interface" with a jurisdiction using different computer hardware; immediately testing software on the second hardware system allowed for the quick identification of problems that might otherwise have reduced the transferability of the finished software package to other jurisdictions.

Table 4. The Diffusion of PROMIS Adoption

Year	PROMIS Adoption
1970	Design of the PROMIS prototype—Washington, D.C.
1973	Redesign of the PROMIS prototype
	Cobb County (Marietta), Ga.
1974	Los Angeles County, Calif.
1975	Marion County (Indianapolis), Ind. Wayne County (Detroit), Mich. State of Rhode Island[a] Orleans Parish (New Orleans), La. New York County (Manhattan), N.Y. Kalamazoo County, Mich. Milwaukee County, Wisc. Salt Lake City, Utah Clark County (Las Vegas), Nev.
1976	Pulaski County (Little Rock), Ark. St. Louis Circuit, Mo. St. Louis County, Mo. Union County (Elizabeth), N.J. Palm Beach County, Fla. Jefferson County (Louisville), Ky. City of San Diego, Calif. San Diego County, Calif. 2nd Judicial District (Tallahassee), Fla.

At the end of 1976, INSLAW reported that an additional sixteen jurisdictions were actively planning the adoption of PROMIS systems. By January 1980 PROMIS was operational in 37 jurisdictions and being planned or implemented in 159 others.

[a]Department of the Attorney General.

NOTE: Research contacts made with each of the twenty PROMIS jurisdictions listed in the table are as follows:

Field visits: Cobb County, Los Angeles County, Orleans Parish, and Wayne County.

Phone interview: Marion County, Milwaukee County, Salt Lake County, Clark County, Pulaski County, Kalamazoo County, New York County, Jefferson County, San Diego County, San Diego City, and Second Judicial Circuit of Florida.

Data provided by INSLAW: State of Rhode Island, Union County, Palm Beach, St. Louis Circuit, and St. Louis County.

Cobb County was not chosen as the first recipient of the PROMIS transfer package as the result of any sophisticated choice process—Cobb County just happened to be interested in PROMIS at the right time. Nevertheless, if an effort had been mounted to find a jurisdiction for testing the transferability of PROMIS with a minimum of implementation complications, a jurisdiction like Cobb County might have been chosen for several reasons.

First, criminal prosecution in the District of Columbia and Cobb County are similar in two aspects relevant to case management information system design: each uses a grand jury system for initial case processing of felonies, and each has a single prosecutor's office without branches. Major differences in criminal procedure or office structure would have dictated greater modification of the PROMIS software. The fewer changes needed, the less chance of design difficulties.

Second, the Cobb County criminal justice system is relatively small in scale, so that a minimum of resources would be required to initiate and manage the implementation effort. The court consists of only three judges. Case load is moderate: about 1,600 to 1,700 cases have the mandatory grand jury presentation per year. The District Attorney's Office has only five prosecutors for criminal cases. Each of these factors suggests that complications related to scale (such as the need to phase the system in rather than begin office-wide operations) would be reduced to a minimum.

Third, it appeared that the project had support from all the local criminal justice agencies, as well as the county administration. Heads of each of the agencies had written letters in support of the initial grant proposal. It thus appeared that implementation problems related to securing interorganizational cooperation would be minimized.

The Los Angeles District Attorney's Office was the second adopter of PROMIS. Like Cobb County, the Los Angeles District Attorney's Office had already secured LEAA funding for the development of a PROMIS-like CMIS when the PROMIS reprogramming was completed. The Los Angeles District Attorney's Office believed that the modification of the PROMIS software would be an easier task than the development of completely new software. Thus by the end of 1974, PROMIS had been adopted by the largest prosecutor's office in the United States.

During 1975, the diffusion of PROMIS adoption accelerated to a rate of nine jurisdictions per year. The inclusion of PROMIS as an optional component of two LEAA discretionary grant programs plays an important role in facilitating the rapid diffusion of PROMIS adoption. The Improved Lower Court Case Handling Program funds the adoption of PROMIS along with seven other projects intended to improve case management in lower (misdemeanor) courts. Administrators of the Career Criminal Program, which funds the creation of special units to prosecute repeat offenders, have allowed a number of jurisdictions to fund PROMIS implementation with Career Criminal Program funds. The supposed capacity of PROMIS to support a case evaluation system is cited as the rationale for its inclusion in Career Criminal Program projects. The securing of PROMIS implementation funds through these LEAA discretionary grant programs eliminates the need to compete for the state block grant funds administered by the state planning agencies. Recently, grants to New Jersey, New York, and Michigan, provided through the Incentive Funding Program, have diffused PROMIS to twenty-five jurisdictions in these states alone.

JUSTIS: A MAJOR MUTATION

The PROMIS prototype was designed to serve the U.S. Attorney's Office in the District of Columbia. Because other prosecutors' offices differ in structure and procedure, each jurisdiction implementing PROMIS must make some alterations in the prototype design. In general, the adaptive changes, though perhaps not trivial for those who had to implement them, have not been of such a degree that they readily distinguish the resulting systems from the PROMIS prototype.

One major mutation of PROMIS has occurred, however. The Milwaukee County District Attorney's Office, in conjunction with county courts, has made a major alteration of the PROMIS prototype that may prove desirable to jurisdictions where there is close cooperation between the prosecution and the courts. Milwaukee County named its system JUSTIS (Judicial Tracking and Information System). It differs from PROMIS in a number of ways, but one difference is of major importance: JUSTIS allows entry of case data directly into case files on a real-time basis, eliminating the twenty-four hour delay in case updates (forty-eight-hour delay for case updates containing syntax errors) associated with PROMIS's batch approach. On-line access to continuously updated files provides the system with a potential for producing logistical support information for the courts. The greater the benefits that can be offered to the courts, the greater the chances of securing their cooperation in data collection.

Although the adoption of JUSTIS will continue to be equated with the adoption of PROMIS (as it is in table 4), it is interesting to note that some of the PROMIS diffusion actually involves (or may involve) the transfer of JUSTIS. Florida's Second Judicial District is implementing the JUSTIS system with technical assistance provided by Milwaukee County through its Judicial Information Systems coordinator. Other jurisdictions listed in table 4 that are considering the adoption of JUSTIS rather than PROMIS are New York County (New York), Palm Beach County (Florida), and Jefferson County (Kentucky). The Systems Development Division included in the 1977 PROMIS Transfer Project grant funds that allowed INSLAW to incorporate the JUSTIS software design as an option in the PROMIS transfer package.

IMPLEMENTATION STUDIES AS A COMPONENT OF EVALUATION

We would be committing a serious error by evaluating the PROMIS Transfer Project solely in terms of its success in diffusing PROMIS. As discussed in chapter 1, programs of induced diffusion run the risk of widely diffusing innovations in the absence of positive evidence, or even in the presence of negative evidence, that their potential benefits can be realized by adopters. Our evaluation must therefore include an assessment of the extent to which adopters have been able to implement PROMIS successfully so as to realize its advertised benefits. The variability and open-ended nature of the implementation process make the inclusion of investigations of post-adoption experiences a necessary part of the implementation assessment.

A brief look at Cobb County's experience with PROMIS will illustrate the approach. As noted in the previous section, Cobb County was the first jurisdiction to begin the transfer of PROMIS. Its small size, the similarity of its criminal procedure to that of the

District of Columbia, and the apparent close cooperation among county agencies made it appear to be an easy testing ground for PROMIS transferability. Despite these advantages, several problems were encountered during the implementation process.

Data collection began in January 1975. Problems were encountered in achieving data quality because police officers and assistant prosecutors sometimes neglected to fill out the data input forms. Although training efforts and the introduction of on-line access led to improved data quality, the court system project manager still viewed the maintenance of data quality as a problem nearly two years later.

During the implementation, a controversy developed between the Cobb County superior court and the other county criminal justice agencies over the control of agency budgets. The excellent cooperation exhibited in the original grant proposals for PROMIS implementation evaporated, and a struggle ensued for control of the PROMIS system. The situation finally stabilized, with control of the system going to the country data processing center. Nevertheless, the unexpected controversy almost stopped the implementation process.

More than a year and a half after data collection had begun, District Attorney George W. Darden was not relying on PROMIS for the generation of management reports. Although several reports were being generated for his office, the district attorney was not actually using them. One reason was that his staff consisted of only five assistant prosecutors—a number easily managed by face-to-face contact. The district attorney indicated that he felt the system had become primarily a court system, offering no essential management benefits to his office.

The Cobb County experience demonstrated the transferability of PROMIS software and enhancements. It suggests, however, that, despite the headstart in system design, maintaining data quality is likely to be a problem, even in relatively small jurisdictions. It also illustrated potential for danger when implementation depends on the cooperation of more than one local agency. In the following chapter we shall investigate the implementation experiences (through the Spring of 1977) of the other PROMIS adopters in an attempt to make a general assessment of the circumstance under which information benefits are most likely to result.

NOTES

1. This estimate was made by William Hamilton, president of INSLAW, in an interview on June 25, 1976.

2. Figures are computed from data collected in phone interviews with the implementing jurisdictions and data provided by Alvin Ash, PROMIS Transfer Project Monitor, National Criminal Justice Information and Statistics Service, LEAA.

3. LEAA has provided the following grants to INSLAW to improve the transferability of PROMIS:

Grant Description	*Amount*	*Fiscal Year*
Reprogramming	$ 89,921	1973
Transferability	212,278	1973
Transfer assistance	219,595	1975
Transfer assistance	324,998	1976
TOTAL	$846,792	

INSLAW has also received $1.5 million in LEAA funds in support of research based on PROMIS-generated data. Since 1976, INSLAW has continued to receive LEAA funding for PROMIS-related activities.

4. See, for example, William A. Hamilton, "Modern Management for the Prosecutor," *The Prosecutor* 7, no. 6 (November-December 1971); Charles R. Work, "A Prosecutor's Guide to Automation," *The Prosecutor* 7, no. 6 (November-December 1971); and Dean C. Merrill, "Using the PROMIS Tracking System for Criminal Justice Evaluation," *International Symposium on Criminal Justice and Statistics Systems,* SEARCH Group, Inc., October 1972; William A. Hamilton and Charles R. Work, "The Prosecutor's Role in the Urban Court System: The Case for Management Consciousness," *The Journal of Criminal Law and Criminology* 64, no. 2 (1973): 188.

5. For a discussion of criticisms of LEAA, see Richard E. Cohen, "Renewal of LEAA Likely Despite Doubts on Crime Impact," *National Journal* 7, no. 38 (September 20, 1975).

6. The project team had been actively searching for sources of funding to improve PROMIS. It had previously attempted to encourage the Justice Department to support the transfer of PROMIS to the local offices of the U.S. Attorney's Office.

7. Office of Technology Transfer, "Exemplary Projects: A Program of the National Institute of Law Enforcement and Criminal Justice," December 1975, p. 1.

8. Ibid., p. 6.

9. INSLAW, "Final Report: PROMIS Transferability Contract," July 1975, pp. 3-5.

10. INSLAW, "Management Overview of PROMIS," PROMIS Briefing Series No. 7, July 1975, pp. 3-5.

11. INSLAW, "Final Report: PROMIS Transferability Contract," p. 24.

12. The six volumes of PROMIS documentation provided by INSLAW are *System Overview, System and Program Descriptions, Data Preparation Guide,*

Software Implementation Guide, Office Paperwork Procedures, and System Options. As the titles indicate, the volumes discuss more than just the PROMIS software.

13. Initially, INSLAW did not wish to prepare a nonautomated version of PROMIS, perhaps because it might undercut the diffusion of the automated version. The institute was persuaded to do so, however, when it learned that LEAA would turn to another contractor for its development. By December 1976, nine jurisdictions were in the process of implementing the nonautomated version of PROMIS.

14. The court system project manager reports that over the first eight months of 1972 he contacted jurisdictions across the country that had received federal grants to develop automated court information systems.

chapter 6

A General Assessment of PROMIS Implementation

An important objective in evaluating any program of induced diffusion is to determine which circumstances actually produce the anticipated benefits so that predictions can be made about the outcomes of future adoptions. When enough adopters have had the innovation long enough to provide reasonable trials of its effectiveness, it becomes more feasible to employ statistical methodologies for measuring and predicting impacts systematically. When the innovation is still in a stage of diffusion, it is difficult to determine when to conduct the evaluation. The longer we wait, the fewer the number of potential adopters remain to be influenced by our findings. Where diffusion is rapid and the implementation period long, the potential market for the innovation might be saturated before an adequate data base for statistical analysis could be assembled.

Such is the case with the PROMIS Transfer Project. By the end of 1978, ninety-one jurisdictions containing one-third of the U.S. population had adopted or were committed to adopting PROMIS. Yet PROMIS was operational in only twenty of the jurisdictions, a number too small to support statistical research for the correlates of success and failure. At the time the study presented here was completed in the spring of 1977, only twenty jurisdictions had actually begun implementing PROMIS.[1] The results, which were qualitative in nature, are presented in terms of the general problem themes developed in the implementation analysis of the PROMIS and DALITE prototypes. Although general observations will be advanced without specific reference to each jurisdiction, anecdotal evidence will be provided for illustrative purposes. Major contradictions to the general observations will also be noted.

THE PROMIS TRANSFER PROJECT AND THE CMIS IMPLEMENTATION PROBLEM THEMES

DESIGN AND COGNITION

Designing and planning the implementation of a case management information system require the application of technical skills unlikely to be found among the personnel regularly employed by prosecutors' offices. The PROMIS and DALITE prototype experiences point to the dangers of relying on outside consultants for the provision of supplementary technical skills. Design inadequacies may result from the consultants' lack of knowledge of the substantive activities of the office, as well as from the office's inexperience in dealing with consultants. Once the consultants have withdrawn with their technical skills, it may not be possible for the office to make major modifications of the system. Unanticipated changes in office procedures or organization may render the CMIS obsolete.

As was discussed in chapter 5, various types of implementation assistance are offered to jurisdictions through the PROMIS Transfer Project. Software and documentation for PROMIS and its enhancements, assistance in dealing with contractors, and direct technical assistance from INSLAW are available at no cost to the jurisdictions adopting PROMIS. Has this assistance been sufficient to allow jurisdictions to avoid the design and modification problems encountered during the PROMIS and DALITE prototype implementations?

It appears that jurisdictions are able to adapt the basic PROMIS design so that its operational characteristics can be achieved in a variety of organizational settings. As might be expected, the greater the amount of change required to fit the prototype design to the organizational characteristics of the jurisdiction, the greater the chances that design difficulties will be encountered. Instead of necessitating major redesigns of the basic prototype or leading to project terminations, the design difficulties encountered are being overcome at the cost of delay. As evidenced by the introduction of the PROMIS enhancements in several of the jurisdictions, it also appears that jurisdictions have been able to modify their systems after the initial implementation period has ended.

Two very different cases illustrate these general observations. At one extreme is the experience of the Marion County Prosecutor's

Office serving Indianapolis, Indiana. Its case handling procedures and office organization were close enough to those of the U.S. Attorney's Office for the District of Columbia to permit the direct transfer of the PROMIS prototype. Without the assistance of an outside consultant, the Marion County Prosecutor's Office was able to begin data collection activities within three months after receiving an LEAA state block grant for PROMIS implementation. Because the only major modifications made were the addition of several data fields, it has been possible for the office to make rapid implementation of the PROMIS enhancements developed by INSLAW.

At the other extreme is the experience of the Milwaukee County District Attorney's Office. Because an information system was desired that would serve the courts as well as the District Attorney's Office, major changes of the PROMIS prototype design were required. A Judicial Information Systems coordinator, assisted by two systems analysts and two programmers, was able to complete the modifications without the assistance of outside contractors. The project director estimates that about 65 percent of the software required major revisions. The resulting system, JUSTIS, was described in chapter 5 as a major mutation of the PROMIS prototype. Although the system modifications took more than a year to complete, the project director estimated that Milwaukee County saved a minimum of eighteen months' time and $800,000 by opting for the transfer of PROMIS rather than developing a separate information system for the courts.[2]

Several jurisdictions report encountering unexpected delays in making modifications of the PROMIS prototype. One project director indicated that the ease with which personnel were able to install and test the basic software package led them to underestimate the time and effort that would be required to make desired modifications. After referring to the difficulties he encountered in making software modifications, another project director warned that jurisdictions should double their initial estimates of the time that would be required to make modifications of the PROMIS prototype.

Even though several of the jurisdictions reported encountering delay in making modifications of the basic PROMIS design, none reported encountering difficulties that could not be overcome or bypassed. The adaptability of the PROMIS prototype design can be directly attributed to the assistance provided through the PROMIS Transfer Project. Project directors generally found the PROMIS documentation to be of excellent quality. One project director with considerable computer systems experience described the PROMIS documentation as the best he had ever seen. When asked about the quality of assistance provided by INSLAW, project directors' responses ranged from "good" to "outstanding." Most offered illustrations of the timeliness and quality of INSLAW's technical assistance. For example, INSLAW was able on occasion to provide answers to technical questions the same day they were asked. Other jurisdictions relied on INSLAW's assistance to overcome more serious problems requiring site visits by the institute's personnel.

An indirect indication of INSLAW's success as a provider of implementation assistance is the satisfaction expressed by the jurisdictions with the services provided by outside consultants. None of the jurisdictions that relied an outside consultants voiced complaints that the services provided were deficient. INSLAW's help in drafting requests for proposals, the existence of standards from the repetition of PROMIS implementations, and the availability of INSLAW's assistance as a backup for the consultants help explain why jurisdictions were able to make effective use of outside consultants.

ORGANIZATIONAL COOPERATION

Modification of the PROMIS prototype design is only the first step of the implementation process. The prosecutor's office may have to secure cooperation from other public agencies in the form of direct services or altered behavior. Within the prosecutor's office, cooperation must be secured from personnel who will be required to collect data or otherwise change their work patterns. The PROMIS and DALITE prototype experiences illustrated how the need to secure these types of internal and external organizational cooperation can lead to delay and undermine the achievement and maintenance of data quality.

Interorganizational Cooperation

First, we shall consider the dimensions of interorganizational cooperation that may be needed to implement an adapted PROMIS design. Dependence may be placed on the police to fill out initial data entry forms or at least to provide source documents containing the desired data. Similar dependence may be placed on the courts for assistance in the collection of update data. Because the prosecutor's office is unlikely to operate its own computer system, computer services must be secured from the county or municipal data processing center, or from some other county agency that maintains its own computer facilities. Once LEAA grants expire, the local legislative body must be convinced of the need to provide funds for continued implementation or operation.

The particular combination of interorganizational cooperation desired, and the difficulties that will be encountered in achieving it, will be unique to each jurisdiction. The PROMIS Transfer Project cannot, and should not, be expected to intervene directly in local bureaucratic politics on behalf of the prosecutor's office. It might be anticipated, however, that PROMIS Transfer Project assistance could reduce the impact of interorganizational cooperation problems by enabling prosecutors' offices to alter designs to bypass bottlenecks.

A major consideration is cooperation with police departments. Prosecutors' offices enjoy several advantages in dealing with police departments. First, police departments must rely on prosecutors' offices for the filing of formal charges. Second, police departments may be interested in sharing information system outputs, such as disposition reports for updating criminal histories. Third, as police departments generally provide the prosecution with all or most of the desired case data in some form, it may be possible to use the prosecutors' office personnel to collect the data for PROMIS input if the police departments refuse to do so.

The Cobb County project director was able to secure the cooperation of local police departments by redesigning the PROMIS intake form so that it replaced several forms then in use. A similar pattern was followed in several other jurisdictions: consolidation of multiple forms allowed the police to provide PROMIS data without significant increases in time costs. The experience of the Los Angeles District Attorney's Office in gaining police cooperation by promising access to PROMIS data also appears to have been repeated in a number of jurisdictions.

Lack of cooperation with the police department contributed to the inability of the New Orleans District Attorney's Office to realize its plans for collecting data directly from the police booking system. At least five other prosecutors' offices have encountered problems in securing police cooperation. Two offices report encountering major delays before agreements could be reached with local police agencies. (One of the prosecutors' offices had to deal with twenty-three independent law enforcement agencies.) Another prosecutor's office now collecting data, and yet another in the design stage, decided to bear the additional clerical costs required to avoid reliance on the police for the completion of data input forms. Finally, one prosecutor's office reports that plans for computation of case evaluation scores had to be dropped because the police department would not order its officers to complete the necessary data input forms. In these instances, lack of cooperation with the police hindered, rather than blocked, the implementation process.

The courts are a second major consideration in interorganizational cooperation. Prosecutors' offices are generally in a less favorable position in dealing with the courts than with the police. In most jurisdictions, the prosecution depends on the court's goodwill for favorable treatment in matters of calendaring as well as for evenhanded treatment in the adversary process. Given the general relational advantage enjoyed, the courts are free to decide the level of cooperation they will provide primarily on the costs and benefits of the CMIS that they will directly bear. The major cost the courts envision is the potential use of the CMIS as a tool for monitoring sentencing decisions. Automation of case docketing is the most obvious benefit the courts might expect from participation in a CMIS project.

Only three of the PROMIS systems have developed with full participation of the courts. As noted previously, a battle between courts and other county criminal justice agencies over its control resulted in the Cobb County PROMIS becoming more a tool of the court than a tool of the District Attorney's Office. The Milwaukee County District Attorney's Office began its PROMIS project with the full cooperation of the courts. (Cooperation was probably facilitated by the first assistant district attorney's prior employment with the courts' administration.) In order to provide calendaring benefits, however, it was necessary to make major changes in the PROMIS prototype design; the resulting JUSTIS system constitutes the most radical PROMIS mutation. A joint prosecution and courts venture is under way in the Second Judicial Circuit of Florida. After originally evaluating the PROMIS prototype as being incapable of providing the desired court docketing information, the Second Judicial Circuit decided to adopt the JUSTIS mutation.

With the exception of one jurisdiction where court opposition may have been responsible for delaying local funding for over a year, courts have generally exhibited either partial cooperation or nonopposition. Several courts provide copies of their dockets to serve as sources of data on court appearances. (One prosecutor's office complained that it received the docket copies after sometimes as long as a week's delay.) Despite initial opposition from the court to the introduction of PROMIS, one prosecutor's office now receives court appearance data from the court's information system that can be automatically copied into the PROMIS data base. Even without receiving any data collection assistance from the courts, several prosecutors' offices have provided their courts with on-line access to PROMIS case data.

Local data processing centers also play a major role in interorganizational cooperation. Failure to secure full cooperation from the police and the courts will generally result in either project delay or increased data collection costs. Failure to secure full cooperation from the local data processing center not only can result in delay and higher costs but also can threaten the successful completion of the PROMIS implementation.

Consider the experience of the New Orleans District Attorney's Office with the local municipal data processing center. After giving an initial guarantee of cooperation, the municipal data processing center withdrew permission for use of its facilities when the city government refused to fund a major budget increase. If it had not been possible to transfer PROMIS software to an in-house computer, the New Orleans District Attorney's Office would have had to abort its PROMIS project.

The poor reputation of the county data processing center in the early 1970s prompted the Los Angeles District Attorney's Office to seek permission from the Board of Supervisors to contract with private vendors for computer services. Only the untimely death of the district attorney the day before the final vote was to be taken prevented the circumvention of the data processing department. The project director expressed the view that, despite the improvement in the services provided by the data processing department in recent years, the multi-year implementation period could have been shortened if the office had been allowed to operate its own computer system or that of a vendor.

With the exception of New Orleans, one prosecutor's office that is using a private vendor because its county does not operate a computer center, and another prosecutor's office that anticipates use of computer facilities maintained by the local police department, all the PROMIS jurisdictions must rely upon services provided by shared computer centers operated by local governments. At least six jurisdictions attribute project delays directly to unsatisfactory services provided by the data processing centers. In one case, excellent services deteriorated when the data processing center directed its attention to dealing with a major problem that had developed with another county management information system. Dissatisfaction with the services of data processing centers may persist for several prosecutors' offices as regular operations begin. There may be delays in the generation of regular reports and the provision of programming resources for conducting special studies or making system modifications.

Securing local funding is another aspect of interorganizational cooperation. With the New York City fiscal crisis of recent years, it is not surprising that the New York District Attorney's Office encountered considerable difficulties in securing local matching funds for its PROMIS implementation grant. Substantial delay was encountered when funding requests had to be filtered through New York City's formidable bureaucracy. Eventual success was facilitated by a favorable benefit-cost analysis of anticipated system operations that was prepared with INSLAW assistance.

Fear of a New York-style financial crisis led to fiscal conservatism in Los Angeles County and several times threatened renewal of local funding. The problem was exacerbated when local recipients were no longer allowed to count employee time ("soft match") as contributions to matching funds. As in New York, the submission of optimistic benefit-cost analyses helped secure local funding.

To date, all the PROMIS jurisdictions whose implementation grants expired have been successful in securing operating funds from their local legislative bodies. Several have used benefit-cost analyses prepared with INSLAW's assistance to justify continued operations. Other jurisdictions indicated that they also were planning to use benefit-cost analyses as part of requests for local funding of operations. It is likely that many of the offices would not have been capable of producing convincing benefit-cost analyses without INSLAW assistance.

Intraorganizational Cooperation

In general, those who are responsible for collecting PROMIS data are not the primary beneficiaries of the management information produced. In particular, line prosecutors who directly handle case screening and court appearances may view data collection tasks as a hindrance to the execution of their primary job responsibilities. Other line prosecutors may view data collection tasks as an affront to their professional training: "Lawyers aren't clerks!" Some may even see the use of the data they collect by office management as a threat to the exercise of their professional judgment in case handling. It is no wonder that the implementation experiences of the PROMIS and DALITE prototypes involved problems related to compelling line prosecutors to complete data input forms conscientiously.

Of the ten jurisdictions that have begun data collection and rely on line prosecutors for completing data collection forms, only three reported not encountering problems in getting the line prosecutors to complete the requested data collection tasks conscientiously. Of the three jurisdictions reporting no major problems, two were not yet collecting case update data and the third had just begun data collection the week of the interviews. The problems cited ranged from complaints by line prosecutors to department heads, to the need for "constant vigilance and keeping the secretaries on their [the prosecutors'] backs." Resistance from line prosecutors makes it difficult to achieve and maintain a complete and accurate data base.

Two jurisdictions opted to bypass line prosecutors almost completely for data collection, and at least one other office is currently planning to do the same. The Marion County Prosecutor's Office uses paralegal personnel to collect initial case data through interviews with police officers. Clerical personnel collect case update data from copies of the court docket. Although relieving line prosecutors of data collection responsibilities has placed a strain on the office's clerical staff, the chief deputy prosecutor indicated that reliance on line prosecutors would probably have resulted in an unacceptable level of incompleteness in the data base. A similar opinion was expressed by the first assistant district attorney in Milwaukee: "I wouldn't recommend doing it [adopting PROMIS] if the courts weren't providing case update data. We couldn't get the staff to do an adequate job of data input. It's too easy for the assistants to subtly undermine the integrity of the data."[3]

ACHIEVING AND MAINTAINING DATA QUALITY

The preceding discussion has indicated how design, external cooperation, and internal cooperation problems can undermine the achievement or maintenance of complete and accurate data. Because each jurisdiction that has begun data collection has faced one or more of these types of problems, it is not surprising that they all report difficulties in achieving data quality. Data quality problems appear most serious for the larger jurisdictions, especially in terms of maintaining the completeness of the data base. For example, the Los Angeles project team reports that extensive data error enters the system each time efforts are concentrated on beginning data collection in another of the eight branch offices. Errors arise not only from the added branch, but also from the others already collecting data that must be neglected during the expansion. Poor data quality has blocked the realization of anticipated benefits in Los Angeles and other jurisdictions.

Several project directors hoped that the introduction of on-line access to PROMIS data would lead to better data quality by providing line prosecutors, who collect data, with direct benefits. Another project director, who had hoped to accomplish the same by introducing calendars for line prosecutors, appears to be caught in the vicious circle of data quality and use. Incomplete data have made the introduction of the calendars impractical. Without the introduction and use of calendars, however, it may not be possible to correct errors of omission. This contrasts with the New Orleans experience, where the vicious circle was broken by forcing deputies to rely on PROMIS-generated calendars by forbidding them to maintain their own manual calendars.

ACCEPTANCE AND USE

Poor data quality and lack of in-house resources for generating nonroutine reports were previously identified as major impediments to the production of information outputs by the PROMIS and DALITE prototypes. Because the maintenance of data quality appears to be a problem among the PROMIS jurisdictions, it should not be surprising that some of the anticipated information benefits have not yet been achieved by any of the jurisdictions. On the other hand, by introducing the Management Report Package and the Generalized Inquiry Package as PROMIS enhancements, it appears that INSLAW has successfully reduced the programming costs of conducting nonroutine analysis, thus increasing the feasibility of in-house special studies.

In attempting to determine whether or not it is likely that most jurisdictions will be successful in realizing a particular information benefit from PROMIS, it should be recognized that the conversion of PROMIS data to information that will support decision making is the final stage of the implementation process. Consequently, it may not be possible to distinguish at any particular time the jurisdictions that have not yet realized a type of information benefit from those that never will. Nevertheless, if no jurisdiction has been successful in achieving a particular information benefit, other jurisdictions would be wise to reevaluate their expectations of ever achieving it. When only a small number of jurisdictions are successful in achieving a particular information benefit, an explanation for their success may also be helpful to other jurisdictions in determining the chances that they too will be able to realize the information benefit.

First, let us consider the use of PROMIS for generating operational and logistical support information outputs. Jurisdictions that have adopted the on-line access capability have been successful in realizing some operational information benefits in the form of answered requests for case specific data. In Milwaukee, the District

Attorney's Office and the courts are currently averaging 40,000 such inquiries per month. (Most of these inquiries are from the court that uses the system for case docketing.) Utilization by prosecutors of on-line capability in several of the jurisdictions appears to be low because line prosecutors were unenthusiastic about participating in training sessions on the use of on-line terminals.

Poor data quality (particularly incompleteness) and unreliability in the timely arrival of batch reports produced by data processing centers have generally prevented prosecutors' offices from relying on PROMIS-generated calendars. The major exception is New Orleans, where the district attorney ordered his assistants to stop keeping manual calendars, and the computer facilities are completely in-house, ensuring the timely completion of calendars.

Poor data quality has also been a major factor in the failure of jurisdictions to achieve fully automated subpoena generation. To date, not one jurisdiction has been successful in achieving this capability. Yet the anticipated benefits from automatic subpoena generation figure heavily in a number of the jurisdictions' benefit-cost analyses.

Next, let us consider the generation of management control information. It includes two of the PROMIS management objectives advanced in the PROMIS Briefing Series: the identification of serious cases and the monitoring and enforcing of evenhandedness in the exercise of prosecutorial discretion.[4]

Not a single jurisdiction is currently using PROMIS's capability for identifying serious cases. Only two of the prosecutors' offices were considering using the revised case evaluation capability currently being developed by INSLAW. Lack of use of the case evalution capability is interesting for two reasons. First, the major justification for naming PROMIS an exemplary project was the capability it offered for singling out serious cases for special attention. Second, those who administer Career Criminal Program grants have allowed funds to be used for PROMIS implementation in several jurisdictions on the grounds that the case evaluation capability would assist in the identification of repeat offenders. The following chapter will attempt to explain why the case evaluation capability has not actually been used by PROMIS jurisdictions.

Some instances of the use of PROMIS in the monitoring and enforcing of evenhandedness in the exercise of prosecutorial discretion can be identified. The New Orleans District Attorney's Office uses PROMIS reports to support its clearance system (described in chapter 2). The other jurisdiction that could cite examples of administrative action resulting from the use of PROMIS reports is the Marion County Prosecutor's Office. For example, one report indicated that an assistant had not taken a case to trial in three months. Further investigations revealed that the assistant had been avoiding trials by offering plea bargains contrary to office policy, leading the prosecutor to fire the assistant.

What factors explain the realization of management control benefits from PROMIS by the Marion County Prosecutor's Office? Unlike the experience of the Los Angeles District Attorney's Office, where the same office characteristics (large size and spatial decentralization) that made PROMIS desirable also made it difficult to implement, the circumstances of the Marion County Prosecutor's Office were favorable for both use and implementation. First, the office's large size and small management staff made the potential of increased management control information appear very desirable. A criminal prosecution staff of seventy assistants is managed by only four supervisory personnel (including the prosecutor and his chief deputy). Although a clearance system has been established that requires assistants to secure prior approval of felony dispositions from one of the four supervisors, before the introduction of PROMIS there was no way of determining whether the clearance procedure was being followed in all cases. Second, design problems were minimized because very few changes were made in PROMIS prototype software, and intraorganizational cooperation problems were avoided by relying on paralegal and clerical personnel instead of prosecutors for data collection. Because few changes were made in the prototype design, it was possible for the office to begin rapid implementation of the Management Report Package enhancement when it became available. Finally, both the use and implementation of PROMIS were facilitated by the prosecutor's willingness to play a strong management role (as evidenced by his firing of the assistant who was not following office policies).

Finally, the introduction of the Management Report Package has helped several jurisdictions to begin using PROMIS as a resource for assisting in problem analysis and strategic planning. Most of the applications appear to be in response to external stimuli rather than as part of a reassessment of office policies. INSLAW has attempted to encourage use by having a number of jurisdictions present the results of suggested analyses at PROMIS Users Group meetings. Other applications might be termed "firefighting": using reports based on PROMIS data to counter criticisms of office policies or practices. It appears that the Wayne County Office of the Prosecuting Attorney may be currently making the greatest use of PROMIS for the examination of office policies. Active use of PROMIS in this capacity has been encouraged by the project manager, who has had experience as a social science researcher.

SUMMARY OF THE PROMIS IMPLEMENTATION EXPERIENCES

As of the spring of 1977 it is still too early to tell whether the majority of those jurisdictions that have adopted PROMIS will be able to realize fully the case management information system benefits initially anticipated. It does appear that implementation assistance provided through the PROMIS Transfer Project has helped to mitigate some of the problems encountered during the development of the PROMIS and DALITE prototypes. With the exception of benefits from the utilization of PROMIS's case evaluation capability, examples of the realization of each of the other types of advertised PROMIS benefits can be found. In general, however, poor data quality has hindered the use of PROMIS for producing operational and logistical support information. Two jurisdictions have demonstrated that PROMIS can be used to produce management control information in support of case disposition clearance systems. Several other jurisdictions have demonstrated that PROMIS can be used to provide information in support of problem analysis and strategic planning—though it appears that these uses may be primarily in response to external stimuli rather than from requests by office management for information to help improve office policy.

THE CMIS CATCH-22

The Los Angeles District Attorney's Office began designing a CMIS as a result of a 1972 Rand Corporation study that recommended the adoption of a PROMIS-like system to enable the district attorney to better control idiosyncratic prosecution.[5] The three district attorneys who have held office during the implementation of PROMIS have been enthusiastic and supportive because of the potential the system offers for increasing their control over the staff of six hundred assistants spread over twenty-five separate area and branch offices. Yet the same factors of large size and spatial decentralization have contributed to a long and uncompleted implementation process that has yielded only minimal information benefits.[6]

Minimal information benefits have resulted in other jurisdictions for different reasons. In Cobb County, small size made it relatively easy to overcome implementation problems, but also meant that the district attorney placed a low value on the information PROMIS could provide. In New Orleans, cited by the vice president of INSLAW at the time that this study was being planned as the most successful PROMIS jurisdiction, the management benefits that have resulted have been marginal compared with the benefits of other management changes the district attorney was able to accomplish. These implementation experiences suggest a catch-22. The same factors that make a CMIS desirable also make it difficult to implement, or, conversely, the same factors that facilitate CMIS implementation reduce the magnitude of the resulting benefits.

The New Orleans experience illustrates the converse of the CMIS catch-22. The implementation of PROMIS could not have been completed without strong leadership from the district attorney. He exhibited an ability and willingness to secure external resources and administer internal rewards and punishments. For example, once the computer had been leased for PROMIS, the district attorney had to lobby the City Council to maintain control of the system. When the PROMIS staff was falling behind schedule, the district attorney withheld pay increases. Trial section deputies who maintained their own calendars rather than use the PROMIS calendars were threatened with firing.

But the ability and willingness to secure external resources and administer internal rewards and punishments also allowed the district attorney to reorganize the office (as described in chapter 2). The district attorney was able to more than double his staff (and require all assistants to work full time), allowing more trials to be held in support of a tighter plea-bargaining policy. The Screening Division, without which the clearance system would not be practical, is viewed as a choice assignment by deputies in part because of the salary increases deputies receive when they join it. The clearance system itself requires strong management control to ensure that it is actually used in all cases. These organizational changes have resulted in less potential for management control benefits from PROMIS than there would have been under the old office organization, in which discretion was much more decentralized. PROMIS is as much a symptom as it is a tool of management control.

There are several circumstances that, if different, might have made implementation both more difficult and more desirable. For example, prior to the implementation of PROMIS, the number of active cases on the court docket was reduced to a third of its former level. A greater number of cases on the docket would have made PROMIS calendars much more useful. A tripling of the already high costs of the data collection start-up costs actually encountered probably would have seriously hampered PROMIS implementation.

The existence of multiple courts and police agencies probably would have made case tracking information much more valuable. PROMIS implementation probably would have been more difficult, however, if it had involved the tracking of cases through spatially separated courts rather than through one central court or the monitoring of case filings from a number of police departments rather than from only the New Orleans Police Department.

As a final example, consider the manual statistical system developed prior to PROMIS implementation. As the first assistant used the manual statistical reports in the weekly staff meetings, he was easily able to modify them to improve their usefulness. When PROMIS reports were being designed, the manual statistical system was available as a well-developed prototype. The resulting PROMIS reports were only marginal improvements over the manual statistical reports. If the statistical system had not existed, PROMIS implementation might have involved the use of a less rigorously tested design that would have required reprogramming to improve. On the other hand, if a manual statistical system had not previously existed, there probably would have been major information benefits from the introduction of PROMIS reports.

THE PROMIS TRANSFER PROJECT AND PROGRAMS OF INDUCED DIFFUSION

Drawing on the experiences of the jurisdictions that have adopted PROMIS, we can formulate suggestions that relate to prosecutors, LEAA, and the study of programs of induced diffusion.

PROSECUTORS AND PROMIS ADOPTION

First, prior to making a commitment to automation, prosecutors would be wise to adopt the nonautomated version of PROMIS. Once the nonautomated version of PROMIS has been adopted, the benefit-cost methodology can be computed comparing the improved manual information system with the fully automated PROMIS, and the office will be in a strong position to begin automation. As the PROMIS project director in one jurisdiction recommended: "Don't get fooled by the bells and whistles. Don't get fooled by the hardware. Concentrate on paper flow and be sure the manual system is working first."[7] If it is decided that the fully automated PROMIS will not be implemented, the office still gains from improved manual procedures. As suggested by Charles Work, the process of thinking through the system may provide a large part of the benefits of the final system.[8]

In addition to offering benefits without precluding (or requiring) the eventual adoption of the fully automated PROMIS, implementation of the nonautomated PROMIS can be carried out by office personnel using a handbook prepared by INSLAW.[9] Elimination of the need for outside consultants reduces the amount of funds needed to begin implementation and allows the office to proceed at its own pace.

Second, in conducting benefit-cost analyses, prosecutors should be skeptical of including benefits that have not yet been achieved in any PROMIS jurisdiction. For example, many of the PROMIS jurisdictions have included savings from the automation of subpoena preparation as a major benefit. As of the spring of 1977, however, not a single jurisdiction had yet realized these savings. Another example is benefits anticipated to result from the automatic production of schedules. It appears, however, that the basic PROMIS prototype design employing batch updates and operated on a shared computer facility will be unlikely to produce schedules that replace their manual counterparts because of data quality problems. Perhaps it will be more reasonable to include such benefits for PROMIS systems employing on-line data updating (as with the JUSTIS mutation).

It should also be remembered that although costs begin accruing at close to their steady-state level as soon as data collection begins, the anticipated benefits may be phased in over a number of years. The prosecutor should discount the anticipated benefits likely to be realized only after a considerable period of time has elapsed.

Third, once it has been decided to adopt PROMIS, all the data elements should be reviewed to determine their relevance to office operations. Because data collection costs are a function of the amount of data collected per case and because limited data collection resources often hamper PROMIS implementation, it is desirable to eliminate data elements that will not be used regularly. Although it may be noble to attempt to collect data solely because it may be of interest in the future to some researcher, collecting data that is not regularly used makes implementation more difficult. In addition, because errors are not corrected through regular use, such data may not be of sufficient quality to support research even if it is collected.

Fourth, it is best to avoid reliance on prosecutors for data collection tasks whenever possible. Costs should be anticipated in training (and retraining) prosecutors in data collection tasks. Costs should also be anticipated in the form of management effort that must be expended to ensure that prosecutors are fulfilling their data collection responsibilities. In some situations (such as in the collection of case update data), it may be desirable to allow prosecutors to record data in written form that can later be coded by clerical personnel.

Fifth, shortages in clerical personnel should be anticipated during the initiation of data collection. To minimize start-up problems, it may be desirable to begin data collection in an office subunit. This may be particularly helpful if the case load of the subunit is sufficiently independent from the rest of office operations to permit the generation of reports for the subunit. If it is not possible to phase in the initiation of data collection, efforts should be made to secure extra clerical personnel during the start-up period.

LEAA AND PROMIS ADOPTION

Support for PROMIS implementations should no longer be provided to jurisdictions through LEAA discretionary grant funds. In particular, funds for PROMIS implementations should not be provided in connection with grants awarded under the Career Criminal Program. The rationale for the connection between PROMIS and the Career Criminal Program was based on PROMIS's capacity for identifying defendants having serious criminal histories. Because this capacity has not been used by any of the PROMIS jurisdictions, the two programs should not be linked.

The introduction of the Management Report Package has helped to encourage prosecutors to make greater use of their PROMIS data bases by lowering the programming costs of producing special reports. Further use might be encouraged by helping prosecutors to hire individuals with methodological training in the social sciences. For example, at relatively low cost, LEAA could fund the hiring of an in-house researcher for jurisdictions that have been collecting data for over a year. The in-house researcher, hired for one to two years, would have graduate training, or undergraduate training with a strong methodological background, in the social sciences. The in-house researcher would be required to spend the first months of employment directly observing the various phases of office operations. The grant would also require that the in-house researcher meet regularly with the district attorney or his chief assistant.

The major objective of the in-house researcher would be to produce analyses based on the PROMIS data that are of direct interest to office management. This objective contrasts with the goal of the PROMIS Research Project to produce research of general interest to criminal justice practitioners. A second objective of the in-house researcher would be to develop research skills among office personnel by example and through working directly with office managers.

A CONCLUDING COMMENT

The history of the PROMIS Transfer Project suggests that programs of induced diffusion can be highly effective in encouraging the adoption of complex technologies by local public agencies. The majority of the PROMIS jurisdictions would not have attempted to adopt case management information systems without PROMIS Transfer Project support. It also appears, however, that programs of induced diffusion run the risk of spreading technologies without proven benefits: the initial designation of PROMIS as an exemplary project was on questionable grounds, and jurisdictions continue to advance benefit-cost analyses involving benefits that have either not yet been achieved by any PROMIS user or been achieved only under very special circumstances. Chapter 9 will explore the advantages and dangers of programs of induced diffusion by illustrating the analytical framework developed in chapter 1 with the history of the PROMIS Transfer Project.

NOTES

1. Four of the jurisdictions were actually visited by the author. In each of the others the district attorney was sent a letter describing the author's research interest in the implementation of PROMIS systems. The letter included a request for the names and telephone numbers of office personnel directly involved in PROMIS implementation or management use. Eleven of the sixteen jurisdictions responded and subsequently participated in telephone interviews. INSLAW provided previously collected questionnaires as well as other background information concerning the five jurisdictions that did not participate in the telephone interviews. Only one of the five jurisdictions not directly contacted had actually begun data collection.

Two biases in this approach are worthy of note. First, because contact was limited to jurisdictions that had secured LEAA grants to support PROMIS implementation, the problems encountered in securing LEAA funding may be underestimated. To correct for this bias it would be necessary to include jurisdictions that wanted PROMIS but were unable to secure LEAA funding. Second, it is likely that personnel in the jurisdictions will be biased toward presenting their implementation efforts in the best possible light. To guard against this bias, the more successful a jurisdiction appeared, the greater the number of personnel interviewed. One or two individuals were interviewed in the jurisdictions that had not yet begun to collect data; four or five were interviewed in jurisdictions that reported actually making use of PROMIS outputs.

2. Trip Report, Alvin Ash, PROMIS Users Group Meeting, New Orleans, Louisiana, April 22-23, 1976, p. 2.

3. Telephone interview with first assistant district attorney, April 28, 1977.

4. INSLAW, "Management Overview of PROMIS," PROMIS Briefing Series no. 7, July 1975, pp. 3-5.

5. Peter W. Greenwood, Sorrell Wildhorn, Eugene C. Poggio, Michael J. Strumwasser, and Peter DeLeon, *Prosecution of Adult Felony Defendants in Los Angeles County: A Policy Perspective,* Rand R-1127-DOJ (Santa Monica, Calif., March 1973).

6. Referring to the approximately eighteen staff members who meet to discuss office management questions, the project director speculates that "a secret ballot today whether or not PROMIS is a boondoggle would be about 50/50. Three years ago, only the District Attorney would have voted to keep it."

7. As might be expected, this comment was made by the project director of one of the smaller jurisdictions. Nevertheless, the project director of one of the large jurisdictions specifically recommended that the nonautomated PROMIS be installed before the automated version.

8. Charles R. Work, "A Prosecutor's Guide to Automation," *The Prosecutor* 7, no. 6 (November-December 1970): 480.

9. Robert H. Cain and John R. Ours, "PROMIS and the Nonautomated or Semiautomated Office," Institute for Law and Social Research, April 1976.

chapter 7

The Centerpiece Alone: Case Ranking Systems

The PROMIS prototype included a case ranking system as one of its major components. Use of the case ranking system in support of the Special Litigation Unit operated by the U.S. Attorney's Office during the early 1970s is cited by LEAA as a major reason for the designation of PROMIS as an exemplary project. The potential use of the PROMIS case ranking capability to identify defendants with serious criminal histories continues to be advanced as one of the major management benefits that can be expected from PROMIS. As discussed in the preceding chapter, the case ranking capability is not being used by the PROMIS jurisdictions. In fact, none of the jurisdictions cited the case evaluation capability as a major consideration in its decision to adopt PROMIS. It appears that only the LEAA administrators of the Career Criminal Program (who helped facilitate the use of LEAA discretionary grant funds for several PROMIS implementations) acted on the assumption that the PROMIS case ranking capability could and would be realized in practice.

The case ranking system, however, gained a life of its own as an innovation independent of the PROMIS case management information system. A manual version of the prototype case ranking system was transferred to the Wayne County (Michigan) Office of the Prosecuting Attorney shortly after it had become operational in the U.S. Attorney's Office. In the second half of 1973, the prototype's design methodology was employed to customize a case ranking system for use by the Bronx District Attorney's Office. Although the Wayne County case ranking system never reached a satisfactory level of operation, the Bronx case ranking system continues to be used to help select cases for the office's Major Offense Bureau (MOB), which applies enhanced prosecutorial effort to a restricted case load.

The first two sections of this chapter will review the implementation and use of case ranking systems by the Wayne County Office of the Prosecuting Attorney and the Bronx District Attorney's Office. Drawing on these experiences, as well as that of the U.S. Attorney's Office with the case ranking system prototype, the third section of the chapter will discuss the basic issues underlying the design, implementation, and use of case ranking systems. An attempt will be made to answer the question: Would it be desirable to facilitate the spread of case ranking systems through a program of induced diffusion?

OPERATION PREPARE

The Wayne County (Michigan) Office of the Prosecuting Attorney is responsible for the prosecution of defendants in the Detroit Recorder's Court, which has jurisdiction over violations of the laws of the state of Michigan occurring within the boundaries of the city of Detroit. By 1970, there was a division of labor in the Office of the Prosecuting Attorney for the handling of felonies. The Warrant Section employed a number of deputies whose task it was to screen requests made by the police for the issue of arrest warrants. The Pre-Trial Division of three deputies held pretrial conferences with defense attorneys to facilitate plea bargaining. Four or five deputies made up a homicide team and were assigned murder cases (and on rare occasions other cases of a notorious nature) on an individualized basis at the beginning of each month. A single deputy handled all plea negotiations on the day of trial. The deputies whose job it was actually to try cases were assigned to specific trial courts: each deputy (or team of deputies) presented the state's case in all the nonhomicide trials held in the court they covered.

The Warrant Section was instituted to increase the uniformity in case charging and to screen out weak cases before they entered the court system. The Pre-Trial Division (and the limiting of trial day plea bargaining to a single deputy) was designed to increase the uniformity in plea bargaining by limiting the number of deputies bargaining and thus preventing defense attorneys from "shopping for the best bargain" among a large number of deputies. The assignment of trial deputies to courts was primarily a response to the trial docketing system used by the Recorder's Court.

In 1970, the Recorder's Court employed a central docketing system for felonies: each court day the presiding judge would work through a list of roughly one hundred cases, assigning as many as possible of those in which both the state and the defense were ready for trial to openings in the eight or nine courts used for trials. The list of cases used by the presiding judge included all cases that were ever assigned for trial that day. It was not updated with respect to cases that reached disposition through guilty pleas or dismissals. The list also often included cases that had been continued to a new trial date at a prior court appearance. The police officer handling the case would answer when the presiding judge asked if the state was ready for trial. If the defense was also ready for trial, the case would be assigned to a trial court if any was available. If no trial courts were available, or the defense had a legitimate reason for delay, the case would be continued to a new date. A common reason for defense requests for delay was "to see Deputy Prosecutor Flanagan," who handled the trial day plea negotiations. Under the central docketing system, only a few of the one hundred cases scheduled for trial would actually go to trial on a given court day.

When a trial deputy received a case, he would have only about fifteen minutes to prepare it; the preparation was usually limited to reviewing the police file and talking with the police officer handling the case. The uncertainty in the central docketing system with respect to which of the one hundred cases would actually go to trial hindered more extensive pretrial preparation: Why prepare all or most of the one hundred cases when only a few would actually go to trial? In addition, the Office of the Prosecuting Attorney did not maintain its own case records for the majority of defendants, but instead relied on the police case file maintained by the police officer assigned to the case. Lack of case files prevented the weeding out of cases scheduled for trial that had already reached dispositions or had been continued.

The homicide team was one response to the lack of trial preparation. Each homicide was singled out and given extensive pretrial preparation by the deputy assigned to handle its trial. The Office of the Prosecuting Attorney did not have sufficient manpower to provide similar preparation for a large number of cases. It was felt that resources were available to provide extensive pretrial preparation for some additional cases. Because the prosecuting attorney was concerned about the deficiency of preparation for trial cases, it would have been desirable to develop a method for identifying those cases most likely to go to trial so they could be given extra preparation. Failing to identify cases most likely to go to trial, an alternate strategy was to identify the most serious cases (in terms of the crime and the defendant's prior conviction record) so that the office would be adequately prepared in the event these more serious cases actually went to trial.

In the autumn of 1970, James Garber, then chief of the Criminal Division of the Wayne County Office of the Prosecuting Attorney, met Joan Jacoby and Charles Work at a National District Attorneys Association convention. Jacoby and Work explained their efforts then under way to design the PROMIS Case Evaluation System (described in chapter 3). It was suggested that a manual version of the PROMIS Case Evaluation System might be used by the Wayne County Office of the Prosecuting Attorney to identify cases for special pretrial preparation. Garber became interested in the manual PROMIS Case Evaluation System and convinced the prosecuting attorney, William Cahalan, to institute Operation PREPARE (Prosecutors' Evaluation, Preparation, and Response).

Operation PREPARE involved the installation of a manual version of the PROMIS Case Evaluation System that was prepared by the National Center for Prosecution Management (headed by Jacoby when she left the District of Columbia Office of Crime Analysis at the beginning of 1972).[1] The case evaluation system was intended to be used as a means of identifying cases most deserving of preparation prior to trial date so that they could be assigned to more experienced deputies before the days of trial. Those involved in Operation PREPARE envisioned other future uses of the case ranks generated by the evaluation system: as an index of case seriousness, the case ranks might serve as a device for the specification, monitoring, and control of office plea bargaining and bail hearing actions.

The case evaluation system required the collection of defendant and offense data by the Warrant Section at the time cases were screened. A filing sheet was introduced to collect the deputy's estimate of the probability of gaining a conviction in the case, data required for an evaluation of the seriousness of the offense as measured by a modified version of Thorsten Sellin's and Marvin Wolfgang's Seriousness Scale, and data required for an evaluation of the seriousness of the defendant's conviction and arrest record as measured by a modified version of Gottfredson's Base Expectation Score (as described in chapter 3). Comments noting any special circumstances of the case were also collected (and is the only one of the foregoing features of the filing sheet surviving to this day). A reestimation of the probability of gaining a conviction and additional comments on special circumstances were made after the cases had preliminary hearings.

The filing sheets were sent to a clerk who computed the case ranks using a calculator programmed with weights for combining the probability of conviction, the seriousness of the offense, and the seriousness of the defendant's arrest and conviction record. The weights were taken directly from the automated PROMIS Case Evaluation System, with the exception of the elimination of the case age from the formula because the case ranks would be computed only once for each case. These weights not only reflected the policies of a different prosecutor's office (the U.S. Attorney's Office) but also the interpretation of the policies by a particular deputy (the chief of the U.S. Attorney's Office Misdemeanor Section) at a particular point in time.

During the planning of Operation PREPARE, the reaction of the staff was, in general, interest with some enthusiasm for the prospects of the evaluation system. As soon as a set of ranks became available for comparison, however, the general reaction turned to skepticism. The case evaluation system tended to give high ranks to many cases in little need of extensive pretrial preparation.

One source of inappropriate ranks was the way the conviction probability entered the ranking equation. The ranking equation gave positive weights to all the terms involving the conviction probability.

That is, the greater the conviction probability, the higher the ranking. There were two reasons why cases with high conviction probabilities tended not to be the type of cases the office wished to identify for special trial preparation. First, there is less room for increasing the conviction probability of an already strong case than there is for increasing the conviction probability of a weaker case. Contacting a second or third witness may have a greater impact than contacting a fourth or fifth witness. Second, at the time it appeared that, other things being equal, the weaker the case, the more likely the defense would demand a trial. Effort allocated to stronger cases was thus less likely to result in a payoff at trial.

It was soon realized that for the purposes of Operation PREPARE the cumulative weight given to the conviction probability should have been negative rather than positive. Such a change would have required a complete reestimation of the case evaluation equation, a task beyond the scope of office resources and expertise. The deputies attempting to implement Operation PREPARE attempted to improve the ranks by "tinkering" with the case evaluation equation and the defendant and offense seriousness measures. (For example, when manslaughter cases appeared to receive too high a rank, the number of points assigned to a case involving the death of a victim was reduced in the measure of the seriousness of the offense.) After about a year of experimentation, Operation PREPARE was abandoned.

Why did Operation PREPARE fail? Probably the major reason was that the case evaluation system was designed to meet a different set of needs than those of the Wayne County Office of the Prosecuting Attorney. The system was designed to identify the most serious misdemeanor cases, whereas the Wayne County Office desired a system that would identify felonies most deserving of special pretrial preparation. Lacking a specific theory as to which cases will go to trial or which cases should receive the added pretrial preparation, it was not unreasonable to attempt to use the manual version of the PROMIS Case Evaluation System. When the system proved inadequate, however, its complexity prevented its successful modification to better fit the needs of the Wayne County Office of the Prosecuting Attorney.

POSTSCRIPT FOR OPERATION PREPARE

In April 1974 a new deputy chief of the Trial Division was appointed. He noticed a secretary operating a calculating machine. When he inquired the purpose of her activity, she responded that she computed case ranks, which she then attached to the filing sheet used by the deputies. When the new Trial Division chief questioned the trial deputies about how they used the ranks, they all responded that they did not know what the ranks meant. The Trial Division chief, deciding he could better employ his secretarial help, eliminated the computation of ranks, which had lingered more than a year past the termination of Operation PREPARE.

At least one other lingering aspect of Operation PREPARE has proved useful and beneficial to case handling. Even though the data needed for the calculation of the case ranks are no longer collected, the use of the filing sheet to record written comments concerning special characteristics of the case has continued. These comments are useful to the deputy preparing the case for preliminary hearings and, along with the comments added after the preliminary hearings, aid in the preparation of the case for trial.

THE BRONX COUNTY MAJOR OFFENSE BUREAU (MOB)

During the past decade, the case load of the Bronx County District Attorney's Office grew at a faster pace than its case handling resources. By 1973, despite the fact that over 90 percent of case dispositions had resulted from guilty pleas or dismissals, delays of two or more years between arrests and trials were typical.[2] With the exception of homicide and narcotics cases, which were handled by special units within the office, cases reached disposition through decisions made by a staff of over 150 assistant prosecutors who received only minimal managerial supervision. The recurrence of rearrests of defendants awaiting trial and of defendants who had previously avoided long prison terms through plea bargaining suggested to some of the office personnel that persistent delay and administrative laxness (resulting from heavy case loads) over case dispositions were allowing repeat offenders to avoid their just punishments by taking advantage of the weaknesses in the case handling system.[3]

In January 1973 Mario Merola took office as the Bronx County district attorney. The prospect of only limited increases in office resources led him to adopt a policy of selective prosecution. Instead of continuing to allocate prosecutorial resources uniformly across the office case load (exclusive of the homicide and narcotics cases, which were already being handled by special units), special attention would be given to cases involving the most serious offenses and defendants with the most serious criminal histories. One objective of the selective prosecution policy was to provide swifter, surer, and more severe punishment for repeat offenders who were believed to be responsible for an amount of crime disproportionately large for their number. A second objective was to increase the correspondence between the seriousness of the committed offense and the resulting level of punishment by ensuring that the most serious offense received greater prosecutorial effort and administrative review.

In April 1973 the Bronx County District Attorney's Office received an LEAA grant of $461,551 (with an additional $312,556 in state and local matching funds) to fund the development of a selective prosecution unit. Assistant District Attorney Paul Gentile was assigned to direct the development of the special prosecution unit, which has been named the Major Offense Bureau (MOB). Gentile was appointed chief of MOB when it began operations in July 1973. A deputy bureau chief, nine assistant district attorneys, an administrative clerk, and a legal secretary are full-time members of MOB. Seven law students are also employed on a part-time basis to assist in case screening and trial preparation.

All requests for prosecution are scored in terms of the case evaluation form presented in exhibit 1. The form is completed by a clerk who notifies an assistant district attorney assigned to MOB if any of three criteria is satisfied: (1) a total of twenty or more points are scored under Part A ("Nature of Case") and the offense is a Class A felony (punishable by life imprisonment) or a Class B felony (punishable by up to twenty-five years imprisonment); (2) a total of fifteen or more points are scored under Part B ("Nature of Defendant"); or (3) the case involves forcible sexual offenses between unrelated parties, arson where there is substantial damage, child abuse involving children under the age of eight, or multiple robberies or burglaries. Besides referral by the clerks who rank the cases, a procedure has been established for direct referral of cases to MOB by the New York City Police Department, the Housing Authority Police, and the Transit Authority Police. When an arrest is made involving one of the specified types of offenses (such as robbery in which the defendant was armed with a firearm), the arresting agency will telephone the MOB assistant on duty. If the assistant on duty cannot be reached by telephone immediately, he will be contacted through the use of an electronic beeper similar to those used by doctors on call.

If the assistant district attorney on duty evaluates the case as acceptable for MOB, work begins immediately to prepare the case for grand jury presentation. Many of the accepted cases are presented to the grand jury within twenty-four hours of arrest, and most are presented within seventy-two hours.[4] Grand jury presentations for cases not handled by MOB are generally made as long as a month after the arrest.

The case evaluation forms of all cases referred to MOB are reviewed by the bureau chief within twenty-four hours of their receipt. After all the major facts of the case have been determined and the defendant's complete criminal history has been reviewed, a final decision is made concerning whether or not the case will be handled by MOB. If a positive decision is made, the assistant who made the grand jury presentation of the case will stay with the case until its disposition. If the case is not accepted for MOB handling, it is referred to one of the other bureaus within the office, including the Supreme Court Bureau, which handles all the cases not referred to the homicide, arson, narcotics, or rackets bureaus.

Through an agreement reached with the Appellate Division of the State Supreme Court, two trial courts were designated for exclusive use by MOB. Access to these courts permits MOB trial dates much closer to the time of arrest than otherwise possible. In order to take full advantage of this resource, a policy of full disclosure

Exhibit 1. Bronx Case Evaluation Form

DOCKET NO.____________________ INDICTMENT NO.________________

PEOPLE v.______________ CHARGE______________ DATE____________

Please record those points which apply to your case. Where there are multiple defendants, compute a base on the defendant with the most serious offense(s).

A. NATURE OF CASE	check if applicable	pts.
VICTIM		
one or more persons	☐	2.0
VICTIM INJURY		
received minor injury	☐	2.4
treated and released	☐	3.0
hospitalized	☐	4.2
INTIMIDATION		
one or more persons	☐	1.3
WEAPON		
defendant armed	☐	7.4
defendant fired shot or carried gun, or carried explosives	☐	15.7
STOLEN PROPERTY		
any value	☐	7.5
PRIOR RELATIONSHIP		
victim and defendant - same family	☐	−2.8
ARREST		
at scene	☐	4.6
within 24 hours	☐	2.9
EVIDENCE		
admission or statement	☐	1.4
additional witnesses	☐	3.1

C. REFER TO M.O.B. IF ANY OF THE FOLLOWING CONDITIONS APPLY:
(check those applicable-offense is most serious charge)

☐ FORCIBLE SEXUAL OFFENSES BETWEEN UNRELATED PARTIES

☐ ARSON WITH SUBSTANTIAL DAMAGE OR HIGH POTENTIAL FOR INJURY

☐ CHILD ABUSE, CHILD SEVEN OR UNDER

☐ MULTIPLE ROBBERIES OR BURGLARIES

D. SUMMARY INFORMATION

NO. OF VICTIMS ________

☐ received minor injury
☐ treated and hospitalized
☐ hospitalized and/or permanent injury
☐ law officer
☐ attempted murder of officer

WEAPON

☐ gun
☐ knife
☐ bomb or explosive
☐ other________

BURGLARY

☐ night-time
☐ evidence of forcible entry
☐ Church, School, Public Bldg.
☐ no. of premises burglarized

IDENTIFICATION

line-up	☐	3.3

TOTAL CASE SCORE ______

B. NATURE OF DEFENDANT

FELONY CONVICTIONS

one	☐	9.7
more than one	☐	18.7

MISDEMEANOR CONVICTIONS

one	☐	3.6
more than one	☐	8.3

PRIOR ARRESTS - SAME CHARGE

one	☐	4.5
more than	☐	7.2

PRIOR ARRESTS

one	☐	2.2
more than one	☐	4.2

PRIOR ARREST-WEAPONS TOP CHARGE

more than one	☐	6.4

STATUS WHEN ARRESTED

state parole	☐	7.1
wanted	☐	4.2

TOTAL DEFENDANT SCORE ______

VALUE OF STOLEN PROPERTY

		recovered	not
☐	under $250	☐	☐
☐	$250 to $1499	☐	☐
☐	$1500 to $25,000	☐	☐
☐	over $25,000	☐	☐

PRIOR RELATIONSHIP

☐ other family
☐ neighbor
☐ friend
☐ acquaintance
☐ other

IDENTIFICATION

☐ photograph
☐ on or nearby scene
☐ other
☐ no. of persons making I.D. ______
☐ time delay of I.D. ______

SUPPORTING EVIDENCE

☐ crime observed by police officer
☐ fingerprints recovered

E. DISTRICT ATTORNEY'S EVALUATION ______

TOTAL SCORE ______

RANKING CLERK ______

A.D.A. NOTICED yes☐ no☐

ACTION BY A.D.A.:

☐ accepted ☐ furthered
☐ rejected ☐ referred to M.O.B.

reasons: ______

______

______

______

66

BCDA FORM -53 9/74

was established to avoid delay that might be caused by the filing of discovery motions by the defense. When the MOB assistant and the defense counsel meet to discuss the potential plea bargains, the defense is advised of all the evidence available to the prosecution.

The MOB chief and the assistant district attorney handling the case decide on the most lenient plea bargain that will be offered to the defense. The MOB policy is that a defendant must plea to the top count of the indictment or one count below. It is also a MOB policy to make a plea bargain offer as soon as possible and not to restart plea negotiations once trial proceedings have begun.

In November 1976 LEAA designated MOB as an exemplary project to serve as a model for prosecutors' offices wishing to establish Career Criminal Bureaus for concentrating prosecutorial resources on repeat offenders. The designation was based on the following results from the first three years of MOB operation:

> The MOB has a median time of 97 days from arrest to case disposition compared to a median time of 400 days for other bureaus within the D.A.'s office;
>
> The MOB has an overall conviction rate of 96 percent. Though not strictly comparable to MOB cases, a comparison group selected from the case load of the D.A.'s Supreme Court Bureau has a rate of 84 percent. Similarly, the MOB has a conviction rate at trial at 92 percent, while the comparison group has a 52 percent rate of conviction at trial;
>
> 94 percent of MOB convictions result in sentences of incarceration as contrasted with 79 percent of the comparison group cases. In 1975, the MOB defendant's average maximum sentence was 10 years while the defendant from the comparison group had an average maximum of 3-5 years.
>
> . . . In short, the MOB approach clearly represents a practical means of identifying career criminal cases for special prosecutorial attention, telescoping the time from arrest to disposition for these cases, and sustaining a high conviction rate.[5]

These findings are not surprising: the greater the prosecutorial and managerial resources applied to a given set of cases, the more favorable the outcomes expected for the prosecution. Given this effectiveness, however, the selection of cases for inclusion in the set receiving the special handling becomes an important consideration in determining whether the special attention is leading to outcomes more consistent with the district attorney's policies than would otherwise be the case. Let us take a closer look at the implementation and use of the case evaluation system that is employed to assist in the selection of cases for MOB.

THE BRONX CASE EVALUATION SYSTEM

The grant that was received to support MOB design and implementation included funding for the services of a consultant to help develop an objective case evaluation system for selecting serious cases. The consulting contract was awarded to the National Center for Prosecution Management because of the role of its executive director, Joan Jacoby, in pioneering the development of the case evaluation system used in conjunction with PROMIS. The National Center for Prosecution Management began its work in June 1973 and completed its work in November 1974.

The delay between the beginning of MOB operations and the completion of implementation of a case evaluation system designed by the National Center for Prosecution Management was anticipated and led the office to design its own case evaluation system for interim use. Gentile began this task by visiting the U.S. Attorney's Office for the District of Columbia and the Wayne County Office of the Prosecuting Attorney to get a firsthand look at the use of the PROMIS case evaluation system prototype and its manual version. When he discovered that neither office actually used its case evaluation system in routine operations, Gentile began developing a case evaluation system in cooperation with an assistant district attorney from the New York County District Attorney's Office, which was involved in a similar project. After identifying factors related to the seriousness of the offense, the seriousness of the defendant's prior criminal record, and the strength of the case, weights were assigned to the factors according to Gentile's subjective valuation of their relationship to office policy. The form presented in exhibit 2 was developed for use by clerks who handled case screening. A total point score above the established cutoff point indicated to the ranking clerk that an assistant district attorney from MOB should

Exhibit 2. Intuitively Designed Case Ranking System

Please circle those points which apply to your case. Where there are multiple defendants compute on base of major defendant, (Most serious record).

1. <u>NATURE OF CASE</u>

A. Victims	
1. Number: (for each)	1 pt.
2. Intimidate (physical or verbal)	1 pt.
3. Hospitalized (not including treated and released or permanent injury	10 pts.
4. Police Officer	2 pts.
5. Attempted murder of Police Officer	10 pts.
A. Total	______
B. Weapon	
1. Gun	
*A. Loaded (any not recovered)	10 pts.
2. Knife	5 pts.
3. Other (Club, billy, etc.)	3 pts.
4. Bomb or explosive	10 pts.
B. Total	______
C. Burglary (Must be Dwelling)	
1. Night-time	10 pts.
2. Evidence of forcible entry	5 pts.
3. Church, School, public building	5 pts.
C. Total	______
D. Arson	
1. Dwelling or Public Building	10 pts.
2. Person Present	10 pts.
3. Extensive Property Damage	5 pts.
D. Total	______
E. Value of Stolen Property	
1. Under $250	1 pt.
2. Up to $1500	2 pts.
3. Over $1500	3 pts.
4. Over $25,000	10 pts.
E. Total	______

III. <u>STRENGTH OF CASE</u>

A. Weapon recovered	5 pts.
1. At scene	3 pts.
2. From defendant	5 pts.
A. Total	______
B. Property recovered	1 pt.
1. At scene	5 pts.
*2. From defendant's person	10 pts.
*3. Elsewhere, but connected to defendant.	5 pts.
B. Total	______
C. Prior Relationship between Defendant and Complainant *Not to be deducted if relationship is only relevant on issue of identity.	5 pts.
C. Total	______
D. Arrest	
1. At scene	10 pts.
2. Shortly after occurrence (within 24 hours)	3 pts.
3. Crime observed by Police Officer	5 pts.
D. Total	______
E. Supporting Evidence	
1. Admission or Statement	5 pts.
2. Additional witnesses	5 pts.
3. Fingerprints recovered	10 pts.
E. Total	______

F. Kidnapping 10 pts.
1. Time of Abduction (In excess of 12 hours) 5 pts.
2. Pansom Demanded 10 pts.
3. Sexually abused 5 pts.
4. Victim under 12 years 5 pts.

F. Total________

1. TOTAL

II. DEFENDANT EVALUATION

A. Prior Criminal Record
1. Felony conviction (for each) 10 pts.
2. Misdemeanor convictions (for each) 5 pts.
3. Prior Arrests
   a) Same as charged (for each) 5 pts.
   b) Violent crimes (for each) 5 pts.
   c) Weapon (top charge) 3 pts.

A. Total________

B. Evidence of Drug Addiction 1 pt.

B. Total________

C. Principal Participant (multiple defendant cases) 3 pts.

C. Total________

D. Defendant's Status When Arrested
1. Pending cases 4 pts.
2. Probation 2 pts.
3. State Parole 3 pts.
4. Wanted 1 pt.

D. Total________

II. TOTAL

III. TOTAL

IV. DISTRICT ATTORNEY'S EVALUATION OF CASES (Range= +15 to -15)

Consider the following: Credibility of Witness(es), Certainty of identification, Search and Seizure problems, Wade issues, Miranda, Motive, Prior relationship between parties and probability of success.

IV. TOTAL

FINAL SCORE________

RANKING CLERK

A.D.A. NOTIFIED

ACTION BY A.D.A.:
[ ] Accepted for M.O.B.
[ ] Rejected - Reasons:

review the case. The assistant district attorney could modify the score by a specified number of points to reflect factors not scored by the screening clerk. If the total point score was thirty-five or greater, the case would receive at least initial preparation by MOB.

This intuitively developed case evaluation system was used until the design of its replacement was completed by the National Center for Prosecution Management. Gentile reports that in his role as chief of MOB he was satisfied with the case selection characteristics of the initially used system. In fact, Gentile suggests that the contract with the National Center for Prosecution Management was executed because of stipulations in the original grant proposal rather than out of dissatisfaction with the intuitively developed case evaluation system.

The National Center for Prosecution Management began its design effort by preparing a sample of 254 cases drawn from the cases presented to the Indictment Bureau, which handles case screening.[6] Data for seventy-two observable variables were recorded for each case. In addition, the chief of MOB ranked each case in terms of the seriousness of the offense, the seriousness of the criminal record of the defendant, and whether or not cases should be referred to MOB. The general methodology employed involved relating the revealed preferences of the MOB chief to the directly observable case characteristics by means of multivariate statistical techniques.

The initially used case evaluation scores were found to have very little power for predicting the MOB chief's direct evaluation of urgency for MOB assignment. For example, the crime score (part A of exhibit 2) was found to explain only 5 percent of the variation in the MOB chief's direct evaluation of offense seriousness. The defendant and case strength components similarly had low predictive power.

The National Center for Prosecution Management attempted to develop a model with greater predictive power by using step-wise linear regression techniques to select a more effective set of independent variables from the seventy-two observable case characteristics. An attempt was also made to test alternate functional forms of the independent variable candidates. Eventually it was found that predictive power could be increased by using an indicator variable (which takes on the value of one if a condition, such as having more than one prior felony conviction, holds, and zero otherwise) in place of linear functional forms. This modification not only facilitated greater predictive power for the model, but also made the calculation of scores easier than before by eliminating the need for multiplication to obtain the component scores of the case weight.

The National Center for Prosecution Management was able to develop a model that predicted the MOB chief's decision to select or reject a case for MOB handling correctly in approximately 75 percent of the cases when all rape cases were automatically selected. Despite several methodological objections that might be raised,[7] it appears that the new system would be much more successful in correctly selecting cases for MOB handling than the intuitively developed system it was designed to replace. The district attorney agreed to adopt the new system with two modifications. First, in addition to forcible sexual offenses between unrelated parties, cases involving arson with substantial damage or high potential for injury, child abuse if the victim is under eight years of age, and multiple robberies or burglaries would be automatically referred to MOB for review no matter what point score resulted. Second, a variable representing the existence of "exculpatory evidence" was eliminated from the evaluation form because it was felt that the clerks who would be completing the evaluation could not be relied upon to make such a legal judgment accurately. The discussion that accompanied exhibit 1 described the procedural use of the new case evaluation system.

The case evaluation system designed by the National Center for Prosecution Management has been in use for over two years. It serves as the first stage of a two-stage selection process for MOB cases. The case evaluation system brings about 25 percent of the requests for felony prosecution to the attention of MOB personnel. Of the twenty to twenty-five cases singled out by the case evaluation system for review each day, one or two of the cases are actually selected for permanent assignment to MOB after review by the MOB chief. (MOB accepts about four hundred cases per year for permanent assignment.) The cases that are selected by the case evaluation system but are not accepted for permanent assignment to MOB often receive case preparation through indictment before being turned over to other bureaus within the office.

One way to analyze the effectiveness of the case evaluation system is in terms of the two types of error it can make. The error of omission involves not selecting a case that should receive MOB handling. The error of unnecessary inclusion involves selecting a case that should not be handled by MOB. Unfortunately, if an attempt is made to alter the selection criteria so as to reduce the occurrence of one type of error, the occurrence of the other type of error will increase. The selection criteria actually chosen will be efficient if it minimizes the sum of the costs expected to result from errors of omission and errors of unnecessary inclusion.

The cost of an error of unnecessary inclusion is a function of the time spent by MOB personnel in the preparation and review of cases not permanently assigned to MOB. The cost per unit of time spent on unnecessarily included cases would be measured as the difference in the value to the office of the time in other MOB activities less the value to the office of the time spent in preparation of cases not permanently assigned to MOB. This difference is probably small for two reasons. First, the initial case preparation displaces case preparation time that would otherwise be expended by the bureaus handling the case. Second, under the assumption that the unnecessarily included cases are in fact more serious than the cases rejected by the case evaluation system, the added advantage of timely preparation by MOB personnel is directed at an appropriate portion of the case load. Cases selected by the case evaluation system and passing the review of the MOB chief receive maximum prosecutorial effort under MOB handling. Cases selected by the case evaluation system and rejected by the MOB chief receive the normal level of prosecutorial effort enhanced by early case preparation by MOB personnel. Cases rejected by the case evaluation system receive only the normal level of prosecutorial effort involving assembly-line handling by teams of prosecutors.

The cost of an error of omission stems from the consequences of a serious case receiving only the normal level of prosecutorial effort.

One component of this cost is the lack of uniformity that results from the serious case receiving the same prosecutorial effort (which will influence the speed and severity of disposition) as less serious cases rather than that given to cases of comparable seriousness. If case seriousness is an indication of propensity for future criminal activity, failure to assign a serious case to MOB may involve costs in the form of criminal activity that could have been avoided by MOB's handling the case in place of one that is less serious.

The National Center for Prosecution Management did not explicitly take into consideration the relative costs of errors of omission or unnecessary inclusion during the construction of the case weighting formula. Although the system initially presented to the district attorney correctly classified over 75 percent of the cases in the data set, it allowed more errors of omission than the district attorney's staff felt desirable. In other words, given the distribution of errors produced by the case evaluation system initially presented by the National Center for Prosecution Management, it can be inferred that the staff felt that the total costs of errors could be reduced by decreasing the number of errors of omission at the expense of an increase in the number of errors of unnecessary inclusion. The inference is based on the observation that the staff initiated two modifications to shift the error distribution toward fewer errors of omission. The first modification was the addition of several offense types for automatic referral to MOB. The second was the decision to refer cases to MOB if either the case or defendant score reached certain cutoff levels, rather than referring cases only if the product of the scores reached a specified cutoff level. Assuming that these changes have reduced the occurrence of errors of omission to a negligible level, the rate of correct classification under these modifications is approximately 5 percent (one or two cases accepted each day for permanent MOB assignment out of the twenty to twenty-five referred by the case evaluation system). Thus after adjustment of the selection criteria to reduce errors of omission, the case evaluation system designed by the National Center for Prosecution Management appears to be operating at approximately the same level of accuracy as the intuitively designed system it replaces. The preceding discussion helps to reconcile the belief of the MOB chief that the intuitively designed system operated satisfactorily, with the apparently contradictory report of the National Center for Prosecution Management that the new system represented a "quantum jump" in predictive power.

TRANSFER OF THE SELECTIVE PROSECUTION MODEL: THE CAREER CRIMINAL PROGRAM

In 1975 LEAA began providing discretionary grant funds to local prosecutors' offices to support the establishment of units that would allow prosecutorial resources to be directed at defendants with extensive criminal histories who might be assumed to be involved with crime as a way of life. The discretionary grant program was named the Career Criminal Program. By the end of 1976, eighteen prosecutors' offices were operating career criminal bureaus that were started with LEAA discretionary funds. Ten other jurisdictions had established career criminal bureaus with LEAA state block grants or strictly local funding, by the same date. The diffusion of career criminal bureaus has been encouraged through information dissemination and technical assistance provided and administered for LEAA initially by the National Legal Data Center, a nonprofit corporation, and more recently by INSLAW.[8] The National Legal Data Center published a quarterly newsletter for prosecutors who have established, or are interested in establishing, career criminal bureaus. The center administered conferences for offices participating in the Career Criminal Program. Site visits were made by National Legal Data Center personnel to assist jurisdictions in designing procedures for the collection of data needed to meet LEAA evaluation requirements.

What is the origin of the Career Criminal Program? In 1974 Charles Work, the deputy administrator of LEAA, formed a committee within LEAA to study the concept of selective prosecution. He was prompted to consider selective prosecution units as a potential improvement in prosecution management by his own experience in the U.S. Attorney's Office with the Special Litigation Unit as well as the experience of the Bronx District Attorney's

Office with MOB. Research findings suggesting that a small number of defendants may be responsible for a disproportionate number of serious crimes directed the committee's attention toward selective prosecution of repeat offenders.

The majority of the career criminal bureaus select cases according to clearly defined criteria. For example, the New Orleans Career Criminal Bureau accepts all cases when defendants have two prior felony convictions or five prior felony arrests. Five offices, however, employ numerical case evaluation systems to aid in the selection of cases. Several of the numerical case evaluations systems are modeled after the defendant section of the Bronx case evaluation system. In general, it appears that the numerical case evaluation systems are used as backups for manual case screening performed by career criminal bureau personnel. It thus appears that case ranking systems have not become essential or highly valued tools for supporting career criminal bureau operations.

CASE RANKING SYSTEMS IN PRACTICE

The case ranking system, developed in conjunction with the PROMIS case management information system prototype, fell into operational disuse well before the unit it supported was discontinued. Despite the availability of its measure of offense and defendant seriousness as part of the PROMIS Transfer Project, not a single jurisdiction has adopted this use. The attempt to transfer a manual version of the case ranking system to the Wayne County Office of the Prosecuting Attorney ended in failure. Only the case ranking system that was tailored to meet the needs of the Bronx District Attorney's Office and several simplified versions of it used to support selection of cases for handling by career criminal bureaus have actually seen operational use for extended periods of time. What do these experiences suggest about the design and use of case ranking systems?

In order to focus the discussion, let us assume that the apparent success of the Career Criminal Program leads LEAA to expand the support of the selective prosecution concept beyond concentration on repeat offenders to selective prosecution of cases according to overall case seriousness. Three approaches can be envisioned for developing case ranking systems to help select cases for the special prosecution units: (1) encourage the transfer of the Bronx Case Evaluation System, (2) help jurisdictions set up statistically based case evaluation systems through a program of induced diffusion, or (3) encourage each jurisdiction to design its own case evaluation system intuitively.

The Wayne County experience with Operation PREPARE should serve as a warning against encouraging the direct transfer of the Bronx Case Evaluation System. It would be unreasonable to assume that the preferences of a single assistant prosecutor in a single office at a particular point in time that are captured in the Bronx Case Evaluation System, will accurately reflect the assessment of case seriousness that would be made by the chief prosecutors of other jurisdictions. It is likely that there would be wide disagreement over which predictor variables should be included. For example, the Bronx Case Evaluation System weights three case strength measures (arrest, evidence, and identification methods). Other prosecutors may even wish to assure that of all the serious cases that are accepted for prosecution, the weakest ones receive the most prosecutorial attention. Although the Bronx Case Evaluation System might serve as a model for other jurisdictions, it is unlikely that its wholesale transfer could operate satisfactorily for other jurisdictions.

The second alternative, encouraging the adoption of case evaluation systems through a program of induced diffusion, would involve sending teams of researchers to participating offices to apply the methodology used by the National Center for Prosecution Management in developing the Bronx Case Evaluation System. Such a program would involve great cost in terms of the time expended by the researchers. Even if the costs were not judged exorbitant, such a program would be unwise because it would leave the jurisdictions with a system they could not easily modify. The inability of the U.S. Attorney's Office and the Wayne County Office of the Prosecuting Attorney to modify the PROMIS prototype case evaluation system illustrates the danger of introducing a technology into an organization that cannot be easily modified by regular personnel. As the environment and resources of the offices changed, the custom-made case evaluation systems would be likely to become obsolete. The task of the induced diffusion sponsor would probably have to develop into a permanent support role.

The third alternative, encouraging prosecutors' offices to design their own case evaluation systems intuitively, is probably the most realistic approach. It offers several advantages. It forces the prosecutor and his top assistants to state explicitly what factors they feel determine the seriousness of cases. Because it is internally designed, it should be possible for the office to easily adjust weights or criteria as conditions change or the prosecutor recognizes deficiencies in the original factors or their weights. The major objection that has been raised to the intuitively developed case evaluation system is that it is less objective than statistically constructed case evaluation systems. Statistically constructed systems start with the subjective ranking of cases made by the prosecutor or one of his chief assistants. Given this ranking, weights for factors can be estimated objectively. The intuitive design method involves the prosecutor (or one of his chief assistants) directly choosing factor weights according to his subjective estimation of factor importance. Both systems thus attempt to measure a subjective estimation of case seriousness. The statistically constructed systems may be more systematic and accurate than intuitively developed ones, but they are not less subjective. The observation that in actual operation the intuitively designed and statistically designed case evaluation system used by the Bronx District Attorney's Office had similar accuracy levels suggests that little improvement in accuracy is likely from statistically designed systems given currently used procedures. Before the adaptability and simplicity of intuitively designed systems are sacrificed, a more convincing demonstration of the accuracy improvements of statistically constructed systems is needed.

NOTES

1. National Center for Prosecution Management, "A System for Manual Evaluation of Case Processing in the Prosecutor's Office," March 1972.

2. Daniel McGillis, "An Exemplary Project: Major Offenses Bureau, Bronx County District Attorney's Office," prepared by ABT Associates, Inc., for the National Institute of Law Enforcement and Criminal Justice, November 1976, p. 9.

3. Joan E. Jacoby, "Case Evaluation: Quantifying Prosecutorial Policy," *Judicature* 58, no. 10 (May 1975): 489.

4. McGillis, "An Exemplary Project," p. 33.

5. Ibid., pp. 5-6.

6. For a detailed description of the methodology employed, see "Report to the Bronx County District Attorney on the Case Evaluation System," National Center for Prosecution Management, November 30, 1974.

7. At least two methodological objections might be raised to the conclusion that the new procedure would actually be able to classify 75 percent of future cases correctly: First, the repeated use of step-wise regression analysis means that it is not valid simply to use the total number of observations less the number of estimated coefficients as the degrees of freedom for calculating multiple R^2 statistics. Something has to be given up for repeatedly estimating coefficients while looking for the best structure. Second, use of a dichotomous dependent variable (accepted/not accepted) in linear regression analysis prevents the normality assumptions on the distribution of the errors from being satisfied so that confidence intervals cannot be constructed with certainty.

8. In 1979, INSLAW was named as the technical assistance provider for the Career Criminal Program.

PART 3

Induced Diffusion: The Local and Federal Perspectives

In a certain village lived a number of people who took pleasure in pointing out the stupidity of others. They often offered the village idiot the choice of either a nickel or a dime and were delighted when the idiot invariably chose the nickel. One day a kind villager took the idiot aside and explained that even though the nickel is larger the dime is worth more. When the idiot responded that he knew, the villager asked him why he always chose the nickel. The idiot replied, "If I choose the dime, they won't do it anymore."

—an old anecdote—
a story commonly told during the 1930s
about a resident of an upstate
New York community

chapter 8

Appropriate Management Innovations in Local Public Agencies

There is a growing awareness among students of the process of innovation that cumulative progress in improving productivity is not solely a function of the adoption of innovations; it also depends on the extent to which the adopted innovations can actually be used.[1] Their work suggests an important question for practitioners who seek to encourage innovation: A priori, how can the likely extent of successful implementation be predicted? The purpose of this chapter is to generalize the insights from our study of innovations in prosecution management to better understand the implementation of innovations in other types of local agencies. Although the empirical focus of this book has been exclusively on prosecution, we shall argue that agencies of various types share characteristics likely to influence their ability to implement new technologies or organizational routines.[2]

The process of foreign aid to less developed nations will serve as a metaphor for our discussion.[3] Local agencies play the role of less developed nations; they are underdeveloped in terms of the management or service delivery technologies they employ and the resources available to improve them. The federal government plays the role of the nation willing to provide economic assistance. This chapter is written from a local perspective, developing the analogy between local public agencies and less developed nations. The next chapter is written from a federal perspective, developing the analogy between assistance to less developed nations and federal efforts to induce innovation.

Less developed nations share with local agencies at least three characteristics that are relevant to the process of innovation. First, both are generally poor. Minimal internally generated discretionary funds are available for major innovative efforts. It may be politically costly for less developed nations to increase the availability of discretionary funds through taxation. It may be economically unsound for them to raise investment funds through increased taxation because their small tax bases necessitate high tax rates that can interfere with work incentives or otherwise distort incentives in the private economy. Similarly, it may be administratively costly for managers of local agencies to generate resources for innovation by "squeezing out" organizational slack such as the work-time of personnel that is not being utilized during periods of routine operations. Some agencies may be seeking innovation primarily because they have little slack available to deal with changes in their environment. Less developed nations face the prospects of delay, uncertainty, and foreign interference when they seek capital from international lending institutions such as the World Bank. Local agencies face the same prospect of delay, uncertainty, and scrutiny from their local funding sources.

Second, the ability to evaluate, implement, and maintain innovative technologies is limited by a lack of internal expertise. Less developed nations often lack the engineering and management infrastructure needed to implement and operate technologically complex innovations independently. Similarly, local agencies are unlikely to employ individuals with technical skills not needed for accomplishing standard operations. They may also lack individuals with the management training or experiences to direct major organizational changes. Reliance on externally provided expertise may facilitate the initial implementation of an innovation. Continued reliance on externally provided expertise, however, may limit the extent to which the innovation can be modified to deal with changing circumstances.

Third, there is wide variability in available resources and institutional structures. Less developed nations differ along dimensions such as population size, culture, political institutions, and available economic resources; these dimensions may all influence the ability to implement an innovation and its effectiveness once implemented. There are obviously differences in the internal structure and organization of even like-functioned groups (or industries) of agencies, such as prosecutors offices, welfare departments, public health agencies, and police departments. There is also wide variation in the demographic characteristics and preferences of the jurisdictions served, the legal and administrative rules constraining the agencies' operation, and other factors in the environment of the agencies. Variation in local circumstances constrains the transferability of innovations from one local public agency to others. What has apparently succeeded in one agency may flounder in another because the agencies differ in some factor relevant to the implementation process. Even more fundamental to the horizontal transfer of innovations, variability among agencies may make it difficult for one agency to determine whether net benefits would result from the adoption of an innovation that has provided net benefits to another agency. It may even be difficult to determine whether the innovation actually has produced net benefits for the other agency.

Severe shortages of investment funds and technical expertise prevent less developed nations from rapidly adopting innovations that have diffused throughout the industries of the developed nations. Over the past thirty years, developed nations have devoted considerable resources to foreign aid programs, which directly through technical assistance and indirectly through financial assistance have been aimed at promoting the modernization of production processes. Indeed, many involved in the conduct and study of foreign aid programs have come to equate development with modernization.[4] Implicit in these modernization projects is the assumption that the most advanced technology is best for the less developed nation.

Recently, attention has been given to the question: Are the advanced technologies of the developed nations "appropriate" for developing nations? E. F. Schumacher has raised the question for the general public in his popular book, *Small Is Beautiful.*[5] On a more scholarly level, the question has been raised by the National Research Council's Panel on Appropriate Technologies for Developing Countries. The major report prepared for that panel recognizes that there are multiple criteria for evaluating development efforts.[6] The determination of the appropriateness of a particular technology depends upon the emphasis placed on the various criteria. For example, assume that regional development and reduction of unemployment are emphasized along with the more conventional criteria of maximizing net national income. The most highly advanced technology that is economically efficient in the developed nations might not be as appropriate for the less developed nation, in light of the multiple criteria, as a less advanced technology that permits greater decentralization or contributes more to expanded employment.

Reports of development projects that fail to achieve anticipated benefits suggest that the ability of the less developed nation to implement and maintain innovations should also enter into the determination of appropriateness. Lack of expertise might be overcome during the initial stages of implementation through the technical assistance from the developed nation offering the technology. Once the technical assistance is withdrawn, however, the innovation may be discontinued through lack of the skilled labor needed to maintain it. For example, a study of manufacturing firms in Indonesia reports that firms had difficulty maintaining and operating advanced equipment and in some cases discontinued its use.[7] It seems unreasonable to define appropriateness solely in terms of the theoretical contribution an innovation can make to various goals; the likelihood that the theoretical contributions can be realized in practice should also be considered. The following section presents implementation as the key to determining appropriate technology for local public agencies.

APPROPRIATE PUBLIC MANAGEMENT INNOVATIONS

Analogous to the concept of appropriate technologies for less developed nations is the concept of appropriate management innovations for local public agencies. An innovation will be considered appropriate when there is a high probability that its implementation will result in the realization of benefits equal to or in excess of costs. The greater the probability of reaching or exceeding the break-even point where benefits equal costs, the more appropriate the innovation. Local public managers are urged to choose the innovations that are most appropriate for their agencies.

The standard decision rule of applied welfare economics is to choose the project (innovation) that offers the greatest net benefits.[8] Use of the appropriateness criterion, which is an alternative decision rule, leads, however, to more conservative choices of innovations. It is possible that an innovation might have large expected net benefits because it offers some chance of producing an outcome yielding large net benefits, yet be inappropriate because other outcomes involving net costs are much more likely. For example, consider two projects each costing $1 million. If the first had a 10 percent chance of yielding $18 million in benefits and a 90 percent chance of yielding no benefits, it would have positive net expected benefits but only a 10 percent chance of yielding net benefits greater than zero. If the second project had a 90 percent chance of yielding $2 million in net benefits and a 10 percent chance of yielding no benefits, it also would have positive expected benefits but a 90 percent chance of yielding net benefits greater than zero. The projects would be ranked equally by the net benefits criterion, but only the second project would pass the criterion of appropriateness.

Why is the more conservative decision rule desirable? It would be presumptuous to challenge the accumulated wisdom of welfare economics by arguing that the appropriateness criterion is desirable on theoretical grounds. Instead, the appropriateness critrion can be justified on practical grounds: local public managers rarely have sufficient analytical resources or information to permit the systematic estimation of expected net benefits. In situations of limited and perhaps biased information, the criterion of appropriateness may provide a better focus for analysis than the theoretically preferable but impractical criteria of expected net benefits.

On the other hand, the two-step application of the appropriateness criterion encourages local public managers to confront directly the possibility that anticipated benefits might not be achieved because of problems encountered during implementation. First, the manager must determine what portion of the innovation's potential benefit must be secured to cover the costs of its implementation and use. Second, he must address the question: How likely is it that the minimum level of benefits needed to break even can actually be achieved?

Urging consideration of appropriateness is the same as asking public managers to be more skeptical of claims made about the benefits of management innovations. Limited discretionary funds and expertise make it unlikely that local public agencies can conduct their own research and development of management innovations. At the same time, variability among local public agencies makes it difficult to judge independently the expected success of innovations that appear to have been successful in other agencies. As will be discussed in the next chapter, bureaucratic incentives may bias the information provided to local public agencies from federal sources. Another source of bias may be the natural tendency of innovators to take an overly optimistic view of the potential of their inventions and innovations. When decisions must be made on the basis of incomplete and perhaps biased information, caution, if not skepticism, is warranted.

Determination of appropriateness is by no means an easy task. Although much of the literature dealing with implementation has focused on problems of an interorganizational nature, the insights provided by some works are helpful in understanding problems of an intraorganizational nature that are likely to be encountered during implementation. At a general level, Eugene Bardach's view of the implementation process (that is, as the attempted assembly of the program elements needed to produce desired outcomes) can serve as a starting point.[9] The types of elements typically needed to implement management innovations and the difficulties likely to be encountered in their assembly are factors that will be included in the framework for determining appropriateness.

The task at hand is complicated by the wide variability among local public agencies. The discussion of appropriateness must of necessity be general. Because implementation will be influenced by the characteristics of the adopting agency as well as by those of the innovation, an innovation might be appropriate for one set of agencies, but not for another. Consequently, the following analysis will focus on two dimensions of appropriateness that reflect the requirements for successful implementation relative to the capacity of the adopting agency to satisfy them: the amount of organizational behavior that must be managed during the innovation's implementation and the need for externally supplied resources and expertise.

The case management information system catch-22 was introduced in chapter 6. The same factors that make a case management information system desirable also make it difficult to implement. Large, decentralized prosecutors' offices with weak management systems would find the benefits of a fully implemented case management information system very desirable. At the same time, the prosecutors' offices, because they are large, decentralized, and weakly managed, would face great difficulty in bringing about the organizational change necessary to implement fully case management information systems. With respect to this particular innovation, the factors making it desirable are colinear with factors hindering implementation. Because a general goal of management innovations is to increase the agency head's control over subordinates and because the implementation of the management innovations often requires responsive and responsible behavior from subordinates to be successful, it is likely that many management innovations will be subject to the catch-22. The determination of appropriateness should include an assessment of the organizational change necessary to reach the break-even point in net benfits, given the resources available to accomplish the necessary change.

At least three factors should be considered in the estimation of the amount of management needed to implement an innovation.[10] First, the greater the number of subordinates who must participate in the change, the greater the managerial effort needed to accomplish the change. Second, the more the subordinates view the innovation or its implementation as a source of net costs (which may include more work, the need to learn new routines, or loss of discretion), the greater the need for managerial effort. Third, the greater the ability of subordinates to withdraw their cooperation either during the implementation of the innovation or during its subsequent use, the greater the need for managerial effort. In terms of the implementation as an assembly process, these three factors correspond to the questions: Which subordinates hold elements necessary for the assembly of the innovation? How willing will they be to provide the elements? Will they be able to withdraw elements during or after the assembly?

After estimating the magnitudes and types of management effort that are likely to be needed during implementation, an inventory of available management resources should be made. The less formal authority, personal influence, and monitoring capability that will be available to the personnel supervising the implementation, the greater is the amount of direct inducement that will be needed to secure necessary behavioral changes.[11] Direct inducement through pay increases or direct coercion through threats of pay reductions, dismissals, or unfavorable transfers may be limited in local public agencies by tight budgets and civil service regulations. The availability of rewards for inducing needed behavioral change may be further reduced by the drain on resources caused by the need to operate dual systems, the innovation and the system it is replacing, during the early stages of implementation.

The greater the gap between the managerial effort needed to secure necessary organizational change and the amount of managerial effort actually available in the agency, the less likely it is that the innovation can be successfully implemented. The managerial gap (specific to a particular innovation and potential adopter) is advanced as a major dimension of appropriateness.

A second dimension for judging appropriateness is the extent to which the innovation requires the local public agency to rely upon externally provided expertise. Successful implementation of management innovations may require skills such as the preparation of proposals for state and federal grants, the writing of requests for proposals for contractor work, statistical analysis, forms design, computer software design, project planning and management, and personnel training—skills that usually are not found among the staffs of substantively oriented local public agencies such as prosecutors' offices, welfare departments, public health agencies, and police departments. Limited discretionary funds and civil service pay scales for professionals that are below private-sector earnings for comparable services make it difficult for local public agencies to hire full-time employees with the needed technical skills for a period long enough to allow them to learn the substantive business of the agency and participate in the choice of an innovation, its implementation, and its use. Instead, expertise must usually be secured from consultants and other local public agencies in the jurisdiction.

Reliance on consultants for technical expertise may involve two major problems. First, if no one in the agency has knowledge of the skills being sought, it may not be possible to prepare a request for proposals that will fully communicate the nature of the required services. If the consultant does not fully understand the substantive business of the office, there is a danger that the purchased services may be inadequate for the project as it was initially conceived. Funds may not be available for remedial work, and the request for proposals may have been insufficiently specific to admit redress through civil action against the consultant. The less agency personnel know about the expertise being sought, the greater the danger that the services provided by the consultant will be inadequate. Garry D. Brewer's study of the failure of large-scale simulation models developed by consultants for local governments provides an extreme illustration of this proposition.[12]

Second, even if the services of the consultant are adequate to allow the implementation of the innovation, the agency may encounter another problem. The consultant's work may be directly tied to the structure, policies, and environment of the agency prevailing at the time of the implementation of the innovation. What will happen when the circumstances of the agency change? If the agency has not developed its own expertise, it may have either to rehire consultants to make the necessary changes or to discontinue use of the innovation. Without readily available funds for maintenance work by consultants, the innovation is always in danger of becoming obsolete.

Some expertise may be available through other local public agencies in the jurisdiction. The executive office for the city or county may be able to provide assistance in securing grants, writing requests for proposals and project management. City or county data processing centers may be able to provide computer-related expertise. Personnel may be borrowed from other agencies that have tried to implement similar innovations. Although it may be possible to secure the nominal cooperation of other local public agencies for the provision of expertise, the innovating agency may have little leverage to ensure that the assistance will be timely and of sufficient quantity and quality. If the agency supplying the expertise does not, for its own successful operation, have to rely upon the goodwill of the innovating agency, then the experts may give technical assistance a low priority. If so, then assistance will perhaps be delayed or eliminated whenever the donor's direct interests could be furthered by its own use of the expertise. The innovating agency may have no carrot or stick to secure the full cooperation of the donor agency, thereby increasing the chances that the implementation will be delayed or discontinued.

The greater the divergence between the expertise needed to implement an innovation and the expertise actually available within the agency, the less likely the innovation is appropriate for the agency. Before adopting an innovation requiring major contributions of externally provided expertise, the innovating manager should be assured that consultants can be effectively communicated with and monitored, that other local public agencies can be persuaded to make and fulfill commitments of assistance, and that it will be possible to modify the innovation as the policies, structure, and environment of the agency change. Without these assurances, the innovating manager would be well advised to consider alternative innovations that require less externally provided expertise to be implemented successfully.

The two dimensions of appropriateness discussed previously are presented schematically in figure 3. The vertical dimension represents the amount of organizational behavior that must be managed by a particular agency to implement and use a particular innovation successfully. The horizontal dimension represents the amount of externally provided expertise that must be secured by the agency during the implementation, maintenance, and use of the innovation. The labeled regions reflect the chances that the present value of net benefits will be greater than or equal to zero; the greater the chances of reaching the break-even point, the more appropriate the innovation for the agency.[13]

Figure 3. Appropriate Innovations for Local Agencies

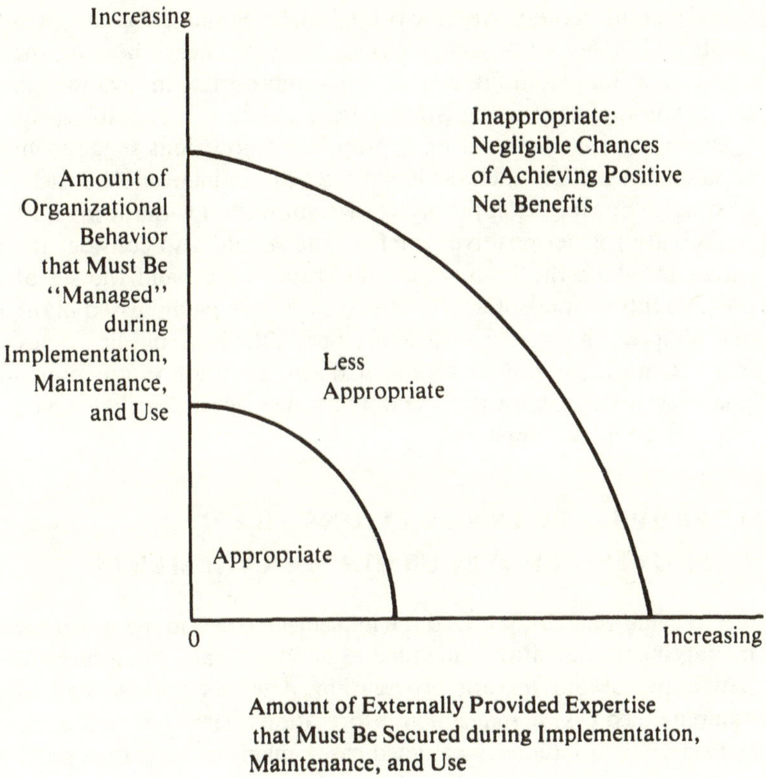

It is important to note that the appropriateness of an innovation is a function of its requirements for successful implementation in a particular agency relative to the capabilities of the agency at a specific point in *time.* An innovation might be judged as inappropriate today, but wholly appropriate five years hence because the agency has adopted a number of other appropriate innovations in the meantime, thereby bolstering its capabilities. The ability of agencies to expand the set of appropriate innovations suggests an additional element to the calculus of choosing an innovation. Instead of simply choosing as appropriate that innovation with the greatest probability for net positive benefits, one should also consider the extent to which the innovation will reduce or expand the set of possible future appropriate innovations. As will be discussed in the next chapter, the incentive structure facing the local public agency manager may lead him to give insufficient attention to the appropriateness of the innovation adopted today, let alone that which might be adopted tomorrow.

APPROPRIATE INNOVATIONS FOR IMPROVING PROSECUTION MANAGEMENT

Preceding chapters analyzed the implementation and use of several management innovations intended to allow the chief prosecutor to better control idiosyncratic prosecution. Attention was focused on computerized case management information systems, as well as on statistically and intuitively designed case ranking systems to support special prosecution units. We also encountered other management innovations: enhanced case screening, clearance procedures, and nonautomated case management information systems. There is wide variation among the policies, organization, and environment of prosecutors' offices, and the appropriateness of the earlier mentioned management innovations will be related to these factors. Consequently, discussion of the appropriateness of the innovations for prosecutors' offices in general must remain somewhat abstract. With this caveat, the following discussion considers the appropriateness of the innovations encountered in this work.

Of all the innovations encountered, enhanced case screening units are most appropriate. Their implementation and use do not require the use of unfamiliar technologies, but rather the reassignment of tasks already performed. The major managerial effort required during implementation is the development of incentives to secure the cooperation of experienced assistant prosecutors in the reassignment. The Alameda County and New Orleans experiences with enhanced case screening units demonstrated how such incentives could be developed. Once implemented, enhanced case screening units continue to operate with a minimum of managerial supervision. Consequently, the equity and efficiency benefits outlined in chapter 2 have a high probability of being routinely realized in practice.

We have previously discussed how the increased uniformity in case charging afforded by enhanced screening units facilitates the operation of systems of clearance procedures. Enhanced case screening units could also increase the chances of successful implementation and use of the other innovations: by improving the selection of cases for special prosecution units, by permitting the inclusion of subjective estimates of the strength of evidence in case ranking systems, and by reducing the number of assistants who have to be trained in the collection of initial case data for case management information systems. In these ways, enhanced case screening units extend the range of appropriate innovations for their adopters.

Clearance procedures and special prosecution units are at the next level of appropriateness. Although neither involves unfamiliar technology, each requires a continuing expenditure of managerial effort. The operation of clearances necessitates managerial review of requests for clearances as well as spot checking to ensure that the restrictions on dispositions are being followed. In addition to the increased cost per case handled, special prosecution units must be continually monitored to ensure that they are selecting the correct set of cases—especially in light of the bias, described in chapter 2, toward selecting cases that are already easy to win at trial. The appropriateness of the clearance procedures and special prosecution units rests on the certain and direct way they produce benefits.

Consequently, planning their implementation can reasonably revolve around choosing how many and which cases will fall in their domains so as to maximize the net benefits from their use.

The appropriateness of a case ranking system designed to assist case selection probably depends on whether it is intuitively developed by office personnel or developed statistically by outside researchers. Although each approach is capable of yielding a system that can be routinely employed with minimal managerial supervision, the intuitive approach is much more amenable to modification without resort to externally provided technical assistance. Because of the inherent difficulty in capturing multidimensional preferences in a numerical scale, case ranking systems will be more appropriate for applications where the ranks can be interpreted as general reflections of the chief prosecutor's preferences rather than as exact representations.

The computerized case management information system is the least appropriate of the innovations studied. Implementation requires several types of expertise rarely found in prosecutors' offices. Information system analysis, forms design, computer programming, large project planning and management, and data base management skills must generally be secured from external sources. In the absence of major increases in clerical personnel, the implementation of computerized case management information systems requires the management of extensive changes in the behavior of assistant prosecutors, who are required to collect complete and accurate case data on a timely basis. Without the full cooperation of those who are required to collect the data, the data base may never reach a sufficient level of accuracy to permit the realization of the anticipated logistical and management benefits. The experience of PROMIS in the District of Columbia and DALITE in Alameda County underlies the prediction that other case management information system implementers would face difficulty in achieving and maintaining data quality. The experience of PROMIS jurisdictions appears to confirm this prediction. Levels of utilization below those anticipated reflect the data quality problems.

The more types of expertise needed for implementation that already exist in the office or can be permanently added to the staff, the more likely that the case management information system can be successfully implemented. For example, the direct employment of system managers and the direct control of computer hardware by the Alameda County and New Orleans District Attorney's Office probably made a major contribution to their success in utilizing their case management information systems as a reliable source of reports for logistical support purposes.

Computerized case management information systems are also likely to be more appropriate innovations for offices that already have well-developed manual information systems: less behaviorial modification is needed during implementation if personnel already view conscientious data collection as a legitimate part of their job. It may be desirable for prosecutors' offices to attempt to implement a manual version of the case management information system they wish to adopt before attempting computerization. Any other previously implemented innovations that increase the chief prosecutor's control over those who are to collect data (such as Alameda County's Felony Task Force, which allows case data to be collected by a limited number of experienced assistants) or reduces the amount of behavior change needed (such as the manually prepared disposition reports introduced prior to PROMIS in New Orleans) can help increase the appropriateness of a computerized case management information system.

If case management information systems are the least appropriate of the innovations considered, why has LEAA spent more on their diffusion than on any other innovation? The following chapter reviews the answer to this question.

NOTES

1. In particular, see Neal C. Gross, Joseph B. Giaquinta, and Marilyn Bernstein, *Implementing Organizational Innovations* (New York: Basic Books, 1971), pp. 29-40. Paul Berman and Milbrey Wallis McLaughlin, *Federal Programs Supporting Educational Change, Vol. 1: A Model of Educational Change,* Rand R-1589/1-HEW (Santa Monica, Calif., September 1974), pp. v-vi. Robert K. Yin, Karen A. Heald, and Mary E. Vogel, *Tinkering with the System* (Lexington, Mass.: Lexington Books, 1977). Richard R. Nelson and Douglas Yates, eds., *Innovations and Implementation in Public Organizations* (Lexington, Mass.: Lexington Books, 1978).

2. The innovations studied in this work all involved the increased centralization of decision making. The framework that is developed in this chapter, however, can

be applied to innovations that involve greater decentralization of decision making. As noted by Yates in "Decentralization: Innovation and Implementation in New York," the successful implementation of decentralization may require strong initiative and leadership, a dimension of the framework in this chapter. Douglas Yates, "Decentralization: Innovation and Implementation in New York," in Nelson and Yates, *Innovations and Implementation,* pp. 147-74.

3. The metaphor is borrowed from Pressman and Wildavsky. See, for example: Jeffrey L. Pressman and Aaron Wildavsky, *Implementation* (Berkeley: University of California Press, 1975), pp. 136-42; Jeffrey L. Pressman, *Federal Programs and City Politics* (Berkeley: University of California Press, 1975), pp. 105-34; and Aaron Wildavsky, *Budgeting: A Comparative Theory of Budgetary Processes* (Boston: Little, Brown, 1975).

4. Robert E. Asher, *Development Assistance in the Seventies* (Washington, D.C.: The Brookings Institution, 1970), pp. 39-41.

5. E. F. Schumacher, *Small Is Beautiful* (New York: Harper & Row, 1973), pt. 3.

6. Richard S. Ekaus, *Appropriate Technologies for Developing Countries,* prepared for the Panel on Appropriate Technologies for Developing Countries of the National Council Research Council (Washington, D.C.: National Academy of Sciences, 1977), p. 37.

7. C. Peter Timmer, John W. Thomas, Louis J. Wells, and David Moravetz, *The Choice of Technology in Developing Countries: Some Cautionary Tales* (Cambridge, Mass.: Center for International Affairs, Harvard University, 1975), p. 84.

8. The expected value of the net benefits of an innovation would be computed by summing all the possible levels of net benefits that might result where each level is multiplied by the probability of its occurrence.

9. Eugene Bardach, *The Implementation Game: What Happens After a Bill Becomes a Law* (Cambridge, Mass.: MIT Press, 1977), p. 37.

10. Several authors have suggested that the conduct of a benefit-cost analysis from the perspective of each interest group can be useful in anticipating implementation problems. It is a logical extension to apply this approach to intraorganizational actors. See Harold S. Luft, "Benefit-Cost Analysis and Public Policy Implementation: From Normative to Positive Analysis," *Public Policy* 24, no. 4 (Fall 1976), and Lee S. Friedman, "An Interim Evaluation of the Supported Work Experiment," *Policy Analysis* 3, no. 2 (Spring 1977).

11. At least with respect to management innovations intended to increase the centralization of authority, the local public manager who can confidently order his or her subordinates to carry out the necessary activities for the successful implementation of a management innovation probably stands to gain only marginal benefits from its use. Rather, it is managers with less secure control who stand to gain the greatest net benefits from the use of management innovations. Yet it is the manager with less effective control who must coerce, induce, and monitor when orders alone will not elicit needed cooperation.

12. Garry D. Brewer, *Politicians, Bureaucrats and the Consultant* (New York: Basic Books, 1973).

13. The arguments of this section can be summarized symbolically as: $Pb\ [PV\ (B - C) \geq 0] = f(M_N - M_A, E_N - E_I)$ where $Pb\ [PV\ (B - C) \geq 0]$ is the probability that the present value of net benefits, $PV\ (B - C)$, is greater than or equal to zero; f is a nonincreasing function of the difference between the level of management effort required to guarantee necessary changes in organizational behavior (M_N) and the level of management activity that will actually be available (M_A). The function f is also a nonincreasing function of the difference between the level of expertise needed for implementation, maintenance, and use of the innovation $E_N)$ and the level of expertise that can be directly supplied by the agency itself (E_I).

In chapter 6, it was argued that the technical assistance provided by INSLAW to PROMIS adopters greatly increased the chances of successful implementation. This finding contradicts the finding of Yin, Heald, and Vogel that federal technical assistance makes a negative contribution to successful implementation. Because their statistical analysis included no variable to control for E_N, it is likely that their results simply reflect the effects of E_N or $E_N - E_I$. A specification, such as that presented here, which explicitly recognizes the importance of considering the requirements for successful implementation relative to the capacity of the adopting agency might have led Yin, Heald, and Vogel to a different conclusion concerning the value of federal technical assistance. Yin, Heald, and Vogel, *Tinkering with the System*, pp. 115-22.

chapter 9

The Mixed Blessings of Induced Diffusion

Local public agencies face limitations in the availability of investment funds and expertise which inhibits endogenous invention and hinders the identification, adoption, and implementation of innovations that could improve the services provided by these agencies. Local agencies do not have access to capital markets; investment funds must be obtained from increases in local budgets or from state or federal grants. Financially strapped local governments may be unwilling to provide budget increases to agencies for the adoption of innovations unless persuasive arguments can be made that the innovations are very likely to yield cost reductions. It may be difficult to secure locally generated funds for management and service delivery innovations that have the potential for improving the quality and equity of the services provided; quality and equity are much more difficult for local budget makers to observe and value than changes in monetary operating costs. Sole reliance on locally generated funds is likely to result in less than a socially optimal rate of adoption of innovations by local agencies. Therefore, it may be socially desirable for the federal government to provide local agencies with assistance that will increase their ability to identify, adopt, and implement potentially beneficial innovations.

In a metaphor that compares local public agencies to less developed nations in terms of the difficulty of innovation, federal assistance is analogous to foreign aid. Those who study foreign programs have extensively explored the normative and positive distributional questions: Who should get how much? Who will get how much? Students of the foreign aid process have also realized that the form in which the aid is given is of practical import.[1] Grants-in-aid, soft loans, technical assistance, and other forms of foreign aid not only differ in their effectiveness for achieving various foreign aid program goals, but also in the behavioral responses they elicit from recipients and donors. It should also be expected that the form federal assistance to local public agencies takes will likewise be of importance in explaining outcomes that result.

A federal program for which the goal is to increase the rate of innovation by local public agencies would include one or more of three components: the dissemination of information, the granting of funds, and the provision of technical assistance. Information is disseminated in an attempt to generate interest among potential adopters and assist them in selecting a particular innovation. Grants are made available to help defray costs incurred during implementation. Technical assistance is provided to compensate for deficiencies in expertise that hinder the adopting agency's ability to plan and manage the implementation of the innovation.[2] A program that included all three of these components would increase not only the chances that an innovation is adopted, but also the chances that it is successfully implemented.[3]

Consider the problem of designing a federal assistance program intended to increase the rate of management and service delivery innovation among a set of like-functioned local public agencies (such as prosecutors' offices). Assuming limited resources, how many different types of innovations should the program support? On the one hand, recognition of the wide variability of needs and capabilities among even like-functioned local agencies suggests that the more types of alternative innovations supported, the greater the likelihood that potential recipients will be able to choose innovations appropriate to their needs and capabilities. On the other hand, the more types of alternative innovations supported, the less likely that the federal program will be able to provide the assistance of high-quality expertise that recipients need to implement the innovation. The fewer the number of selections offered, the more specialization and the accumulation of experience will allow the federal program to develop and deliver assistance and thereby increase the chances of successful implementation by the program recipients.[4]

At the extreme, a federal assistance program could selectively disseminate information, funding, and technical assistance for one particular innovation. Chapter 1 developed a framework for analyzing the advantages and disadvantages of such programs of induced diffusion. The purpose of this chapter is to illustrate the important aspects of the theory of induced diffusion with the history of the PROMIS Transfer Project. We shall argue that programs of induced diffusion offer mixed blessings. Rapid diffusion and greater chances for successful implementations are purchased as the price of establishing organizational incentives that may inhibit the search for and selection of more appropriate innovations.

THE ADVANTAGE: INCREASED CAPACITY TO UTILIZE EXPERTISE

Programs of induced diffusion can provide incentives to the managers of local agencies so as to facilitate the rapid diffusion of the supported innovations. Such diffusion is desirable when it leads to the realization of net benefits through improvements in the services delivered by the adopting agency; it is undesirable when it leads to net costs, implementation failures, or the displacement of alternative innovations that could have produced greater net benefits. Before dealing with the question of the desirability of the induced diffusion, however, we shall discuss a characteristic of such an approach with less equivocal value: the provision of direct managerial and technical assistance. This can greatly increase the ability of adopting agencies to utilize effectively expertise that must be secured from extra-agency sources. By helping to close the gap between requirements and capabilities in expertise, programs of induced diffusion increase the likelihood that adopted innovations will be implemented successfully.

The technical assistance provided by INSLAW to prosecutors' offices participating in LEAA's PROMIS Transfer Project illustrates the vital role that can be played in the implementation process by the expertise made available through programs of induced diffusion. INSLAW provides continuous support to prosecutors' offices that have adopted PROMIS. Direct involvement in the planning and management of implementation of PROMIS has enabled INSLAW to complement its detailed knowledge of the PROMIS system with an awareness of the types of assistance most needed by prosecutors' offices for its successful implementation. As a result, implementation failures as a result of purely technical reasons have been avoided.

A brief comparison of the PROMIS prototype experience with the general observations on subsequent PROMIS implementations indicates the benefits from direct technical assistance. Whereas problems with contractor-provided technical services delayed and then necessitated the eventual redesign of the PROMIS prototype, none of the other PROMIS jurisdictions surveyed reported major problems with contractor-provided services. The nonrecurrence of contractor-related problems might be attributed to the well-documented software provided by INSLAW. Because all jurisdictions had to modify the software package to some extent, it is not unreasonable to attribute at least part of the absence of contractor-related problems to the active role played by INSLAW. The assistance provided by INSLAW in the preparation and evaluation of requests for proposals probably was instrumental in enabling many jurisdictions to utilize contractor-provided services effectively. Once projects were begun, INSLAW's response to technical questions through telephone conversations and site visits enabled jurisdictions to overcome problems that might otherwise have resulted in long delays or cost overruns. Even the general project planning and management advice given by INSLAW probably made a major contribution to success for most of the participating jurisdictions in assembling the technical components needed for PROMIS implementation.

INSLAW's dedication to and continual involvement with the basic PROMIS design also resulted in the development and diffusion of enhancements that helped mitigate the organizational problems in PROMIS implementation. (On the other hand, it will be suggested in the next section that dedication to the basic PROMIS design may have led INSLAW to exclude consideration of some potentially beneficial changes that would require major redesign.) INSLAW recognized the importance of providing information benefits to those who collect PROMIS data. To facilitate the use of PROMIS by line prosecutors, INSLAW introduced on-line access to case data. Recognition that office managers were being frustrated in their attempts to utilize PROMIS data led to the introduction of software packages that offered the potential for offices to generate nonroutine reports with minimal programming costs. Involvement in training programs for data collection personnel and attempts to encourage management use of PROMIS through demonstrations and testimonials at the regular PROMIS Users Group meetings also indicate an awareness of the nontechnical problems that must be addressed to achieve the successful implementation and use of case management information systems.

As discussed previously, none of the jurisdictions surveyed has achieved all of the information benefits PROMIS is said to offer. In fact, at the time of the survey, none of the jurisdictions was using PROMIS for case ranking or the automatic generation of subpoenas, and only one was relying on PROMIS for the exclusive generation of calendars. The detection of deviations from office policies and other management uses of PROMIS appeared to be realized only on a sporadic rather than routine basis. Problems with achieving and maintaining data quality appeared to be a problem for most jurisdictions, preventing the realization of promised benefits. Nevertheless, without the expertise provided by INSLAW, it is unlikely that even the limited benefits so far realized by PROMIS jurisdictions could have been achieved. Even if INSLAW provided documented software, but without direct technical assistance, it is easy to imagine that many of the PROMIS jurisdictions would have encountered delays or outright failures achieving the levels of data quality and use that they actually have achieved. Although one cannot actually prove that the contributions of INSLAW's technical assistance made a difference, still that contribution should not be underestimated.

THE DISADVANTAGE: DANGEROUS INCENTIVES

We argued in Chapter 1 that the use of programs of induced diffusion is likely to involve organizational incentives for diffision of the supported innovations even in the absence of positive evidence (or perhaps even in the presence of negative evidence) that the advertised benefits of the innovations can be obtained. In less than four years, the PROMIS Transfer Project has succeeded in diffusing PROMIS to over twenty jurisdictions. PROMIS continues to spread even though it is yet to be demonstrated that its advertised benefits can be routinely achieved by adopting agencies. Some of its advertised benefits have not yet been achieved by a single jurisdiction. In fact, the PROMIS prototype had ceased producing the management benefits that were advanced as rationales for diffusion at the time the PROMIS Transfer Project was begun. The incentives that have led to the rapid diffusion of PROMIS will be used to illustrate the danger that programs of induced diffusion create undesirable incentives.

Three actors are affected by incentives stemming from programs of induced diffusion. They are managers considering the adoption of the innovations, organizations providing marketing and technical assistance, and budgetary sponsors.

POTENTIAL ADOPTERS

Programs of induced diffusion can encourage local public agency managers to adopt the supported innovation in a number of ways. The primary inducement is a grant of funds to cover the costs of start-up and initial operation of the innovation. In the absence of federal financial assistance, socially desirable innovations may not be adopted because local managers have insufficient funds for investment in new technologies. Federal financial assistance may, however, lead to socially undesirable innovation by putting a wedge between the total social costs of the innovation and the costs actually borne by the local public agency. When the local public manager bears the full cost of the innovation, he compares the sum of the present value of the expected monetary costs (C_m) and the present value of the expected non-monetary organizational costs (C_o) with the present value of the expected benefits (B). If total costs $(C_m + C_o)$ are greater than benefits (B), the manager would presumably reject the innovation. With financial assistance, however, the local public agency does not bear the full monetary costs of the project (C_m). In his calculation of net benefits the manager is likely to ignore the portion of costs covered by federal funds because a negligible portion of these federal dollars are paid by residents in the local public agency's jurisdiction. If the decision is made primarily on the basis of comparison of organizational costs (C_o) and benefits (B), projects that are sociably undesirable may be undertaken.

The danger of diffusing innovations with net social costs is not limited to programs of induced innovation.[5] Programs that simply provide funding for innovations chosen by the local agency on its own can also result in the diffusion of innovations with net social costs. Programs of induced diffusion, however, interfere with the choice of the best innovation by each local public agency by lowering the price of the supported innovations relative to other innovations that are not being supported. The local public agency manager may decide to take what the program of induced diffusion is offering rather than face the uncertainties of trying to secure local funding for a better innovation. For example, one district attorney related that after he had been elected, he sought funding for almost all LEAA-sponsored projects relevant to prosecution. The projects were viewed not only in terms of the particular benefits they might yield, but also as a way of increasing the total level of resources available to the office.

The incentive to take what is being offered is enhanced by the local public agency manager's assumption that the federal sponsor would not be advocating the adoption of the innovation without determining that it would be good for the adopters. Reliance on the sponsor's imprimatur limits the amount of analysis the local public agency manager must do to convince himself, his agency, and the local legislature that the innovation is desirable. A prosecutor, for example, may feel he can take claims about the benefits of PROMIS at face value: If LEAA, with all the expertise it can command, has concluded that PROMIS will yield certain benefits, why should much additional effort be expended in trying to determine the accuracy of these claims? But if LEAA's conclusions are not fully accurate, the prosecutor may make a decision to adopt PROMIS on the basis of overestimated benefits, underestimated costs, or unanticipated implementation problems.

The prestige of being considered an innovator may encourage local public agency managers to join and remain in programs of induced diffusion. The managers may wish the citizens and other officials in their jurisdictions to view them as progressive; public announcements about federal grants for innovative projects can help build reputations for progressive management. The programs of induced diffusion can enhance—and may even be designed to enhance—the prestige of adopters among their professional colleagues. For example, PROMIS Users Group meetings and newsletters provide prosecutors with an opportunity to tell other adopters and potential adopters about the progress they have made in implementing and utilizing PROMIS.

Local public agency managers who have participated in programs of induced diffusion may be reluctant to admit that anticipated benefits have not been realized. There is much to lose and little to gain from such an admission. In addition to losing prestige as an innovator, the manager may be forced to give up resources, such as specially skilled employees, which were secured during the attempted implementation of the innovation. Resources released from the implementation project are not necessarily available for other uses within the agency; it is possible that the local legislature may attempt to restore the agency to resource levels that prevailed prior to the innovation.

It may not be necessary for the local public agency manager to admit defeat for two reasons. First, it may be difficult for those external to the agency to discover that the innovation has not produced anticipated benefits. Service delivery and management innovations are intended to provide changes in the quality and equity of services produced, as well as changes in the quantity. Quality and equity may be very difficult to measure, and no benchmark may exist for comparison. An innovation such as PROMIS may appear to the casual external observer to have been implemented (data are being collected and reports are being generated), and yet not be producing any information benefits. Second, there may be no clear point at which to judge that an innovation has failed. The implementation of a complex innovation may be protracted. The implementing agency may assert that benefits not yet realized will soon be achieved. Observers from outside the agency may have difficulty determining the validity of these claims. It may not even be clear to those implementing the innovation that anticipated benefits will not be realized some time in the future. Most jurisdictions adopting PROMIS have experienced, and continue to experience, delay in achieving sufficient data quality to permit the realization of many of the anticipated information benefits. At what point in time should prosecutors conclude that the necessary level of data quality will probably never be obtained? This is a difficult question to answer. Rather than admit failure, an easier path may be to continue trying.

THE PROGRAM ADMINISTRATOR

Once a federal agency has decided to establish a program of induced diffusion, it must select an organization to administer marketing activity and technical assistance. The program administrator becomes the major source of information about the innovation and its implementation, not only to potential adopters, but also to the federal sponsor. If the information provided by the program administrator is biased, adoption and funding decisions that lead to diffusion may be inefficient. Unfortunately, the program administrator is likely to have a strong incentive to provide an overly optimistic assessment of the extent to which the innovation can be successfully implemented and used by potential adopters. As a result, there is danger that the supported innovation will be diffused to local agencies when an alternate innovation or even the status quo would have produced greater net benefits.

The incentive to provide overly optimistic information about the innovation and its implementation arises from the assumption that the program administrator wishes to increase, or at least hold constant, the level of funding received from the federal sponsor. (Organizations do not welcome budget cuts. Furthermore, the greater the portion of the total budget provided by the program, the greater the importance of maintaining it.) Continued funding depends on how well the program administrator can demonstrate that the innovation is being diffused. One way of doing this is to overestimate the benefits and underestimate the costs and implementation problems in information provided to potential adopters.

INSLAW has administered the PROMIS Transfer Project from its inception. During the first few years of its existence, INSLAW's budget was made up almost entirely of PROMIS-related grants.

INSLAW's continued existence depended in large part on the willingness of prosecutors to adopt PROMIS. It is not surprising, then, that the institute did at times paint an overly optimistic picture of the potential of PROMIS.

For example, according to a statement in the PROMIS Briefing Series, the "centerpiece of PROMIS" is its ability to rate cases according to seriousness. But in fact the PROMIS prototype was no longer being used for case ranking at the time the Briefing Series was first written. Even though none of the first twenty PROMIS adopters was using, or planned to use, PROMIS for case ranking, the claim continued to be made. Although the information may not have been misleading to adopters, it appears to have misled LEAA. The LEAA personnel responsible for the Career Criminal Program took the claim at face value, citing the capacity of PROMIS to help identify defendants with serious prior records as a rationale for supporting the use of LEAA discretionary funds for PROMIS implementations. In general, the PROMIS Briefing Series gives the impression that many transient information benefits that resulted from use of the prototype continued to be provided routinely. No mention was made of the problems encountered with the prototype in achieving and maintaining data quality.

INSLAW's introduction of a benefit-cost methodology also suggests a bias toward providing information that will lead to adoption. Ideally, the benefit-cost methodology should help the potential adopter to determine whether a project is desirable. The rationale for the introduction of the benefit-cost methodology emphasized by INSLAW, however, is its value in helping convince the local legislature that funds to match implementation grants or cover operating costs should be appropriated. The inclusion of benefits in the benefit-cost analysis that have not yet been realized in any PROMIS jurisdiction, again suggests an overly optimistic presentation. The apparent objectivity and comprehensiveness of the benefit-cost approach may even serve to hide such unwarranted assumptions from the local legislature.

There is another danger for potential adopters in addition to receiving optimistically biased information. The program administrator may become committed to a particular technological form of the innovation (PROMIS) rather than to the development and propagation of the larger class of innovations to which it belongs (case management information systems). The technological "lock-in" is partially a by-product of the program administrator's desire to spread the innovation rapidly. No reward will be gained if a potential adopter chooses an alternative over the innovation that is being promoted. Another reason for the technological lock-in is that the investments made by the organization administering the program in developing technical assistance services and marketing activities are specific to the innovation being supported. Major changes in the technological form of the innovation could involve substantial costs to the program administrator that might not be completely reimbursed by the sponsor. It might also increase the chances of another organization being chosen as project administrator because of greater familiarity with the new technological form.

INSLAW's administration of the PROMIS Transfer Project illustrates the danger of technological lock-in. On the one hand, the continuous involvement of INSLAW personnel with the basic PROMIS prototype design has enabled them to provide high-quality technical assistance to the PROMIS jurisdictions. They have also been highly successful in introducing enhancements of the basic PROMIS prototype design. On the other hand, INSLAW did not initiate efforts to use on-line data entry as a replacement for the batch data entry used by the PROMIS prototype. An independent evaluator, perhaps after reviewing DALITE's success in producing scheduling information, might have reached the same conclusion as the jurisdictions adopting the JUSTIS mutation of PROMIS: the basic PROMIS prototype design operated on a shared computer facility is unlikely to produce scheduling benefits. Another example may be INSLAW's initial reluctance to prepare a nonautomated version of PROMIS, perhaps because of fear that it might compete with the diffusion of the basic PROMIS prototype.

THE PROGRAM SPONSOR

Consider a federal agency whose putative goal is to contribute to the improvement of some service delivered by a like-functioned set of local public agencies. Assume the federal agency identifies an innovation it believes will improve the services provided by the set of local agencies. If the federal agency also believes that the local agencies would not be willing or able to adopt and implement the innovation without external assistance, it may decide to sponsor a program of induced diffusion. The federal agency believes that the program of induced diffusion will permit the diffusion and implementation of the innovation so that the desired service improvements will result.

The federal agency may also have other goals (such as maintaining or increasing its budget), whose achievement can be furthered by sponsoring a program of induced diffusion. Jeffrey L. Pressman notes that federal agencies providing domestic grants to local governments, like agencies providing assistance to less developed countries, seek ways of ensuring the disbursement of appropriations in a justifiable manner.[6] If appropriated money is not being spent or the spending lacks apparent justification, the federal agency will be accused by its budgetary sponsor of not doing its job. The program of induced diffusion is one way to ensure a steady flow of grant applications that the federal agency will find acceptable. As long as the federal agency's budgetary sponsors believe that the innovation provides desirable benefits, the number of jurisdictions adopting the innovation is a readily observable measure of performance, encouraging the federal agency to continue funding the program of induced diffusion.

The federal agency sponsoring the program may be reluctant to reevaluate the desirability of the innovation in light of the experiences of the first adopters. Although positive findings would only help support the already established contention that the innovation is desirable, negative findings could destroy the federal agency's credibility both with its budgetary sponsor and with the local agencies that have adopted the innovation on its recommendation. The more the innovation has diffused, the greater the organizational costs of negative evaluation findings. Thus once the innovation has begun to diffuse, the sponsor of the program of induced diffusion has little incentive to conduct an evaluation that might produce negative findings. Because neither the adopting agencies nor the program administrator is likely to draw attention to failures of the innovation to produce its advertised benefits, an undesirable innovation may be widely diffused.

The danger that a program of induced diffusion, once started, may result in the diffusion of an undesirable innovation points to the importance of beginning such a program only when the program sponsor is very confident that the anticipated benefits can actually be realized by future adopters. As indicated in Chapter 5 there are reasons to doubt the propriety of LEAA's designation of PROMIS as an exemplary project. Most of the claimed uses of the PROMIS prototype had been discontinued by the time the decision was made. Instead of contracting with an external evaluator to provide information on the advantages and disadvantages of PROMIS, information was obtained from personnel of the future program administrator. LEAA continues to rely on INSLAW as a source of information on the success of PROMIS in the adopting agencies. LEAA has contracted for no external evaluation of the PROMIS Transfer Project.

What factors might explain LEAA's willingness to begin the project in the absence of strong evidence that the claimed benefits of PROMIS were likely to be realized? Perhaps the decision was influenced by criticism that LEAA was placing too much emphasis on support for police agencies relative to the courts. Or the decision may have been influenced by the potential of PROMIS to contribute to the development of comprehensive offender-based criminal statistics, a goal pursued by LEAA's National Criminal Justice Information and Statistics Service, which serves as the PROMIS Transfer Project monitor. Perhaps the favorable publicity generated by those involved in the development of the PROMIS prototype contributed to a presumption that it is a desirable innovation. Whatever the reasons, the PROMIS Transfer Project illustrates the dangerous incentives that accompany the creation of programs of induced diffusion.

CAN PROGRAMS OF INDUCED DIFFUSION BE CONTROLLED?

Programs of induced diffusion are a highly effective mechanism for rapidly spreading a particular innovation and maximizing the chances that the innovation will be successfully implemented. The incentives in such programs, however, present the danger that adoption will be induced in local agencies where the status quo or an alternative innovation would provide greater net benefits to society. Are there ways to design the program of induced diffusion so that its advantages can be obtained and its dangers avoided? A brief exploration of this question follows.

Some approaches can be suggested as starting points for further research. The importance of selecting only innovations that have a high probability of yielding net benefits to potential adopters is obvious. If the program sponsor relies on experimental projects executed by local public agencies as a source of candidates for induced diffusion, it is likely that the selection will have to be made on the basis of incomplete evaluations. We have previously discussed the limitations to evaluating experimental projects that have agency-wide effects. In particular, it is unlikely that evaluations will contain any strong evidence concerning the impact of the experimental project. Lack of strong evidence concerning impact adds to the importance of conducting a thorough implementation analysis. An independent evaluator should review the implementation experience, with the aim of predicting the types of problems likely to be encountered by other agencies adopting the innovation. An attempt should be made to place the historical observations in the context of anticipated organizational behavior.

There is wide variability in the organization and environment of even like-functioned local public agencies. An innovation might be appropriate for some local agencies and inappropriate for others. The implementation analysis should include consideration of the conditions under which the innovation is most likely to be implemented successfully and used. If a set of necessary conditions can be identified by the implementation analysis, the program of induced diffusion should be designed so that the adoption of the innovation would not be encouraged or funded where these conditions do not hold.

The program of induced diffusion should be designed with a mandatory requirement for reevaluation of the desirability of the innovation's continued diffusion in light of the experience of the first few adopters. Because the program sponsor and program administrator have incentives to be biased in favor of continued diffusion, the reevaluation should be carried out by an independent contractor or federal agency. The program sponsor should have no veto power over publication of the resulting report. If it appears that major anticipated benefits have not been achieved by the first few adopters, efforts to diffuse the innovation further should be terminated until achievement of the benefits has been demonstrated. At the least, the dissemination of information about the innovation should clearly distinguish between those benefits that are being routinely realized by adopters and those benefits that have not yet been demonstrated to be attainable by adopters on a routine basis.

It might be desirable to conduct a two-stage testing procedure before unleashing a program of induced diffusion. If the results of a demonstration project look promising, the innovation would then be diffused to a strictly limited number of additional agencies. Only if the innovation appears to be yielding anticipated net benefits in the limited set of adopting agencies would a decision be made to continue the program of induced diffusion. Two-stage testing procedures decrease the probability that bad innovations will be widely diffused at the cost of delaying the diffusion of good innovations. If the limited set of adopters is carefully chosen, however, the second-stage testing may help identify local conditions that either hinder or enhance the chances for successful implementation. A two-stage testing procedure is illustrated by the replication of the New York Supported Work Experiment in thirteen cities before committing resources to encourage widespread diffusion.[7]

Even with the safeguards discussed previously, there still exists the danger that the induced innovation will be adopted to the exclusion of alternative innovations that can produce greater net benefits to society. The danger could be reduced by designing the program of induced diffusion so that potential adopters are offered a choice of innovations for which they could receive financial and technical implementation assistance. Offering multiple innovations would encourage a consideration of the relative disadvantages and advantages of each of the innovations. Multiple-innovation programs, however, would probably be less able to provide high-quality technical assistance than the single-innovation program because they would be slower in developing implementation experience with each of the particular innovations. Decreases in the quality of technical assistance that can be provided might be mitigated if the innovations chosen for the program required less externally provided technical expertise for implementation. The supported innovations would have to be more appropriate technologically for the potential adopters to maintain a given level of expected implementation success.

NOTES

1. For example, see Robert F. Asher, *Development Assistance in the Seventies* (Washington, D.C.: The Brookings Institution, 1970).

2. Perry and Kraemer predict extremely limited diffusion of PROMIS marked by only occasional adoptions. This incorrect prediction demonstrates the need to build models that have explanatory variables describing the type of federal assistance rather than simply indicating whether or not there was federal financial assistance. James Perry and Kenneth Kraemer, "Innovation Attributes, Policy Intervention and the Diffusion of Computer Applications Among Local Governments," *Policy Sciences* 9, no. 2 (April 1978): 179-205.

3. A caveat related to the assertion that technical assistance can increase the chances of successful implementation is worthy of note. If technical assistance substitutes for local agency investment in human capital, the likelihood that the innovation can be used effectively and maintained after initial implementation may be lower than in the case where expertise is developed within the implementing agencies. When technical assistance will not be available to adopters on a continuing basis after initial implementation, it should include efforts to transfer the expertise needed for use and maintenance of the innovation to agency personnel.

4. Let us imagine that the loss resulting from decreases in appropriateness could be measured as a decreasing function of the number of alternative innovations supported. Let us also assume that the loss resulting from decreases in the adequacy of the expertise and technical assistance provided could be measured (in similar units) as an increasing function of the number of alternative innovations supported. An "optimal" number of alternative innovations to be supported would be found as the minimum point of the sum of the two loss functions. Unfortuantely, the difficulties involved in operationalizing concepts such as appropriateness of innovations and adequacy of expertise and technical assistance render application of such a model impractical.

5. Yin, Heald, and Vogel attempt to show that bureaucratic self-interest and a desire by local managers for productive efficiency are interrelated motives that must be considered to understand the innovative process. Robert K. Yin, Karen A. Heald, and Mary E. Vogel, *Tinkering with the System* (Lexington, Mass.: Lexington Books, 1977), pp. 91-108.

6. Jeffrey L. Pressman, *Federal Programs and City Politics* (Berkeley: University of California Press, 1975), pp. 107-8.

7. Lee S. Friedman, "An Interim Evaluation of the Supported Work Experiment," *Policy Analysis* 3, no. 2 (Spring 1977): 147-70.

chapter 10

PROMIS and the Study of PROMIS: What Have We Learned?

The organization and emphasis of the preceding chapters reflect the central concern of this volume with the study of the induced diffusion of innovations among local public agencies. In addition, two aspects of the study deserve further comment. First, some remarks will be directed to the substantive focus on innovations in prosecution management. Second, an attempt will be made to place the approach to the study of induced diffusion in the general context of the study of innovation. The following discussion highlights these points.

PROMIS AND IMPROVED PROSECUTION

The PROMIS Transfer Project has served as the primary empirical base for our analysis. At the time the PROMIS Transfer Project was launched, it was yet to be demonstrated that the advertised benefits could be routinely achieved—the U.S. Attorney's Office had largely discontinued use of the prototype. Three years later, at the time this empirical research was completed, some of the major advertised benefits were yet to be achieved routinely by any of the adopters. The difficulties of maintaining accurate and complete data make it unlikely that the batch update versions of PROMIS implemented on shared computers will ever be able to produce all the advertised information benefits. Our implementation analysis of the CMIS prototypes would lead us to be somewhat more optimistic about the prospects for the real-time mini-computer version of PROMIS now being developed.

Of course, even if all the PROMIS adopters eventually achieved net benefits, it would not necessarily follow that the initial decision to begin the PROMIS Transfer Project will be justified in terms of total social costs and benefits. Large and certain costs that begin immediately are not easily offset by benefits of uncertain magnitude that will begin accruing at some uncertain time in the future. The proper federal role in such situations would seem to be continued research and development, perhaps coupled with tightly controlled and monitored diffusion, rather than the launching of programs of induced diffusion. Where such caution is lacking, the local prosecutor must be a skeptical consumer. It is hoped that the recommendations offered at the end of chapter 6 will help prosecutors decide whether PROMIS, or some other case management information system, is appropriate for their offices.

It might be argued that the entire PROMIS Transfer Project should be viewed as a research and development effort; PROMIS has been continuously improved and even if net social benefits have not been achieved, many prosecutors' offices have probably realized benefits in excess of their share of PROMIS costs. An evaluation of this argument must take into account the opportunity costs associated with the PROMIS Transfer Project. Local prosecutors could have invested the managerial effort expended on PROMIS on innovations with much more certain payoffs. For example, enhanced screening and the selective use of clearance procedures seem to be much steadier steps toward reducing idiosyncratic prosecution than the unfamiliar technology of computerized management information systems.

The PROMIS Transfer Project also involved substantial opportunity costs for LEAA. The stated reason for the selection of of PROMIS as an exemplary project, the apparent success of the Special Litigation Unit, was in reality an argument in support of the concept of the vertical prosecution unit. This concept was eventually developed into the Career Criminal Program, which is now considered by LEAA to be one of its most successful programs. Had the success of the Special Litigation Unit not been incorrectly attributed to PROMIS, attention might have focused on the vertical prosecution concept much sooner. Although they are expensive and invoke organizational incentives that discourage optimal case selection, career criminal units provide a direct conversion of prosecutorial resources into observable case outcomes without extended or uncertain periods of implementation.

The choice of PROMIS had the consequence of foreclosing the consideration of alternative case management information system designs. About the time PROMIS was being prepared for transfer, DALITE began operation. Yet no effort was made to determine whether it might provide a better prototype for diffusion than PROMIS. Such a study might have led to adoption of the minicomputer concept that has contributed to the greater success of DALITE in producing logistical support information. Instead, this modification was forced on the PROMIS Transfer Project administrators after several years by the research and development efforts of one of the PROMIS adopters. Although our study would lead us to believe that the PROMIS Transfer Project will continue to improve the prototype through incremental changes, it raises the prospect that major changes of a desirable nature will be avoided.

Has the PROMIS Transfer Project improved prosecution? That PROMIS adopters achieve at least some benefits suggests an affirmative answer. But at what cost? Both in terms of expended resources and opportunity costs, the cost is very high indeed.

INDUCED DIFFUSION IN A GENERAL CONTEXT

Consistent with a growing literature from a variety of substantive fields, we observed that innovations in prosecution management often fail to yield their potential benefits because of unanticipated difficulties that arise during their implementation. Such a finding is no longer surprising and perhaps is of little general interest. At several points, however, observations that should be of general interest were made concerning the importance of not excluding consideration of implementation questions in the study of innovative processes. Three observations about the study of the implementation of innovations are worth noting here.

First, the process by which local public agencies select innovations is likely to involve social inefficiency when the choice set consists of innovations requiring implementation efforts of extended duration, high cost, and uncertain outcome. The benefits of desirable innovations may be forgone if reliance is placed solely on local financial sources because of the difficulty local public agencies face in securing investment funds to cover high start-up costs for risky or unproven innovations. Federal assistance linked to the adoption of specific innovations may result in the socially inefficient adoption of these innovations if potential adopters compare anticipated benefits with the portion of the cost borne by their agencies rather than with the total social costs of implementation and use. The situation is complicated by the open-ended and agency-specific nature of implementation efforts; it is difficult to distinguish between the anticipated benefits that have been delayed and those that will never be realized. Even in the absence of bureaucratic incentives to provide overly optimistic information, the experiences of actual adopters may make only a small contribution to the quality of decisions made by potential adopters, federal funding agencies, or local budgetary sponsors. Students of the innovation process have already begun to pay attention to implementation and the post-adoption stage. It also appears that nontrivial implementation requirements will influence the process by which innovations are selected. Greater research attention to the latter seems desirable.

Second, a demonstration of how one might conduct an implementation analysis was provided. Although recent literature on the policy sciences abounds with calls for the inclusion of implementation analysis as a component of program planning, discussions of how to do it are rare and actual examples are even rarer. The implementation analysis that was presented attempted to predict the implementation problems that would be encountered by adopters of PROMIS. The analysis proceeded inductively from the implementation histories of two case management information system prototypes and deductively from the simple behavioral proposition that individuals attempt to avoid net costs and to gain net benefits. The predictions of the implementation analysis were generally verified by a subsequent investigation of the implementation experiences of the first set of PROMIS adopters. Those who study and practice policy analysis would benefit from the presentation of additional examples of implementation analysis.

A third view of the implementation process worth recalling is the general framework that was advanced for estimating the appropriateness of innovations for local agencies. Appropriateness was defined in terms of the probability that implementation of the innovation would result in the realization of net benefits. It was argued that appropriateness is a function of the resources needed for the innovation's implementation relative to the resources internally available to the implementing agency. Acceptance of this simple proposition has implications for empirical research into the factors related to successful implementation. Namely, studies employing statistical methodologies that focus on characteristics of the innovations or characteristics of the implementing agencies but not on the combinations of these explanatory variables are misspecified and may lead to erroneous conclusions.

The investigation of the implementation and use of two types of management control technologies formed the empirical path of the study. The rapid and widespread diffusion of one of the innovations would not have occurred in the absence of the marketing, funding, and technical assistance provided through a federal program of induced diffusion. General predictions were made concerning the operation of programs of induced diffusion. The history of the program of induced diffusion encountered in the preceding pages is consistent with the general predictions: fast diffusion and an increased probability of successful implementations are obtained at the cost of creating organizational incentives that may lead to the adoption of the innovation where the status quo or an alternative innovation would have provided greater net benefits to society. If, as suggested by the case study presented, these predictions are indeed valid, they indicate the importance of giving attention not only to the amount of federal aid provided in support of local public agency innovation, but also to the form and manner in which it is delivered.

Two important questions must be addressed if the federal government is to play an effective role in fostering efficient innovation among local agencies: What criteria and procedures should be used to select innovations for diffusion? How should the diffusion be induced? Further research, including studies of other federal efforts to diffuse particular innovations, is needed to answer these questions. Several observations might be helpful to other investigators.

First, the recommendation that selection decisions be improved through the conduct of impact evaluations based on random assignment experimental designs is inadequate and generally impractical.

Impact evaluations are inadequate unless they are coupled with implementation analyses that help identify the conditions under which desirable impacts are likely to be replicated and undesirable impacts are likely to be avoided by potential adopters. Because it is difficult to impose experimental designs on already operating programs to evaluate their impact, experimental designs will generally be impractical for evaluating innovations endogenously arising in local public agencies. If these innovations are to be considered as candidates for induced diffusion, indirect measures of impact must be made available to federal agencies sponsoring programs of induced diffusion. Blindly mandating that local projects supported by federal funding be accompanied by experimental design evaluations may stifle the decentralized generation of candidates for induced diffusion by overtaxing the limited analytical resources of local agencies.

A common complaint of students of evaluation is that organizational activity associated with the implementation of innovations frustrates efforts to carry out experimental design evaluations. It would be of dubious value to trade this complaint for the complaint that rigid adherence to experimental design evaluations frustrate efforts to innovate. It is not being suggested that experimental design evaluations should play no role in the selection process. Rather, research is needed to identify the circumstances in which their use is a practical and efficient means of generating information that will lead to better selection decisions.

A second focus for research having practical impact is the study of the design and operation of the programs intended to induce diffusion. How can the advantages of induced diffusion be secured with minimal danger of spreading inappropriate innovations? The development of better procedures for selecting the innovations that will be induced is an incomplete solution because it is unlikely that any single innovation will be appropriate for all the potential adopters.

Attention must be given to determining ways of targeting the inducement to those agencies where the supported innovation is most appropriate. Research directed at determining the desirable forms and combinations of marketing (including information dissemination), funding, and technical assistance is needed. The number of innovations to be supported by each program and the reward structures provided to program administrators are other organizational design questions that should be addressed by researchers. Students of the process of innovation have begun to shift their attention from the study of the diffusion of artifacts and pieces of technical information to the study of innovation necessitating extended implementation efforts; a corresponding shift from the study of the individual change agent to the study of the organizations that induce diffusion is needed.

Appendix A

The DALITE Prototype

DALITE (District Attorney's Automated Legal Information System) is operated by the Alameda County (California) District Attorney's Office. The following discussion of DALITE is based on an evaluation conducted by the author in late 1975 and early 1976. At the time of the evaluation, data had been collected for slightly over two years and management reports had been generated for approximately one year. DALITE development had reached a plateau in two senses of the word. First, DALITE had achieved an important threshold in perceived data quality. Superior court trial managers appointed in January 1975 were the first deputy district attorneys (assistant prosecutors) at this management level to rely on DALITE reports as the main source of logistical support information. Second, major alterations or expansions of DALITE are constrained by limited computer related resources. Current operations consume most of the system manager's efforts.

FOLLOWING A CASE THROUGH DALITE

In Alameda County, requests for criminal prosecution may originate from any one of seventeen local police agencies. DALITE is activated when a police officer makes a request to one of the six municipal court branch offices of the District Attorney's Office for the filing of felony charges against a suspect. The request is handled by a deputy district attorney (assistant prosecutor) who is a member of the Felony Task Force. The Felony Task Force consists of deputies who have had at least some (typically considerable) experience in superior court trial work. The number of Felony Task Force members in an office ranges from five in the largest branch office to one in each of the three smallest branches.

If the deputy handling the request (the charging deputy) declines to file felony charges, he fills out a nonfelony charge decision form. This form records how the case was actually handled (for example, whether it was sent back for further investigation, filed as a misdemeanor instead of as a felony, or closed without filing charges) and the reason for not filing a felony. The form is sent to the main office, where DALITE clerical personnel (more than two full-time employees) use CRT computer input devices to add its data to a file of case rejections. The software for inputting case rejections was the last input program developed. Consequently, there is presently a backlog of data awaiting entry into the case rejection file that has not been used to date.

If the charging deputy decides to file a felony against the suspect, he fills out the first page of a data entry form (the felony charge set). This form records routine data: identifying the defendant, the police agency making the request, the branch office and the deputy filing the charges, the number of codefendants, the charges filed, special penal code sections applicable to the charges filed, witness information, and dates of the alleged offenses, the arrest, and the municipal court filing. The charging deputy makes an analysis of the case with respect to factors such as the type of defense expected and the method of defendant identification. An estimate is made of the probability of winning the case if it goes to jury trial (the win probability) and the length of such a trial (the trial time).

The charging deputy employs, and the felony charge set records, a three-step process for assigning a weight to each case. First, the case is identified as falling into one of ten mutually exclusive classifications in each of three categories: the defendant analysis number dealing with the defendant's criminal history, the victim analysis number dealing with the amount of harm done to the victim of the offense, and the community significance of the offense. Second, the classifications directly translate into one, two, or three points for each of the three categories. The points are added to yield the numerical weight of the case. Finally, a letter weight of "A," "B," or "C" is assigned to the case according to the value of the numerical weight, with a lower limit for certain offenses. For example, a case with a numerical weight of eight or nine points would be classified as an "A" case (the highest case weight). But, if the case was a homicide, it would automatically receive an "A" weight no matter what the value of the numerical weight. In the same manner, a nighttime residential burglary would receive at least a "B" case weight.

The letter weight serves as a *hierarchical control device,* indicating the organizational level having authority to dispose of the case through plea negotiation or dismissal without prior approval from a supervisor. Although municipal court felony department deputies may dispose of "C" cases without prior approval, the disposition of "A" and "B" cases requires prior approval from either the deputy who charged the case or the branch manager, who in turn seeks approval from superior court managers for the disposition of "A" cases. At the superior court level, disposition of "A" cases requires the prior approval of a trial team leader.[1]

In addition to the data coded for computer input, the charging deputy makes written comments on the felony charge set, suggesting specific dispositions or noting unusual aspects of the case. It is important to note that the felony charge set is not in addition to, but rather replaces and supplements the previously used charging forms. The original copy of the felony charge set becomes the summary sheet in the case folder used by the deputy handling the case at each particular court appearance. The carbon copy of the felony charge set is sent to the main office, where it is added to a computer file of felonies currently being processed through the municipal courts.

The deputy handling the case at its municipal court preliminary examination (PX) writes a narrative (short story) on the second sheet of the felony charge set, describing the PX proceedings and identifying factors that might be important in preparing the case for trial. If the PX results in the case being held to answer in superior court, the branch manager reviews and edits the PX short story. In addition, he may modify the win probability estimate or the case weight (possibly because additional information concerning the defendant's criminal history became available). These modifications will not be recorded in the case's computer file unless the branch manager notifies the DALITE personnel.

The actual tracking of cases through municipal court is done with data collected from the court docket by branch office clerical personnel. The results of each court appearance are recorded on a municipal court activity slip: the deputy handling the appearance, the data and type of appearance (including continuances). If a disposition has been reached through plea bargaining, the type of bargain reached is recorded. If the case was dismissed, the reason for dismissal is recorded. The municipal court activity slip is transported to DALITE personnel. When a disposition has been reached, or the case has been reduced to a misdemeanor for municipal court trial, the DALITE record of the case is closed.

When the case file reaches superior court, it is reviewed by one of the two assistant district attorneys who make sure the case has been properly weighted and review "add clauses" related to the use of firearms that require mandatory prison sentences for defendants upon conviction. Although the felony charge set may show corrections in the case weight, these corrections will not be made in the case's computer file record. A blue card is also filled out. This card records data related to the offense and the defendant's prior criminal record. The blue card serves as a link between the municipal court DALITE record of the case and its superior court DALITE record by indicating both the municipal court docket number as well as the newly assigned superior court docket number. The blue-card data allow DALITE to copy municipal court case weight and case analysis data into the superior court case record. It also allows the charges actually filed in superior court to be recorded.

Unlike the tracking of the case in municipal court, data related to superior court appearances are recorded on a superior court activity slip by the deputy who actually handles the court appearance. Disposition data are recorded by the deputy who handled the disposition in narrative as well as coded form. (DALITE clerical personnel use the narrative and court docket records to verify the coded data.) If the case is disposed of through trial, a post-trial analysis (including data similar to that collected in the pretrial analysis by the charging deputy) is made.

COSTS

The direct operating costs of DALITE in Alameda County in 1976 were $92,500 per year. In addition to this monetary cost reflecting computer rental costs and the salaries of DALITE personnel, indirect costs are incurred in the form of employee time diverted to data collection tasks. The largest indirect cost is probably the time expended by charging deputies in filling out the coded data on the felony charge set. This time cost is something less than the five to ten minutes per case needed to fill out the entire felony charge set. The total time costs would add up to approximately one-half a year. Therefore, the time cost is equivalent to using the services of a lawyer for one-half a year.[2] The equivalent of about one full-time secretary is needed to collect municipal court appearance data. The collection of superior court appearance data probably involves only slight time costs to clerical and attorney personnel above that which was required under the previously used manual system. The sum of the direct and the indirect DALITE costs are estimated to be between $110,000 and $120,000 per year. DALITE records data for approximately 10,000 felony requests per year, adding an average of $11 or $12 per case in costs in excess of the previously used manual information system it replaces. (The per case cost appears to be slightly higher than that of PROMIS.)

INFORMATION OUTPUTS

DALITE data are converted to operational, logistical support, and management control information through the generation of regular reports. The following discussion summarizes the information value of the regularly generated reports and indicates the extent to which DALITE has been and is being used as an information source for problem analysis, strategic planning, and general research.

Several of the regular reports produce operational information by simply replacing manually generated lists or by eliminating the need to refer to the manual files. In the municipal court branch offices, clerical personnel use the reports listing upcoming preliminary examinations to indicate which case jackets should be pulled from the files for the following week's court activity. Superior court secretaries use the weekly listing of all cases scheduled for superior court appearances to answer requests made by police officers, witnesses, deputy district attorneys, and defense attorneys for case-specific information. Superior court trial team leaders use the reports listing the cases of each team that are scheduled for the weekly pretrial conferences to ensure that a plea-bargaining stance is prepared for each case. A report listing dispositions is used by the evidence room to clear requests for the release of property to victims. It is also used by DALITE personnel to answer requests from police agencies, municipal court deputies, or witnesses concerning the dispositions of particular cases.

A copy of the felony charge set serves as a summary sheet in the case folder. Felony department deputies refer to the felony charge set when preparing cases for preliminary examinations. The shorter the tenure in the felony department, the greater the time savings felony department deputies reported from its use.[3] These time savings more than offset the time needed to record the summary data on the felony charge set. It should be noted, however, that the operational information outputs resulting from the use of the felony charge set as a summary sheet are independent of computerization and could be achieved by a manual information system.

Several DALITE reports provide logistical support information. In the largest municipal court branch offices, daily reports listing cases scheduled for preliminary hearings seven days later are used by the branch managers to assign deputies to cases. It is also used to monitor deputies' case loads and plan for absences (for illness or vacations). Its use eliminates the need for decoding the absent deputy's calendar of court appearances.

A weekly listing of cases scheduled for superior court trials is produced for each of the trial team managers. It replaces manual calendars, which were previously kept by each of the three trial team managers. It is used to assign deputies and investigators to cases. Trial team managers estimated that the report provides them with information that would require the services of a part-time or full-time secretary to produce manually. It was also suggested by a trial team manager that the six deputy teams (teams previously had consisted of only three deputies) would be too difficult to manage without the report and without additional clerical support. The value of the information in the report might be estimated as the wages needed to hire one or more secretaries.

Two types of DALITE reports produce management control information. The "lag notice" reports help office managers monitor the discretion exercised by deputy district attorneys in dealing with case delay. The disposition reports help monitor superior court plea-bargaining practice. In addition to these reports, the case weighting system operated in conjunction with DALITE produces management control information by providing a summary of case seriousness. However, the benefits of the selective imposition of clearances made possible by the case weighting system will not be counted as DALITE benefits, because the case weighting system could be operated independently.

Each municipal court branch manager receives a monthly report listing all cases handled by the branch office that have not had preliminary examinations within twenty-eight court days of their first court appearance. Managers of the four largest branch offices communicate verbally with their felony department deputies to find out why specific cases are lagging. Deputies may be instructed to object to all continuances requested by defense attorneys who appear to be stalling. If the case is not moving because a key witness is no longer available, the manager may instruct the felony department deputy to dismiss the charges.

A quarterly report listing all cases that have not reached the trial stage within 180 days of the date they were filed in superior court is produced for superior court managers. Like the corresponding municipal court reports, it is used to identify cases in which either the prosecution or defense appears to be delaying the processing of the case purposely. It has been used to detect individual defense attorneys with large numbers of lagging cases so that a request can be made to the court to stop assigning court-appointed cases to the tardy defense attorneys.

A weekly report listing superior court dispositions is produced for superior court managers. The deputy who manages the three superior court trial teams uses the report as a basis for discussion at the weekly trial staff meetings. Dispositions that appear out of line with office policy (such as armed robbery being reduced to a misdemeanor as part of a plea bargain) are discussed with the deputy who has handled the case. Intermittently, the trial department manager manually computes summary statistics (such as the percentage of cases resulting in state prison sentences) from the disposition listings. Changes in the summary statistics over time are used as an overview of the trial department's performance.[4]

DALITE continues to provide information that aids in problem analysis and strategic planning. During 1975 approximately thirty special reports were produced for office managers and other county agencies. As a result of limitations in the DALITE software, the reports were limited to counts or lists of cases sharing a particular characteristic. At the time of the study, one superior court manager suggested that the volume of requests would increase as deputies became aware of reports the system can easily produce that "they would never have dreamed of asking a secretary to do because of the amount of time it would involve." In 1976 the DALITE manager reported that he received two or three requests for special reports each week. Although the majority of the requested reports would be most accurately classified as sources of operational information, some are used as sources of information for problem analysis and strategic planning. As noted previously, PROMIS has also been used to produce these types of information outputs. Unlike the transitory and externally stimulated use of PROMIS, the use of DALITE for problem analysis and strategic planning appears to have been institutionalized within the office.

The use of DALITE to help determine the impact of the 1976 mandatory sentencing laws for defendants convicted of using firearms in the commission of felonies provides an example of strategic planning. A listing of all 1975 cases that would have come under the provisions of the 1976 law was generated. The list indicated to office management the magnitude of the number of cases likely to be affected by the mandatory sentencing law and was used as documentation in support of a request to the California Judicial Council for additional judges.

The major uses of DALITE data in support of general research have evolved from a study of plea bargaining conducted through a

University of California research seminar.[5] DALITE data have also been used by the California Judicial Council to compute statistics on the length of time required for cases to reach disposition after initial charges have been filed. One factor limiting the extent of its use in general research is the difficulty of extracting data from the DALITE system because of the complicated data storage structure and the limited amount of programming resources available within the office for nonroutine activities.

DALITE currently produces at least some output in each of the six information categories described in table 2 of chapter 4. The following description of the history of DALITE design and implementation will help explain why the various levels of information outputs resulted.

ORIGINS

In 1972 the Courts Task Force of the California Council on Criminal Justice Planning (CCJP) compiled a list of court-related projects it considered appropriate for LEAA funding. One of the suggested projects was the design and implementation of a prosecutorial case management information system. The list of suggested projects was presented to the district attorneys of the largest California counties. This presentation led to the submittal of a proposal for a grant for the development of a case management system by D. Lowell Jensen, the Alameda County district attorney.

The proposal was accepted by LEAA. A grant of $100,000 in federal funds was provided for the fifteen-month period of April 1, 1973, to June 30, 1974. The grant required Alameda County to provide $40,396 in matching funds for a total project budget of $140,396. Alameda County provided most of the matching funds in the form of employee time. The grant was used to design and implement the DALITE case management information system.

THE DALITE PROJECT TEAM

Richard Humphrey was chosen to be the DALITE project director. At the time, he had had over two years' experience as a deputy district attorney in Alameda County. Before joining the District

Attorney's Office, he had experience as a systems analyst and computer forms designer while employed by a private firm. Consequently, he brought to his job the rare combination of general knowledge of information systems and specific knowledge of the substantive operations of the organization.

The project director was assisted by consultants from Peat, Marwick, Mitchell and Company, the firm that had been involved in the design of PROMIS. (The personnel provided by Peat, Marwick, Mitchell and Company had not been involved with PROMIS design.) One informant suggested that the consultants were most helpful in the early stages of the project. First, the consultants set the project in motion by helping to develop an interview strategy for the determination of information problems and needs. Second, the consultants' presence as outside experts added legitimacy to the project. Because the consultants had to travel from Los Angeles, office personnel felt obligated to attend design meetings conscientiously. The consultants were interested in having a "clean" operating system fully implemented at the expiration of the federal grant. Consequently, the consultants tended to push for a simpler system than the project team desired. As a result, the consultants played a less active role as the design developed. The consultants later prepared the only DALITE documentation report.

Approval and guidance was provided to the project team by the District Attorney Planning Committee, composed of the district attorney, the chief assistant district attorney, the six municipal court branch managers, and representatives of the Law and Motions, Research and Investigations Divisions of the office.

GENERAL DESIGN PROCEDURE

Recalling his perception of the project team's task, Humphrey states: "It was my understanding, as project director, that we were to review all available data, speak to all available sources, attempt to isolate existing problems and to suggest the solutions." The district attorney had expressed an interest in automation. Although he did not direct the project team to consider only automation, the project team treated it as a possible solution during the assessment of office needs.

The project team's first activity consisted of extensive interviewing of superior and municipal court management personnel. Each manager was asked the following questions: What information would you like an automated system to provide? How often? In what form? How would you use this information?

The interview process not only provided insight into the information desires of office managers but also served a public relations function. Office managers had been trained as lawyers rather than as administrators. It was anticipated that the middle-level managers would be unsympathetic to the change of routine that would accompany the introduction of a computerized CMIS.[6] It was hoped that involving the office managers in the design process would reduce their skepticism. In addition to the professional orientation of the office managers, the decentralization of the municipal courts suggested that a public relations effort was necessary. In many respects each of the six municipal court branch offices is autonomous. For example, the interpretation and implementation of office-wide charging policies are not easily monitored by the district attorney. The introduction of a case management information system would allow greater monitoring and thus tend to limit the autonomy of the branch managers.

DEFINING DALITE OBJECTIVES

The project team classified the objectives of the proposed CMIS into three categories: case tracking, resource management, and policy research/performance evaluation.

In general, case tracking describes the monitoring of case flow from initial filing to disposition. Specifically, it refers to a capability for quickly checking the status of particular cases, in order to answer requests made by deputies, police officers, victims, and witnesses for information about court appearances. This led to the inclusion of court appearance data such as the date and event type of the next scheduled court appearance. Case tracking also refers to the monitoring of charging decisions made by deputies. Before DALITE, no records were kept for cases in which the charging deputy had refused to file charges. To meet this objective the nonfelony charge decision form was introduced.

Resource management describes the expected use of the CMIS in the allocation of personnel to cases and assigning of scheduling priority among cases. This objective led to the inclusion of the case weight data (numerical weight, letter weight, win probability, and trial time), which were discussed previously. The regular DALITE reports (such as the superior court calendar notice) were designed to aid in resource management.

Policy research/performance evaluation refers to the analysis of case data in order to improve policy and its implementation. Detailed data describing the type and circumstances of dispositions were included because of their obvious relevance to the analysis of operations. Because the project team included practitioners, it had a general idea of what data items might be useful for policy research. The pretrial analysis data (such as anticipated defense tactics) and the post-trial analysis data (such as actual defense tactics) were included with the anticipation of use in the assessment of trial performance. Witness data were also considered of potential value for post-disposition analysis.

In the absence of a specific list of questions and methodologies to answer them, the project team attempted to design the data matrix so that detailed data not needed for the resource allocation objective could be recorded. For example, the numerical weight is derived by summing one to three points for each of three categories (community significance, defendant analysis, and victim analysis). The project team developed a schedule to be used by charging deputies that would allow the presentation of ten classifications for each of the three categories. Through the use of this chart, the charging deputy can easily record not only the numerical weight but also a more detailed description of why each weight component has been chosen.

RESTRICTION OF THE SCOPE OF DATA COLLECTION

Each year, Alameda County law enforcement agencies make roughly 12,000 to 13,000 felony arrests. Approximately 9,000 to 10,000 requests for filing of felony charges against defendants are made annually. (About 2,500 of these defendants are actually held to answer in superior court.) A much larger number of requests for the filing of misdemeanor charges are made each year. A decision was made that the CMIS would only track cases for which requests for felony filings had been made. Several factors led to this decision. First, in order to monitor charging practices, it would be necessary to know why requests for felony filings were rejected. This meant that the CMIS could not be limited to tracking just those cases that had actually been filed as felonies. Second, the tracking of misdemeanor requests was rejected because the large number of these cases would greatly increase the amount of computer storage and processing capacity needed. It was also felt that misdemeanor cases often reach disposition so quickly that tracking them would result primarily in historical data rather than management information useful in the handling of active cases.

The project team also realized that it had to limit the amount of data collected for each case. In deciding what data not to collect, the project team employed two principles. First, if the data would not have relevance to office policy, it would not be included. For example, the only demographic data included was defendant age. Age might be of relevance because there exist special age-related sentencing provisions in the California penal code for youthful defendants and sex offenders. Other demographic data such as race and sex were not included because it was felt that they had no direct relevance to office policy. A second reason for the exclusion of certain types of data was the availability of substitute measures. For example, the pretrial custody status of the defendant was not included in the data matrix because waiver of the right to speedy trial is an excellent proxy measure that also has value as case processing information.[7]

In addition to the previously mentioned reasons for limiting the scope of the data to be collected by the CMIS, the project team wanted to increase the chances of achieving an operational system before the project grant expired. This would allow the office to approach the county administrator with a funding request for an operational system rather than for one that was still in the planning stages, especially important because the county data processing center (DPC) might consider the project an intrusion into its domain.

TAKING ADVANTAGE OF EXISTING ORGANIZATIONAL STRUCTURE

Prior to 1970, municipal court arraignments were held in the early morning. In order to have charges ready to file at arraignments, both experienced and inexperienced deputies were required to review requests for prosecution each morning. One deputy described the process in the branch office he was working in at the time:

> There was a long counter. Deputy D.A.'s would line up on one side and police officers would line up on the other. The deputies would charge cases as quickly as possible. . . . Police officers could "shop" for the deputy who would be likely to file the highest charges for a given case.

Deputies also had considerable leeway with respect to case disposition. Although less experienced deputies were expected to consult with more experienced deputies before disposing of a case, one deputy recalls: "In the larger offices, there would always be one deputy who would usually say, 'Send him to prison,' and another who would tell you, 'Get rid of it.' Depending on the answer you wanted, you could go to one or the other of these deputies."

In 1970 the district attorney instituted the Felony Task Force to eliminate these undesirable municipal court charging and disposition practices. Arraignments were switched to afternoons so that a small number of task force deputies could handle all requests for felony prosecution. Inexperienced deputies would consult with the task force member who charged the case when a disposition was being considered. In addition, the Felony Task Force would meet regularly with the district attorney to discuss charging practices and policies in an attempt to achieve greater uniformity in case charging.

Fundamental to the concept underlying the Felony Task Force is the restriction of membership to deputies who have had considerable experience as superior court trial deputies. Although case charging is generally recognized as one of the most discretionary prosecutorial decisions, district attorneys' offices usually are not able to employ highly experienced personnel as charging deputies, partly because of the low status experienced deputies associated with the position. The Felony Task Force vests the position of charging deputy with status so that experienced deputies view service as a charging deputy (alternated with superior court trial work) as acceptable.

In 1972 a case weighting system based on the seriousness of the defendant's criminal record was introduced along with standardized charging forms. Although many of the deputies interviewed remembered the weighting system, conflicting opinions were offered about the extent of its use. Some deputies remember filling out the case weight. Others report that it was generally not used. One explanation for these conflicting recollections is that the weighting system may have been used in some branch offices but not in others. It is also likely that policies concerning the use of the case weights were not fully developed or communicated. In addition, monitoring of case weight use would have required tedious sampling from manual files.

The existence of the Felony Task Force and elementary case weighting system at the time DALITE was being designed offered several benefits to the project team. First, because all Felony Task Force members have had superior court trial experience, it is at least plausible that they are able to estimate the chances of winning cases at trial (win probability) and the lengths of trials (trial time) when they charge cases. Second, because the Felony Task Force consists of a relatively small number of deputies (only about 15 out of approximately 100 deputies employed by the office), it would be easier to control the quality of charging data collected. In addition, the regular meetings of the felony task force could serve as a means of encouraging uniformity in the data collection process. Third, because the concept of a case weighting system had already been introduced, the development of a more complex weighting system that could actually serve as a case disposition control device was made easier. Instead of having to devote energy to convincing deputies that there should be a weighting system, energy could be focused on its design.

COMPUTERIZATION: IN-HOUSE VS. DPC

The project team reached a tentative conclusion that an automated CMIS would be required to solve the problems identified through the interviews with management personnel. It is possible, however, that anticipation of automation influenced the particular set of problems actually identified. Solutions for the identified problems would require multiple indexing of case records allowing access by defendant name and court docket number (for answering questions about the status of particular cases), date of preliminary hearing (for providing notice of hearings scheduled), length of time in municipal court (for identifying lagging cases), trial date (for providing notice of scheduled trials), length of time in superior court (again, for identifying lagging cases), and trial team and deputy assigned to the case. Although in theory these tasks could be handled by a manual system, the project team felt that even a larger clerical staff than would be available could not provide the desired reports on a timely basis. In addition, manual record keeping would not be conducive to the statistical investigation of office performance.

The project team considered two alternative methods of automation: (1) use of the computer facilities operated by the county data processing center (DPC), and (2) installation of a minicomputer that would be totally operated and controlled by the District Attorney's Office. The project team recommended installation of an in-house minicomputer for the following reasons:

1. DPC's then in-depth involvement with the CORPUS Project (an offender-based information system used by Alameda County Law Enforcement Agencies to record criminal histories of "booked" suspects) would mean virtually no DPC personnel would be available to help coordinate the needs of any outside time sharer or to aid in programming.
2. An indication from the DPC that due to "load" periods, processing time for reports, etc., would not meet projected D. A. demands.
3. The Project Team also was aware of problems a "time sharer" has in initiating and coordinating any new or additional programs.
4. Security factors—it was felt that certain base information in the DALITE system should be kept confidential. It was felt security of this type of information could best be effected without going to a large, out-of-office operation for data storage and processing operations.

   It was felt by the Project Team that although DPC had much sophisticated computer equipment, our limited access would mean that this equipment would serve only to provide a historical comparison of D. A. data rather than to aid the D. A. with current case management on a day-to-day basis.[8]

The project consultants helped prepare a request for proposals for an in-house computer system and evaluate the responses. A contract for the leasing of computer hardware was made with a nationally known firm that had recently entered the computer business with the introduction of a line of minicomputers.

SOFTWARE PROBLEMS

The computer hardware vendor recommended a programming consultant who was hired by the District Attorney's Office to write the computer software needed for DALITE. In January 1974 a permanent system manager was hired. The system manager was responsible for the implementation of the software written by the programming consultant, the training of clerical personnel needed to operate the CRT input services, and managing the day-to-day DALITE operations.

Several difficulties and delays were encountered during the implementation of DALITE software. First, although the project team specified what items should be included in the data base, the request for proposal for the software design left considerable leeway to the programming consultant with respect to how the data base would be structured. The system manager had to devote much of his time to interpreting and rewriting the software specifications for the programming consultant. The request for proposal did not prevent the programming consultant from designing a computer file structure that makes access to some "interesting" data difficult. For example, the file structure was so designed that alphanumeric codes for disposition results are stored unordered in a character field that must be searched for specific disposition results. This searching process makes it difficult (in terms of programming and computer time) to locate, say, cases that ended in dismissal or resulted in state prison sentences.

A second problem was related to the operating software provided by the computer vendor. Because the assembler (which interprets simple statements used to write programs) was not available when the hardware was installed, the hardware vendor provided a simpler table processor that would allow some programming until the assembler was delivered. The programming consultant decided to write the DALITE input software for the table processor in order to put the system into operation as quickly as possible. When the assembler was finally delivered, all the programs written by the consultant had to be debugged. Instead of sending most of the programs back to the consultant, the system manager attempted to do most of the debugging to reduce time delays involved in shuttling programs back and forth to the consultant. The last input program did not arrive from the consultant until February 1975, more than fourteen months after the hardware had been installed. This last input program required so much debugging that the DALITE manager discarded it and wrote his own.

A third software problem is that several of the DALITE design features were never implemented. The project team originally planned to have an editing program that would prevent clerical personnel from entering data in an incorrect format. The editor was not written by the consultant because it was not specifically called for in the software specifications. Logic commands (and/or statements) were never implemented. As a result, construction of a simple cross-tabulation requires the programmer to create subsets of the data base on scratch files for each cell of the table. Consequently, providing any output other than listings or counts is a major programming task.

The software difficulties are complicated by the fact that the hardware vendor is quitting the computer business and therefore cannot be called upon to provide support services for dealing with the software deficiencies.

MUNICIPAL COURT APPEARANCE DATA

The importance of considering the organizational roles of those who are to collect data for information systems is illustrated by the history of the collection of DALITE municipal court appearance data.

The data processing center collects municipal court appearance data for the CORPUS system. The project team initially considered the possibility of having the DPC prepare computer tapes from the CORPUS file with the court appearance data needed by DALITE. (The tape would be prepared daily and include data only for the felony cases tracked by DALITE.) The tapes would be manually transported to the DALITE computer, which would copy the desired data. It was not possible, however, to reach an agreement with the DPC for the implementation of these procedures.[9]

Next, an attempt was made to have felony department deputies fill out activity slips after each municipal court appearance. One deputy, who was a branch manager at the time, reports that his deputies accepted the task at first because they thought it would only be temporary until the data would be collected from the DPC tape. When the municipal court felony department deputies discovered they would have to collect the data indefinitely, there was a revolt. The job of municipal court felony department deputy is one of the most hectic in the office. It is understandable that they objected to additional paper work that nearly duplicated the forms they had to fill out for CORPUS. In addition, it was often not possible for them to fill out the activity slips because of judges' requests for errands, which meant they might be out of the courtroom while a continuance was being granted.

Concluding that "lawyers are not clerks," the office trained clerical personnel in each municipal court branch to collect the needed data from the court docket.

The collection of court appearance data in municipal court contrasts with that in superior court, where deputies still fill out activity slips after court appearances. Initially, some superior court deputies coded disposition results incorrectly, but this problem was overcome by having the deputies also write short narratives on the activity slips that the DALITE personnel could compare with the coded results.

There appear to be three reasons why there was no superior court revolt. First, the superior court deputies generally spend more time per case and handle fewer court appearances. Consequently, filling out activity slips does not consume as much effort as it does in the municipal court, where deputies handle more court appearances per day. Second, the superior court deputies filled out similar activity slips prior to the introduction of DALITE, so that only a small change in behavior was required. Third, because the superior court deputies are centrally located in a single office, their compliance could be secured through personal contact with DALITE personnel.

In addition, superior court deputies often request case status information from DALITE, making them more aware of DALITE benefits than municipal court felony department deputies, who rarely make such requests.

This example suggests that lawyers may be clerks *under the right circumstances.* More generally, the organizational role of those required to collect data for an information system should be considered during the design process.

SUPERIOR COURT ORGANIZATIONAL CHANGES

Several organizational and personnel changes were instrumental in bringing about the actual use of DALITE reports by superior court trial team leaders.

Trial teams have been developed to allow several deputies to handle a set of cases so that if one deputy has conflicting trial dates, the other team members can help out. In addition, the trial team leader acts as an instructor to the new deputies assigned to his team. In July 1975 the superior court trial staff was reorganized from five teams of three deputies each to three teams of six deputies each. The change was instituted because the smaller teams often could not cover all of their trial dates and therefore would have to transfer cases to another team.

The change made it necessary to identify which cases were assigned to which teams under each of the trial team systems. During this time, DALITE operations became a primary concern of office management. The DALITE manager took advantage of the increased attention to secure approval of methods for handling data problems that had not been anticipated in the design process. For example, no provisions had been made for the continued tracking of cases that were to be retried after a hung jury. DALITE calendar notices would not list these cases. As far as the trial team leaders were concerned, such an omission meant that DALITE could not be relied upon for calendaring because they might miss the new trial. This problem, and others like it, were solved during the switchover.

The trial team leaders requested that investigators' names be added to the superior court DALITE reports. Inclusion of the investigators' names increased the usefulness of the reports to the trial team leaders because they had to assign investigators as well as deputies to cases.

As a result of the clearing up of most of the accumulated data problems, the accuracy of DALITE reports greatly increased. One deputy, who was a trial team leader at the time, reports that by November 1975 the accuracy of data appearing on DALITE reports became "excellent." Despite the improved accuracy, trial team leaders continued to keep their own trial calendars.

In January 1976 a new set of trial team leaders took over. With them came the first reliance on DALITE as a trial calendar. The reason for the new reliance is probably related to the psychological costs of changes in routine. Even though the old trial team leaders could have relied on DALITE in the last few months of their tenure, they would have had to break with routine to do so. Because the new trial team leaders did not have an established routine, the psychological costs associated with using the new system were lower.

The trial team examples suggest that the disruption of routine behavior associated with organizational change may be favorable to the introduction of information systems. If the personnel will not change their ways, change the personnel.

THE CONTINUING THREAT TO DALITE AUTONOMY

In the autumn of 1975 the District Attorney's Office began considering the possibility of converting DALITE operations to a different computer hardware system. Three factors motivated the investigation of alternate computer hardware systems. First, the vendor providing the original hardware was leaving the computer business, raising the question of the availability of maintenance services in the future. Second, additional hardware capabilities were desired to support a legal research system (which would allow quick reference to case citations) being developed by the office. Third, the conversion process would allow the modification of the DALITE data file structures to permit easier access and facilitate statistical analysis.

In early 1976 the office released a request for proposal (RFP) for a new hardware system. By June the responses had been evaluated and a request was made to the County Board of Supervisors for permission to enter into a contract with the chosen vendor. The Board of Supervisors did not grant permission when objections were raised by the DPC through the county administrator. The county administrator recommended that a consultant be hired to evaluate the District Attorney's Office evaluation of the RFP responses.

When the consultant reported that the review of the RFP had been appropriate, the county administrator directed that the consultant prepare specifications that would allow the interfacing of DALITE with the DPC system. In February 1977 the consultant completed a set of specifications that were acceptable to both the District Attorney's Office and the vendor. The day before the contract was to be signed, however, the county administrator again objected, indicating that he felt DALITE should be operated on the DPC facilities with a remote terminal in the District Attorney's Office for access.

Currently, the District Attorney's Office is faced with the choice of continuing to operate the original hardware or switch to remote operations on DPC hardware. The former option is undesirable for the reasons that prompted the search for a new hardware vendor. The latter option is undesirable for the same reasons that led to the choice of an in-house computer during the design of DALITE: slow turn-around time during DPC peak-load periods, and lack of DPC responsiveness to user needs.

DESIGN AND IMPLEMENTATION: STRENGTHS AND WEAKNESSES

The project team was fortunate to have a director who was familiar with both the substantive business of the office and the design of management information systems. The project had the full support of the district attorney. The project consultants provided a strong beginning through their expert and outside status, which helped overcome organizational inertia. A case weighting system was already in existence. It was not necessary to develop and implement a new case weighting scheme but only to modify the existing system. The project team was able to limit the scope of the CMIS by tracking only felony requests. The existence of the

Felony Task Force allowed the project team to develop a more sophisticated data collection system than might otherwise have been possible. These factors surely contributed to the project team's success in operationalizing a CMIS providing at least some useful management information before the project grant expired.

Several factors hindered the project team's efforts. The project team did not include members experienced in statistical analysis or computer software design. The professional orientation of the office personnel was not conducive to the acceptance and utilization of a CMIS. The interviewing during the early stages of the project helped overcome the negative reactions of office personnel. The impact of organizational change unrelated to DALITE was necessary, however, before DALITE reports began to replace manually kept records. Finally, the introduction of a CMIS employing its own computer threatened to infringe on the domain of the county data processing center. Potential DPC opposition was defused by installing the computer hardware and reaching operational level with grant funds so that the county administrator could be approached for continuing support rather than an outlay for new equipment. This factor, however, greatly increased the time constrains for the project team.

NOTES

1. The hierarchical case evaluation system can be thought of as a device for the selective application of disposition clearances. Although DALITE reports use the case weight as a summary of case priority, the case evaluation system could be operated independently of a case management information system.

2. This figure is based on the assumption of five minutes per case and 10,000 cases per year. Of the approximately 10,000 requests for felony prosecution each year, only about 6,000 actually result in felony charges being filed and the felony charge set being completed. Ten thousand cases at five minutes each requires a total of 833 hours, or 40 percent of a lawyer-year.

3. The copy of the felony charge set that stays in the case folder serves two important functions for the felony department deputies. First, it serves as an educational device by providing an assessment of the case (including the probability of a conviction at trial) made by a more experienced deputy. Second, it reduces the time needed to prepare cases for preliminary hearings. The estimates given by felony department deputies of time savings ranged from a few minutes to sometimes over

fifteen minutes. The longest estimate was given by a deputy who had been in the felony department for only three weeks.

4. The summary statistics also serve an intraorganizational political function. Often when confronted with objections to the reduction of certain felony offenses to misdemeanors, municipal court branch office managers counter that the defendants would have received probation if the case had reached disposition in superior court. To back up their assertions, specific instances or "war stories" of serious felonies resulting in straight probation are cited. The trial division manager called his use of the summary statistics a "war story cutoff program." The summary statistics indicated that the "war stories" were the exception rather than the rule.

5. See "Plea Bargaining: Structure and Process," College of Engineering, University of California, Berkeley, Report 75-3, August 15, 1975.

6. To get an idea of the resistance to change that might have been encountered in the branch offices, let us consider the following possibly exaggerated anecdote related by one deputy: "Several years ago we made an attempt to standardize the forms used in the branch offices for felonies. After the new forms had been distributed, and the deputies told to use them, the old forms kept coming up to superior court. Finally, we had to go to the branch offices at night and take the old forms from their desks."

7. Although data identifying judges with dispositions would be interesting to deputies, they are not included in the data set for political reasons—judges are very sensitive about being monitored. The possible benefits of this data did not outweigh the possible hostility of the judges that might have resulted from its collection.

8. This was communicated in a memorandum from the project director to the author, December 18, 1975.

9. One deputy suggested that the reason why an agreement could not be reached with the DPC was related to the fact that DPC hardware and DALITE hardware were supplied by different computer firms: the DPC vendor did not wish to provide any services that would help its new competitor.

Bibliographic Note

There exists an extensive literature on the topic of innovation. A bibliography of the works dealing with the diffusion of innovations recently compiled by Everett Rogers, Linda Williams, and Rhonda Best (1977) lists 2,750 publications. This vast literature encompasses a wide variety of disciplinary approaches and substantive areas. Our analysis has drawn most heavily from the relatively small fraction of works focusing on innovation in the local public sector and federal efforts to influence it. The most relevant of these come from the economic tradition within the policy sciences. Fortunately, three general reviews provide excellent surveys of the literature and issues relevant to the design of federal programs for inducing innovation: Richard Nelson and Sidney Winter (1977), J. David Roessner (1979), and Lee S. Friedman (1979). The latter two provide general frameworks for viewing economic progress in the public sector as well as illustrations drawn from recent research into innovation in a variety of locally provided public services.

An older and much more extensive literature on the diffusion of innovations arises out of the discipline of sociology. Kenneth Warner (1974) contrasts the economic and sociological approaches to the study of diffusion with an eye toward developing a policy-relevant synthesis. A similar approach is taken by Irwin Feller and Donald Menzel (1977), who draw heavily on the sociological literature to develop the concept of "diffusion milieus" for viewing public sector innovation. We do not draw heavily on the sociological literature in developing our framework for viewing induced diffusion because much of it deals with the diffusion of artifacts, ideas, or other innovations that do not exhibit the implementation problems common to the management and service delivery innovations upon which we focus. Also, much of the literature focuses on the characteristics of adoptors and innovations as explanations of diffusion, ignoring the role of outside agents. A major exception, of course, is the study of the role of change agents reviewed by Everett M. Rogers and F. Floyd Shoemaker (1971). Most of this research, however, deals with individuals rather than institutions as change agents and thus is not directly applicable. Perhaps the most relevant review of the sociological literature is provided by Gerald Zoltman, Robert Duncan, and Jonny Holbeck (1973), who attempt to reconcile the various theories dealing with innovation in organizations. An excellent study focusing explicitly on the sociological aspects of the implementation of innovations in an organizational context is presented by Neal Gross, Joseph Giacquinta, and Marilyn Bernstein (1971).

The number of works by political scientists dealing with the diffusion of innovations is small compared with the voluminous sociological literature. One line of inquiry followed by political scientists is the investigation of policy innovations among the states. Early works in the policy diffusion vein include those of Jack L. Walker (1969) and Virginia Gray (1973). A review of this literature is provided by George W. Downs (1976) in his study of the deinstitutionalization of juvenile corrections. Another line of inquiry, more closely linked to the sociological tradition, attempts to explain why some organizations are more innovative than others. James Q. Wilson (1966) and Lawrence B. Mohr (1969) focus on this question. The most recent line of inquiry, best illustrated by the case studies in Richard Nelson and Douglas Yates (1978) and the approach of Robert K. Yin, Karen Heald, and Mary Vogel (1977), recognizes the importance of distinguishing the decision to adopt from the achievement of successful implementation. Our analysis extends this most recent line of inquiry.

The bibliography that follows is not intended to be comprehensive. It does not repeat all the references cited in the chapter notes. Rather, it provides a set of references that review the various approaches to the study of the diffusion of innovations.

Baer, Walter S., Leland L. Johnson, and Edward N. Merrow. *Analysis of Federally Funded Demonstration Projects: Final Report*, R-1926-DOC (Santa Monica, Calif.: Rand Corporation, April 1976).

Berman, Paul, and Milbrey McLaughlin. *Federal Programs Supporting Educational Change*, vol. 1, R-1589/1-HEW (Santa Monica, Calif.: Rand Corporation, September 1974).

Bingham, Richard D. *The Adoption of Innovation by Local Government* (Lexington, Mass.: Lexington Books, 1976).

Brewer, Garry. *Politicians, Bureaucrats, and the Consultant* (New York: Basic Books, 1973).

Collier, David, and Richard Messick. "Prerequisites Versus Diffusion: Testing Alternative Explanations of Social Security Adoption," *American Political Science Review* 69, no. 4 (December 1975).

Davis, Howard R., and Susan E. Solasin. "Strengthening the Contribution of Social R & D to Policy Making," in *Knowledge and Policy: The Uncertain Connection,* Lawrence E. Lynn, Jr., ed. (Washington, D.C.: National Academy of Sciences, 1978).

Doctors, Samuel I. *The Role of Federal Agencies in Technology Transfer* (Cambridge, Mass.: MIT Press, 1969).

Downs, George W. *Bureaucracy, Innovation, and Public Policy* (Lexington, Mass.: Lexington Books, 1976).

______, and Lawrence B. Mohr. "Conceptual Issues in the Study of Innovation," *Administrative Science Quarterly* 21, no. 4 (December 1976).

Eyestone, Robert. "Confusion, Diffusion, and Innovation," *American Political Science Review* 71, no. 2 (June 1977).

Feller, Irwin, and Donald Menzel. "Diffusion Milieus as a Focus of Research on Innovation in the Public Sector," *Policy Sciences* 8, no. 1 (March 1977).

Friedman, Lee S. "The Evolution of a Bail Reform," *Policy Sciences* 7, no. 3 (September 1976).

______. "An Interim Evaluation of the Supported Work Experiment," *Policy Analysis* 3, no. 2 (Spring 1977).

______. "Economic Progress in the Public Sector: A Review and Synthesis," Graduate School of Public Policy, University of California at Berkeley, August 1979.

Gramlich, Edward M., and Patricia P. Koshel. *Educational Performance Contracting: An Evaluation of an Experiment* (Washington, D.C.: The Brookings Institution, 1975).

Gray, Virginia. "Innovation in the States: A Diffusion Study," *American Political Science Review* 67, no. 4 (December 1973).

Gross, Neal, Joseph Giacquinta, and Marilyn Bernstein. *Implementing Organizational Innovations* (New York: Basic Books, 1971).

Havelock, Ronald G. *Planning for Innovation* (Ann Arbor: Center for Research on Utilization of Scientific Knowledge, University of Michigan, 1970).

Mayer, Robert R. *Social Science and Institutional Change* (Washington, D.C.: U.S. Government Printing Office, 1979).

Mohr, Lawrence B. "Determinants of Innovations in Organizations," *American Political Science Review* 63, no. 1 (March 1969).

Nelson, Richard. "The Allocation of Research and Development Resources: Some Problems of Public Policy," in Ohio State *University Conference on the Economics of Research and Development* (Columbus: Ohio University Press, 1962).

Nelson, Richard, and Sidney Winter. "In Search of a Useful Theory of Innovation," *Research Policy* 6, no. 1 (1977).

Nelson, Richard, and Douglas Yates. *Innovation and Implementation in Public Organizations* (Lexington, Mass.: Lexington Books, 1978).

Oster, Sharon M., and John M. Quigley. "Regulatory Barriers to the Diffusion of Innovation: Some Evidence from Building Codes," *The Bell Journal of Economics* 8, no. 2 (Autumn 1977).

Perry, James, and Kenneth Kraemer, "Innovation Attributes, Policy Intervention, and the Diffusion of Computer Applications Among Local Governments," *Policy Sciences* 9, no. 2 (April 1978).

Roessner, J. David. "Incentives to Innovate in Public and Private Organizations," *Administration and Society* 9, no. 3 (November 1977).

______. "Federal Technology Policy: Innovation and Problem Solving in State and Local Governments," *Policy Analysis* 5, no. 2 (Spring (1979).

______. "The Local Government Market as a Stimulus to Industrial Innovation," *Research Policy* 8 (1979): 340-62.

Rogers, Everett M. *Diffusion of Innovations* (New York: Free Press, 1962).

Rogers, Everett M., and F. Floyd Schoemaker. *Communication of Innovations: A Cross-Cultural Approach* (New York: Free Press, 1971).

Rogers, Everett M., Linda Williams, and Rhonda B. Best. *Bibliography of the Diffusion of Innovations* (Palo Alto, Calif.: Institute for Communication Research, Stanford University, 1977).

Walker, Jack L. "The Diffusion of Innovations Among the American States," *American Political Science Review* 63, no. 3 (September 1969).

Warner, Kenneth. "The Need for Some Innovative Concepts of Innovation: An Examination of Research on the Diffusion of Innovation," *Policy Sciences* 5, no. 4 (December 1974).

Weimer, David L. "The Inducement and Implementation of Innovations for Prosecution Management," Dissertation, University of California at Berkeley, 1978.

Wilson, James Q. "Innovation and Organization: Notes Toward a Theory," in *Approaches to Organizational Design,* James Thompson, ed. (Pittsburgh: University of Pittsburgh Press, 1966).

Yin, Robert K., Karen Heald, and Mary Vogel. *Tinkering with the System for Further Research,* R-2020-DOJ (Santa Monica, Calif.: Rand Corporation, December 1976).

Yin, Robert K., Karen Heald, and Mary Vogel. *Tinkering With the System* (Lexington, Mass.: Lexington Books, 1977).

Zaltman, Gerald, Robert Duncan, and Jonny Holbek. *Innovations and Organizations* (New York: John Wiley & Sons, 1973).

Index

About the Author

DAVID L. WEIMER is assistant professor of Political Science and Public Policy Analysis at the University of Rochester, New York. His articles have appeared in *Policy Sciences, Public Policy, Public Administration Review,* and other journals.

www.ingramcontent.com/pod-product-compliance
Lightning Source LLC
LaVergne TN
LVHW101442200926
848483LV00001B/24